CONFLICTING REALITIES:
FOUR READINGS OF A CHAPTER
BY PEREZ GALDOS
(*Fortunata y Jacinta*, Part III, Chapter IV)

CONFLICTING REALITIES:
FOUR READINGS OF A CHAPTER
BY PEREZ GALDOS
(*Fortunata y Jacinta*, Part III, Chapter IV)

Edited by Peter B. Goldman

TAMESIS BOOKS LIMITED

LONDON

Colección Támesis
SERIE A - MONOGRAFIAS, XC

ISBN 0 7293 0158 3

Depósito legal: M. 30429-1984

Printed in Spain by Talleres Gráficos de SELECCIONES GRÁFICAS
Carretera de Irún, km. 11,500 - Madrid-34

for
TAMESIS BOOKS LIMITED
LONDON

CONTENTS

CONTENTS

PREFACE

In putting this volume together, my intention is twofold: First, to take a long look at Galdós by scrutinizing closely and in detail a single episode in one of his novels. Hopefully, the four attempts to elucidate Part III, Chapter IV of Fortunata y Jacinta will provide galdosistas with new insights about the entire novel and its author; some of these insights, I would like to think, may be applicable also to his other works.

But in the second place, far more important to me has been the methodological exercise. Carlos Blanco's question, «Is there one reading of Galdós [and literature generally] 'more' correct than others?» subsumes another: What are the limits and possibilities of the several critical paths currently followed in literary studies?

These questions have plagued me for many years. They still do. And so, in 1977 while drinking claret on the sunporch of Brian Dendle's house and arguing amiably with my friends whose work graces the pages of this volume, our project, however improbably, began. That April Professor Dendle organized the first of what is now a triennial Galdós Symposium as part of the annual Kentucky Foreign Language Conference. A good number of the faithful descended upon Lexington to hear papers and, following three sessions conducted over two days, lock horns in congenial but intellectually hardnosed debate. On a warm and sunny Saturday afternoon, the formal activities behind us, we repaired to the Dendle household for lunch. There, during the sometimes impassioned discussion, some of us conceived this venture. We were loath to let the argument end with our departure from Lexington. Since I was slated to preside the following December at the annual Galdós Seminar of the Modern Language Association, we were able to keep the debate going. For the December meeting I asked John Kronik and Carlos Blanco to prepare long papers, to be distributed and read by all participants in advance. The meeting itself consisted of brief introductory comments from each, followed by Peter Bly's critique and a general discussion. To give the session maximum focus on the problem of method, we agreed that each paper would take as its point of departure the same episode from one novel. A structuralist examination of Leon Roch, and a sociological view of Realidad, for example, are less successfully compared *than scrutinies of identical material. Peter Bly, who gave a formalist critique of Blanco's historicist and Kronik's semiotic readings, is responsible for suggesting the specific episode to be analyzed: Feijoo's affair with Fortunata.*

Although both Blanco and Kronik subsequently published their papers,[1] they, Bly, and Rodolfo Cardona and Paul Olson encouraged me to put the project together in a single volume. Their only error in judgment occurred two years later when they urged me to add a contribution of my own. The latter was written well after the other papers first were presented and therefore is not specifically directed at them. Nevertheless, all readers will recognize at once the extent of my intellectual indebtedness to the speculations of Blanco, Kronik and Bly. Stricken with the disease of neo-Hegelianism, I should not have been able to write my essay had I not first been stimulated and influenced by these three friends and collaborators.

John Varey, capably, and with patience and good temper, has stewarded the project through its final stages.

In the deepest sense, then, this enterprise from its beginning some seven years ago has been a collaborative venture. I am pleased to have been a part of it, and am grateful for the opportunity to work with some of the most gifted practitioners of the art —and science— of literary criticism in Hispanic letters.[2]

[1] CARLOS BLANCO AGUINAGA, «Entrar por el aro: restauración del 'orden' y educación de Fortunata», pp. 49-94 of his *La historia y el texto literario* (Madrid: Nuestra Cultura, 1978). Professor Blanco's essay has been translated by Peter A. Bly and appears in this volume by permission of the author. JOHN W. KRONIK, «Galdosian Reflections: Feijoo and the Fabrication of Fortunata», *MLN*, XCVII (1982), 272-310; reprinted by arrangement with the Johns Hopkins University Press.

[2] Gershon Vincow, Dean of the College of Arts and Sciences, and Volker Weiss, Vice President for Research and Graduate Affairs, both at Syracuse University, provided considerable financial and moral support for this venture. Publication of John W. Kronik's essay was aided by the Hull Memorial Publication Fund of Cornell University. The publication of Professor Bly's essay was facilitated by Dr. John Bed, Associate Dean, School of Graduate Studies and Research, The Queen's University.

DEDICATORY

To Stephen Gilman, a fifth reader.

Each of us, even in the pages which follow, has disagreed at one time or another with Gilman's readings of Galdós. Yet few scholars have so productively fired the minds of others, even in opposition. Few have proved so well the Cervantine axiom that if it is important to be right, it is no less important to incite others to think critically.

To this remarkable explicator of literature we four dedicate this volume, affectionately and with esteem.

CARLOS BLANCO AGUINAGA

Having No Option:
The Restoration of Order
and the Education of Fortunata

To start an arbitrary and obligatory reading of *Fortunata y Jacinta* at Chapter IV, Part III, has its advantages for, insofar as the chapter deals with the «curso de filosofía práctica» that Feijoo imparts to Fortunata, it is one of the central passages about the dominant theme of the novel: the education that Society-Reality will impose on Nature, especially Nature-Pueblo, in order that the social forms and ideas necessary for civilized coexistence will predominate. And by coexistence in 1886 I mean a kind of social behaviour which is typically bourgeois conservative and which, with its essential cultural variants, is established in the West throughout the second half of the nineteenth century and maintains its structures at least until the First World War.

My treatment of this theme will be duly wide-ranging but within the context of the second advantage to be derived from starting the reading at this chapter. This second advantage has to be our starting point since, as we know that *Fortunata y Jacinta* is a novel that unfolds during years of difficult ups and downs in the political history of the Spanish State, what first catches our attention when we approach Chapter IV, Part III, is that this chapter immediately follows the only chapters in the whole novel whose titles refer directly to this political history. Chapter II, let us remember, is entitled: «La Restauración, vencedora», and Chapter III: «La Revolución, vencida». For further proof, the chapter that follows Feijoo's «curso», Chapter V, is called «Otra Restauración». So, in a surprisingly simple and obvious way, after the complex density of the first two parts of the novel, Galdós refers us directly to the precise political context of his fiction, establishing an analogical relation between the story of the characters he is narrating and the real history of the country in which these fictional characters move. So that we have a clear understanding of what we are talking about, it would not be out of place to

13

recall here the chronological relationship between the novel and the history of the period.

In Part I of the novel, the histories of the Santa Cruz and Arnáiz families are chronicled from the end of the eighteenth century. There are two references to Juanito Santa Cruz's birth in 1845. In fact we see him in action for the first time during the revolt by students and «pueblo» on La Noche de San Daniel, that is to say, on the night of 10 April 1865. The story proper of the novel's title begins when Juanito visits the sick Estupiñá one day in December 1869. Part I closes with the military coup of General Pavía on 2-3 January 1874. This had brought to an end the four long and confusing years of disorder which had followed the break with legality represented by the Glorious Revolution of 1868. During those years the country not only had a surprise king for a short period, but a shorter and even more surprising Republic as well as a Third Carlist War (1872-1876) and a cantonal revolution of very serious proportions in the summer of 1873.

Part II covers less than a year of Spanish history, from Pavía's coup until «lo de Sagunto» (III, i, 6; 55),[1] that is to say, until Martínez Campos's coup of 29 December 1874, which was the prelude to the return of Alfonso XII and the Restoration of the Bourbons.

In Part III, which includes the «curso de filosofía práctica», the time period is barely six months: from Alfonso's entry into Madrid (14 January 1875) until June the same year.

Part IV goes from the same June until the Spring (April) of 1876, some nine or ten months in all.

In short, after the story of the post-1868 ascent of the commercial and financial bourgeoisie, the novel begins towards the end of 1869, the year which witnessed Spain's most liberal constitution prior to 1931. The novel finishes in the Spring of 1876, the year which saw the beginning of the first Conservative parliament of the Restoration, just over a year after Alfonso XII had entered Madrid.

Clearly, then, everything that happens to Fortunata and the others happens within the context of a difficult historical process that goes from the popular-liberal optimism aroused by the Glorious Revolution with its subsequent chaos to the re-establishment of order by the two military coups which will be the bases of the Restoration's legality. On the purely historical level, then, if we view everything from a conservative angle we have a process which, like a classical tragedy or the Golden Age theatre, according to Casalduero, for example, goes from disorder to order restored.

---

[1] BENITO PÉREZ GALDÓS, *Fortunata y Jacinta (Dos historias de casadas)* (Madrid: La Guirnalda, 1887), 4 vols. Each volume is paginated separately. All references to this novel are from the first edition. To facilitate identification in other editions, each reference here indicates part or volume, chapter, and section, followed by page number in the first edition.

From another point of view, of course, the period goes from the highest point of the Spanish people's hopes in the nineteenth century to the temporary destruction by force of those hopes.

In other studies, on *El amigo Manso* and the Torquemada series, I have tried to show how history determines the structure of Galdós's texts. This is just Galdós's own realist application of a principle that is basic to the understanding of the dialectical relationships existing between lite-rature and history, and at another level between superstructure and base. It appears that in *Fortunata y Jacinta,* perhaps more boldly than in the Torquemada series or *El amigo Manso,* more naively and more directly, Galdós is trying to remind us once again of this principle. In fact, if Fortunata, for example, is identified, as we know, over and over again with the «pueblo», anarchy, ignorance, disorder, etc., her story will then be about the failure of her yearning for liberty («su loca ilusión», IV, i, 6; 50), of her insane love and of her increasing claims to respectability. Her story will be about her forced submission to an order within which she is to be only the disciplined quarry for the ruling class which finally after the failure of the 1868 Revolution has once more imposed its laws. The words spoken towards the end by La Santa (Guillermina Pacheco), an aristocrat who is related to the financial bourgeoisie and is also a friend of kings and queens, are illuminating in this regard: «Yo pago y dispongo» (IV, vi, 11; 388). Moreover, when talking of Don Baldomero in Part I, the narrator had already established that «Quien manda, manda» (I, xi, 1; 457).

* * *

Does all this mean that the correct reading of *Fortunata y Jacinta* has to be historical in the commonplace sense that the characters and their actions are perhaps only symbols, analogical excuses for a socio-political discourse? The representativeness of the novel would then be so abstract that all individuality, all aesthetic concreteness would disappear. And in the process the two fundamental rules of artistic reflection, such as we know them in Realist novel-writing and as Lukács has amply explained them, would be violated through excess and deficiency. But every reader of *Fortunata y Jacinta* knows that, fortunately, that is not what happens. So overwhelming is the personality of the characters (and not only Fortu-nata) and such is Galdós's art of storytelling that perhaps what happens is the opposite. It is no surprise then that the best critical readings of the novel stress precisely the specific nature of the characters and their actions without at all omitting the relationship the narrator establishes between Fortunata and the «pueblo», for example.

This situation must be due to the fact that, in spite of the titles of the chapters in Part III which we have already mentioned, the history to which they refer is, if we look closely, mostly presented in an indirect way, by two strangely opposite methods: *a)* the simple mention of the date when certain fictional events are occurring without us being told why that date can or can not be significant outside the fiction itself; *b)* the reference to significant events which at certain moments occurred outside the fiction, in history, without year, month or day being specified. The following are some examples, amongst many, of the first method: «Les conocí [a D. Baldomero y a Barbarita] en 1870» (I, ii, 4; 50); «Por esto sintió mucho Arnáiz que Estupiñá dejara la casa en 1837» (I, iii, 1; 80); «un día de diciembre de 1869» (I, iii, 3; 95); «La boda se verificó en mayo del 71» (I, v, 1; 120); «esto pasaba a fines de 1872» (II, i, 1; 14); «todo esto que cuento se refiere al año 74» (III, i, 3; 22); «En aquellos días de febrero del 76» (IV, iv, 2; 237). As examples of the second technique let the following suffice: «metieron infernal bulla en el célebre alboroto de la noche de San Daniel» (I, i, 1; 6); «voy a ver a Don Amadeo» (I, vii, 1; 221); «el rey se marcha... tira la corona» (I, vii, 2; 230-31); «sobrevino lo de Sagunto» (III, i, 6; 55). A variant of this second procedure is to name the year of some important event without really spelling out the event: «en el verano del 73, cuando la Península, ardiendo por los cuatro costados...» (II, i, 1; 14). Inversely, there may be a concrete mention of the event but not of its timing: «Aquel día había entrado en Madrid el Rey Alfonso XII» (III, ii, 1; 59).

The two procedures and their variants fulfill the same purpose. History, in whose context the events that happen in our story occur, is always there like something so perfectly well-known that it does not prevent anyone at all from going about their business: Don Baldomero to his «tertulias», Guillermina on her canvassing for money, Juanito about his love affairs, Fortunata to Juanito, etc. A great example of this apparent opposition between public history and private life would be the end of Part I. It is the only case in the whole novel of a decisive historical event being named in full detail: «¡El 3 de enero de 1874!... ¡El golpe de Estado de Pavía!» (I, xi, 1; 459). Immediately afterwards Villalonga, a deputy in the Cortes and a participant in the military conspiracy, arrives at the Santa Cruz house and relates the details of the coup as well as telling Juanito at the same time, whilst people keep coming in and out of the rooms, about the real piece of news that has prompted his visit, «la noticia que te traigo» (I, xi, 1; 461): Fortunata is back in Madrid and he, Villalonga, has seen her. We shall have a chance to return to this episode later, but we can note that it is in this episode that the narrator calls Villalonga his buddy. In this respect we could also recall the beginning of Chapter II, Part III, when Jacinta muses as she watches from a balcony the entry of Alfonso XII into Madrid: «¿Qué me importa a mí que haya monarquía o república?»

16

You could say then that as the narrator is constantly referring us back to history he is trying to underline private events, apparently contrasting the individual and the social collectivity. Thus, as has been so often said of Galdós, history would merely be a context, a background within or against which the truly important events take place: the development of private lives, of universal, eternal problems and passions. Therefore, the main point or key to a correct reading of *Fortunata y Jacinta* would be, for example, the theme of love and passion, the desire for children or the question of each character's make-up, the opposition of types, etc.

So the temptation to follow along this path, to gradually divest the novel of history with the utmost logical rigour is indeed very great. Perhaps in this way, in fact, we do succeed in discovering the novel's true, deep structure from which the accumulation of purely circumstantial historical references would presumably distract us. Consequently there are people, for example, who have studied the famous central question of the love triangle from a structural point of view. If we dwell on this question for a little, however, it soon becomes very clear that the lack of attention given the semantics of such a structure misleads us with regard to its very grammar, since the first thing we notice is that by concentrating on such a triangle (consisting of Fortunata-Juanito-Jacinta) one ignores the fact that the growing obsession of Fortunata about the essential respectability of her behaviour and of her very being really breaks out not only when her lover deceives his partner, Jacinta, but also when she, Fortunata, deceives her husband, Maxi, that is to say, when she is living with Maximiliano Rubín. The logical result is that if we take seriously the three volumes following Part I, then what we have is not a love triangle but two married couples and two pairs of opposites in constant interplay: Juanito-Jacinta/Maxi-Fortunata and Jacinta-Fortunata/Juanito-Maxi. These pairs are completely antagonistic: unfaithful husband-faithful wife/faithful husband-unfaithful wife; respectable woman-adulteress/adulterer-respectable man; attractive man/grotesque man, etc. The first pair, Juanito-Jacinta, dominate Part I of the novel and the second, Maxi-Fortunata, Part II at the end of which Juanito reappears just as Fortunata did at the end of Part I. In both Parts there is a wedding; however, there is a honeymoon in one, but not in the other. Both Parts open with a chapter title which contains the name of the corresponding husband: Juanito Santa Cruz and Maximiliano Rubín.

Although these chapter titles have in fact generated a high degree of formal mathematical abstractions,[2] it so happens, however, that Chapter I, Part II, entitled «Maximiliano Rubín» covers in fact the same ground as

---

[2] Cf. AGNES MONCY GULLÓN, «The Bird Motif and the Introductory Motif: Structure in *Fortunata y Jacinta*», *Anales Galdosianos*, IX (1974), 51-75.

Chapters I and II, Part I, since it not only presents the character of the title, the same as Chapter I, Part I does, but also furnishes at the same time the socio-economic history of his family. Moreover, this is the first thing mentioned. In view of this difference, we should not be surprised then to see that the Rubín family history turns out to be the inverse of the Santa Cruz or Arnáiz stories. If Chapter II, Part I narrates the origins and socio-economical progress of Juanito's and Jacinta's families and then a little further on we are told that their business prospered even more with the revitalization of commerce after the events of 1868, we should remember that the chapter on the Rubíns in Part II begins as follows:

> La venerable tienda de tirador de oro que desde inmemorial tiempo estuvo en los soportales de Platerías, entre las calles de la Caza y San Felipe Neri, desapareció, si no estoy equivocado, en los primeros días de la revolución del 68. En una misma fecha cayeron, pues, dos cosas seculares, el trono aquel y la tienda aquella, que si no era tan antigua como la Monarquía española, éralo más que los Borbones, pues su fundación databa de 1640, como lo decía un letrero muy mal pintado en la anaquelería. (II, i, 1; 5)

Thus, in contrast to the Santa Cruzs who during that 1873 Christmas Eve supper are described as «opulentos señores de Santa Cruz» (I, x, 5; 417), the Rubíns, when they appear in our story towards the beginning of 1874, belong to an impoverished petty bourgeoisie which, naturally, has ambitions to move up the social scale: an untalented priest (Nicolás), a travelling salesman (Juan Pablo), a moneylender (Doña Lupe) and a pharmacy student (Maxi). So the meaning of the Juanito-Maxi contrast has deepened since we have now struck into the class question. And, of course, we notice that amongst the pairs of opposites enumerated above we had in fact ignored the class divisions between Fortunata on one side and Juanito and Jacinta on the other. If by chance we might believe that such a contrast is not significant, then in Chapter II of this same Part II we are given the necessary basic information about Fortunata's life-story as proof of her «pueblo» status to which so many people refer. Consequently, the parallelisms and contrasts are deepened, since, if in Part I we are given the long success story of the Arnáizs and Santa Cruzs and nothing about Fortunata's life, in Part II the differently contrasting biographies of the Rubíns and Fortunata are briefly related.

And as Fortunata has been around for several years and a pharmacy student can have his ambitions, the parallel continues when Fortunata becomes Maxi's lover (as she had been Juanito's) because of that excuse about having to live somehow. But, of course, the parallel breaks down when, after a month of this relationship, Maxi tells her one day: «Fortunata, yo me caso contigo» (II, ii, 4; 79). The point is very obvious: a Santa Cruz heir could never marry a woman of the «pueblo». A Rubín, on the other hand, a petty bourgeois aspiring to a decent career in pharmacy, can marry her. It is also natural that Maxi, as a petty bourgeois whose destiny can at certain moments be identified with the «pueblo», should decide to educate Fortunata.

If in this series of opposites we exclude social relationships, that is, the history of the classes in Spain during the last third of the nineteenth century, what is left of the novel or of the interplay of opposites which serves as the structure's frame? The only thing that perhaps could be considered as not historically determined and therefore universal, eternal, is that Fortunata is really in love with Juanito whilst Juanito is not in love with her. One could perhaps regard this fact as sufficient for everything else to happen as it does. Such a simplification, however, would destroy the richness of the work before us which is, in fact, supported by *all* the interplays of opposites mentioned above, the basis of which is precisely the class relationships established between the various pairs of opposites. This relationship is the only necessary and adequate element of the novel's non-triangular structure insofar as in Spain at that historical time it was the cardinal factor above all others.[3]

Fortunata herself must have guessed so when she muses that her fortunes would have been different had she fallen in love with a bricklayer and not a «señorito rico, para que me engañara y no se pudiera casar conmigo» (II, vii, 5; 392). She will repeat this idea a couple of more times, after she has imagined the *«idea blanca* que salía de la custodia» telling her:

> El hombre que me pides es un señor de muchas campanillas y tú una pobre muchacha. ¿Te parece fácil que Yo haga casar a los señoritos con las criadas o que a las muchachas del pueblo las convierta en señoras?

Then the «idea blanca» moves into the second person plural thereby allowing Fortunata's claim to be recognized for what it is: the typical absurd idea of *all* the women of her social class:

---

[3] A counter argument could be made out, however, for the importance of an absolutely essential element in the structure of the pairs of opposites: if the two married couples operate in exactly reverse ways and if Juanito and Maxi are opposites in everything, then the class division that sets Fortunata against Jacinta is often overcome, it seems, by their identification as women. Both the novel's subtitle and especially the copulative conjunction of the title itself indicate at the same time the differences as well as the similarities between the two married women.

It is really, of course, a very old and difficult problem: is there total unity of feminine destinies because of their opposition to male domination, or a permanent unity that is fractured by the class struggle? A relatively coherent feminist, non-Marxist interpretation of *Fortunata y Jacinta* could and should be attempted: each woman identifies with the other on more than one occasion, but again and again they are separated by their class differences. We can not insist too much on this point. Perhaps it is enough to remember for now that while Jacinta does not produce, but buys, Fortunata produces and sells.

¡Qué cosas se os ocurren, hijas! Y, además, tonta, ¿no ves que es casado, casado por mi religión y en mis altares?... Me pedís unos disparates que no sé cómo los oigo... Conque resignarse, hijas mías, que por ser cabras no ha de abandonaros vuestro pastor; tomad ejemplo de las ovejas con quien vivís... Con que cuidadito. (II, vi, 7; 304-06)

The contrast Fortunata-goat/Jacinta(nuns)-sheep is basically inseparable from the contrast «pueblo/señoras» in the Spain of that authoritarian «idea blanca» internalized by Fortunata under the threat of the «careful, now»; these words are hurled out by an internalized God made to the measure of the ruling class which dissolved the Republican Cortes in January 1874.

My assumption is that in a satisfactory work of art the relationships of characters can not be accidental. We have to approach a literary text, then, not like Riffaterre who tells Jakobson, with regard to a Baudelaire sonnet, that if it contains certain relations between phonemes that go unnoticed by the ideal reader they can not be important. The phonemes here are the historical facts and the class relationships systematically established by these facts in the novel. What we have to discover, then, is how they function. And we are particularly interested in their relation to the specific nature of their story. Let us go back then to the question of the historical references.

* * *

And let us begin by realizing that these references are not the context, the extra-literary reality within which the events of our fiction are supposed to occur, but that they are the text itself in which, of course, like all the other material, they are only language. And, of course, we know from Tinianov, for example, that words are never the same thing, that their meaning is different not only inside and outside a literary text, but also that it varies in each context and in each text that the works create. But we also know, from Tinianov again, that it is a question of degree and shade, for otherwise all communication would be impossible. So, inevitably, although the words of a literary text are elements of the internal structure of that text and of no other discourse, they do not thereby lose their recognized referent(s). Thus, contrary to what those people who talk in mystifying tones about language and text think, I shall insist that this internal structure rests dialectically on its relationship with referents outside the text, those to which the text itself refers us as, contradictorily, it separates us from them. If we do not know these referents then we shall never get to the meaning of the text. Therefore, not only do we have to realize that there is no grammar without semantics (the structure of the pairs of opposites has its specific content), but also that the very grammar of the text is determined by the historical structures outside it.

We can provide an easy example from this novel. At the end, with Fortunata already dead, Maxi tells Lupe that he wants to withdraw from the world and enter a monastery. Doña Lupe, so we are told, «vio el cielo abierto» and arranges things so that «al día siguiente tempranito» Ballester takes Maxi «al sosegado retiro que le preparaban»:

> Maxi iba contentísimo y no hizo ninguna resistencia. Pero al llegar, decía en alta voz como si hablara con un ser invisible: «¡Si creerán estos tontos que me engañan! Esto es Leganés. Lo acepto, lo acepto y me callo, en prueba de la sumisión absoluta de mi voluntad a lo que el mundo quiera hacer de mi persona.» (IV, vi, 16; 440-41)

This is nothing less than the last paragraph, the very end of the novel, and we will never understand the sense of the relation established there between monastery and Leganés or between Leganés and Las Micaelas as symbols of absolute submission if we do not realize that Leganés is a mental hospital near Madrid, a place where the mad internal freedom of the individual human being is locked up.

Equally essential for the understanding of the text is a knowledge of the historical facts which, as we have shown, contribute to its production. We can not forget, then, the fact that besides the care with which the rise to success of the Santa Cruz and Arnáiz families (equivalent to the development of the Spanish bourgeoisie during the nineteenth century) [4] is narrated, there are in Part I of *Fortunata y Jacinta* more than thirty references to important dates and events of the century, the first of which, at the beginning of Chapter I, is the already-mentioned famous disturbance of La Noche de San Daniel in which the students Juanito Santa Cruz and Villalonga participate together. Let us remember that Juanito is arrested on this occasion and that he spends the night of the 10th of April in prison. In the same way that we shall understand very little of the ending of the novel if we do not know what Leganés means, what we should realize here is that on the night of 10 April 1865, in the Puerta del Sol and its environs, students and Madrid «pueblo» confronted the police to protest the dismissal of Castelar from his university Chair. The arbitrary, anti-liberal expulsion of Castelar was due to the harsh criticism he made of Isabel II's economic policies. In this sense, then, the famous disturbance is an anticipation of the 1868 Revolution, a proof of the government's instability. The financial crisis of 1866 did justify Castelar's attacks whilst in June of the same year, the insurrection of the San Gil barracks in Madrid and the execution of forty sergeants brought the country closer to the edge of revolution. This disturbance and Juanito's arrest allow the narrator to begin painting the character whose name is

---

[4] Cf. CARLOS BLANCO AGUINAGA, «On 'The Birth of Fortunata'», *Anales Galdosianos*, III (1968), 13-24.

given in the title of the chapter. The narrator calls him «nene» and it is his «papá» «el insigne Santa Cruz» who gets him released from prison. We are told that when «el tal Juanito» «de faz graciosa» got out, his clothes were «llena de sietes y oliendo a pueblo». The sarcastic paragraph ends by calling him «el revolucionario, el anarquista, el descamisado Juanito» (I, i, 1; 7). We are also told here that Don Baldomero «figuraba con timidez en el antiguo partido progresista» but that he was not «socio de la revoltosa *tertulia*» and that therefore he was not «sospechoso al Poder». It is added immediately afterwards that «cuando el niño estudiaba los últimos años de su carrera» his behaviour changed and instead of being «travieso y alborotado» he became «juiciosillo» (I, i, 1; 8). We have therefore, the immediate image of a «progre» young gentleman who for a very short space of time allows himself to be carried beyond his family's political ideas only to return quickly to the fold. And obviously of central importance here is the fact that this «nene» appears at the beginning mixed up with the «pueblo» and that he is rescued by «papá» from its bad smells. This is the first chord in which the theme Juanito/Fortunata is sounded very precisely: we have the concrete class relationships, the inconsistency which will characterize the young gentleman and his return to the fold, which is the meaning of his marriage to Jacinta after his first short fling with Fortunata.

This affair only lasts six months and is hardly mentioned in the chapter in which his parents arrange the wedding to Jacinta. (It will be narrated during the honeymoon.) This chapter is almost as short as the one with Juanito's name and is called «Perdición y salvamento del Delfín». It comes after the chapter which offers us the «vistazo histórico sobre el comercio matritense» during which we have fully understood who the Santa Cruzs and Arnáizs are, and after the chapter on Estupiñá who, we are told amongst other things, was born in 1803 and «fundaba su vanidad en *haber visto toda la historia de España* en el presente siglo» (I, iii, 1; 78). From Estupiñá's perspective, this history is only a confusing succession of disorders and proclamations delivered from various balconies, on the last of which he had recently watched another historical character «diciendo a gritos que se habían acabado los reyes» (I, iii, 1; 79). This detail confirms what I said at the beginning of this study: that disorder and return to order, perdition and salvation at both the personal and collectively historical levels are the central themes of the novel, on a small scale in the first chapter, more fully in all of Part I.

We have already noted that Part I ends on a double note, personal and historical: Fortunata's reappearance (which provokes Juanito's desperate sorties to find her and his resultant pneumonia in Part II) and Pavía's coup and dissolution of the Cortes during the night of 2 January 1874.

Meanwhile, since 10 April 1865 (Noche de San Daniel) many things have happened, for example: the Glorious Revolution, the liberal constitution of 1869, Amadeo's election by the Cortes (16 November 1870), Amadeo's arrival in Madrid (2 January 1871), the attempted assassination of Amadeo and María Victoria (July 1872), the beginning of the Third Carlist War, Amadeo's abdication, the proclamation of the First Republic (11 February 1873) and the cantonal revolt of the same year. We should also remember that in 1871, the First International, accused in fact of provoking disorder and anarchy, was declared illegal.

After his fling with Fortunata in the middle of this post-1868 chaos, Juanito becomes engaged to Jacinta in the same year that the Cortes votes for Amadeo as king and declares the First International illegal. Juanito marries Jacinta a few months after Amadeo's arrival in Madrid. Apart from a few odd visits to help Fortunata bury their child and the occasional fling suspected by Jacinta precisely during the days of Amadeo's abdication and the arrival of the First Republic, Juanito lives decorously, although unoccupied, so we are told.[5] During the same historical period Fortunata goes in the opposite direction: she has been forced to live in sin with Juárez el Negro after whose death in Lérida during the «liberalescos años» she goes to Barcelona where she becomes the very free lover of a couple of painters and a government functionary. Then she goes to Paris in exile under the protection of an old ex-Carlist general only to reappear in Madrid on the arm of an illegal weapons dealer just at the time of Pavía's coup. The narrator calls this the «primera temporada de anarquía moral» of Fortunata (II, ii, 2; 65).

And it is precisely from this point on, after so much disorder and when not only Juanito but also the Progresistas, Federalistas and Libertarios have been brought under control, that the various attempts to educate Fortunata begin, Feijoo's being merely the third one. There is a lot of talk in Part I about the ignorance and savagery of the «pueblo» and the analogy established between Fortunata and this «pueblo» is obvious. But as we know from the end of Part I and from things told us in Part II, the only education Fortunata has received up to that year has to do only with the most external of social forms. For example, when she returns from Paris she is wearing neat, elegant clothes and even a hat, as Villalonga enthusiastically remarks to Juanito. On the other hand, she still hardly knows how to read and she can not write. And although she is a woman who, we are told on several occasions, has the hands of a working woman and loves to do the house-cleaning, Fortunata is so unable to fend for herself that she is forced a couple of times to frequent Doña Paca's brothel. When Maxi turns up in her life, however, there also appears the petty bourgeois desire for order, indissolubly linked to another

[5] Unlike Maxi who works, of course.

desire for domesticity and respectability which will become an obsession for both Fortunata and Maxi. In addition, she is convinced that social forms are also necessary: these are Fortunata's first practical lessons.

A point that is repeatedly underlined throughout the novel (and we do not need to give exact references here) is that for the ruling class, the «pueblo»-quarry is incorrigible and that all one can really hope to do with them is to get them to absorb a few social manners. But Maxi does not see things in the same way. He really wants to educate Fortunata and searches with mad enthusiasm for her «salvación social y moral» (II, ii, 1; 56). This does not mean that Maxi's «curso», like Feijoo's a year later, is not also practical. On the one hand, there will be reading and writing; on the other, as well as advice on discretion in dress, there will be lessons on domestic book-keeping and politeness. Fortunata even manages to learn «la sucesión de los meses del año, que no sabía» (II, ii, 4; 75) as well as a few facts of history and geography. At the same time, Maxi also works on the class consciousness of his girlfriend, «haciendo hincapié en lo malos que son los señoritos y en la necesidad de una ley a la inglesa que proteja a las muchachas inocentes contra los seductores» (II, ii, 1; 59). This, of course, has no effect whatsoever on Fortunata's love or otherwise for a certain charming young gentleman.

Fortunata and Maxi also talk about love's freedom and its social limitations, as opposed to its moral anarchy. Coming quite close to some of the principles on which Feijoo will harp later on, Maxi insists that she has to learn and respect certain formulae. But we should note here that in a typically petty bourgeois contradiction the external formulae only have some value within the context of absolute respect for Fortunata as a human being, within Maxi's conviction about her true worth. None the less, it is true that Maxi's treatment of her as a human being is idealistic, as he is really projecting his own illusions. In this sense, like Feijoo, Maxi will insist that first of all, what should always be educated and saved is one's dignity (II, ii, 2; 62).

It is not just a question, then, of Maxi really wanting to educate Fortunata, unlike Juanito who denies that the «pueblo» has any dignity and who is only interested in Fortunata acquiring the sophisticated charm that Villalonga's girlfriend possesses. Rather Maxi's intentions are clearly based on the conviction that the «pueblo», however savage it is or seems to be, is honourable, upright, intelligent and industrious. In the opinion of the narrator (and at the end of this study we shall have to ask ourselves who is the narrator), Maxi's enthusiasm is mad. Thus there is the ironic remark about the pharmacy student who «Soñaba con redenciones y regeneraciones» (II, ii, 1; 56). This will be the fundamental difference between the «curso» of Maxi the Redeemer and the more sceptical «curso» given by Feijoo.

We should not be surprised, then, that for those around Maxi such stupidities seem inadequate to deal with the real issues. So, as soon as the youngest of the Rubín boys tells his family of his intentions to marry Fortunata, his aunt and brothers decide that the operation is viable (after all, Torquemada, Doña Lupe's great friend, had been «pueblo») so long as Fortunata is educated not, or not only, the way Maxi wants but also with the rigour and discipline needed to subjugate both Fortunata's libertarian bent and the bad habits she has acquired during her years of disorder and moral anarchy. That is how Fortunata's second «curso práctico» begins. It will last for about six months and is nothing less than the lesson imparted in the convent of Las Micaelas.

Religion, physical work, trivial formulae for social co-existence, obedience to superiors: the conservative forces in the country have won and the liberal constitution of 1869 with its laws on the freedom of the press, culture and education has been abolished. Now it is a matter of organizing Fortunata's desire for respectability as well as her liking for domestic work within the traditional ideological model of the ruling class as applied to the women of the «pueblo». In this sense the lesson given Fortunata at Las Micaelas really reaches its climax with the visit of the aristocratic patronesses to the convent. The appearance of Jacinta in this group completely overwhelms Fortunata who is now convinced of the existence of an unattainable model as she had already imagined during her liaisons with Juanito. The ideal is so spotless that in its presence not only distances but order have to be kept so that the ideal will not be disturbed. The counterpoint, as we already know, is Mauricia *la Dura* who is incorrigible, disrespectful, violent and addicted to drink. This is the Mauricia who is expelled from Las Micaelas in triumph shouting: «¡Ay, mi querida calle de mi alma!» (II, vi, 10; 340). This is the same Mauricia who later, on her deathbed, will be given the last sacraments together with a glass or two of sherry in front of a small altar which has its Spanish flag.

However, as we know, this part of Fortunata's education is a complete failure, partly owing to Mauricia: «la cabra tira al monte» we are repeatedly told. Shortly after her departure from Las Micaelas and marriage to Maxi, that is, towards the end of 1874, Fortunata goes back to Juanito and leaves the house of Doña Lupe and Maxi. But, as we see at the end of the novel, there will always be deep down inside Fortunata traces of the ruling class's ideology.

We are thus moving closer to the lesson which ought to be decisive, to the «curso de filosofía práctica» to be offered by Feijoo. But before studying it we still have to consider the immediate context in which it appears since if this «curso» is offered it is because Fortunata becomes Feijoo's lover. And to become Feijoo's lover she has had not only to

remain away from Lupe's house but also to end her love affair with Juanito. How has this happened?

Part III opens with the chapter entitled «Costumbres turcas» which
we could subtitle «la comedia ya no tan nueva o el café». There we not
only get to know Feijoo but also hear some of the adventures of the
eldest Rubín boy, Juan Pablo, before the beginning proper of Part III.
Through these episodes we are told indirectly of some aspects of Spanish
politics between 1872 and the end of 1874 when this Rubín who has been
a Carlist gunrunner, in spite of having also been a Progresista, accepts
a government job from a friend of Feijoo who turns out to be Villalonga.
The chapter ends when with characteristic cynicism Juan Pablo Rubín,
now seeing that the Restoration is on the way, submits to the reality of
the political events engineered well above the level of his involvement
with them: «Cómo ha de ser... paciencia. Tengo que ser alfonsino... a la
fuerza. ¡Vaya un compromiso!... ¡Re-Dios, qué compromiso!» (III, i,
6; 57).

The following chapter is entitled in fact «La Restauración, vencedora»
and opens with Alfonso XII's arrival in Madrid on 14 January 1875. The
Santa Cruzs and Guillermina Pacheco are ecstatic: Guillermina knows
very well (of course!) what she is going to ask the new king to do:
to build a floor of her children's home: «porque le hemos traído con esa
condición: que favorezca la beneficencia y la religión» (III, ii, 1; 61).
Although Jacinta is part and parcel of this first person plural with which
the ruling class through the Santa expresses itself, it is only Jacinta
amongst those cheering Alfonso XII who does not share the happiness
of her family because that same day and that same moment she finds out
that Juanito has gone back to Fortunata once more. Instead Jacinta takes
advantage of the happy disorder of the others to have a confrontation with
her husband. Juanito confesses the truth telling her that really he does
not like Fortunata any more, that he is bored with her because she is
plain and ordinary, too domesticated, useless and ineducable. So, without
much resistance, he agrees to break with Fortunata.

I have already pointed out that this chapter is one of the key moments in the novel for our understanding of the relationship between
history and fiction insofar as it seems to contain the opposition between
socio-political events and personal lives for whose problems the arrival of
Alfonso XII seems to represent only local background colour. But we
must not let ourselves be tricked because, while Jacinta is totally obsessed
with Juanito's latest escapades, Don Baldomero keeps exclaiming: «Veremos a ver si ahora, ¡qué diantres!, hacemos algo; si esta nación entra
por el aro» (III, ii, 1; 59). Here clearly what we have again from the
narrator is not the public history/private life polarity but the existence
of an analogical relationship between the two: what Don Baldomero

thinks of the nation is, for the present, what Jacinta thinks of Juanito. It will also be what Juanito will think of Fortunata since just before we move from «La Restauración, vencedora» to the next chapter, «La Revolución, vencida», once Juanito has decided to leave Fortunata, he tells Jacinta that if Fortunata insists on «perseguirle» (the word is used by Jacinta herself during the conversation with her husband) «seré capaz hasta de recurrir a la policía» (III, ii, 3; 82).

This is an indication of a practical side to reality that will be decisive in the education of Fortunata and the nation: that, if necessary, there is no option but force, for Pavía and Martínez Campos have not just given their lesson in vain. Moreover, it has to be understood that military or police force at no time precludes the need for ideological control, as we have seen in the various lessons given to Fortunata and as we again see when immediately after Juanito's words to Jacinta, they go on to talk briefly about the education of Mauricia *la Dura*'s daughter, Adoración, who is Jacinta's protégée. This is the scene in which Severiana tells Jacinta about the girl's progress. La Delfina (so she is called in this passage) says:

> Eso me gusta... El mes que entra la pondremos en un colegio, interna. Ya es grandecita... es preciso que vaya aprendiendo los buenos modales... su poquito de francés, su poquito de piano... Quiero educarla para maestrita o institutriz, ¿verdad? (III, ii, 4; 85)

This is the ruling class's policy: authoritarian appropriation of other people's property and education in the respect owed social forms; but even here only a little bit is necessary for there is no question of a daughter of the «pueblo» being able to rise to the level of «las señoras» as «la *idea blanca*» explains very well. On the contrary, she has to learn just enough to become a primary or secondary schoolteacher in the service of the ruling classes.

The next chapter, «La Revolución, vencida», has only two parts, brief but fundamental. In the first, Juanito decides that his anarchy is over. In the same analogical way to which we are now used, he explains this decision to himself with the thought that it is necessary «cambiar de forma de gobierno cada poco tiempo». The «anarquista» and «descamisado» young bourgeois of the novel's first chapter continues to be loyal, then, to his opportunistic fickleness. In the last analysis Fortunata «la pobrecilla, no aprende, no adelanta un solo paso en el arte de agradar». She is only a «marmotona». Therefore (and these are the final words of his meditation): «¡Abajo la República!» (III, iii, 1; 97-98).

Thus, Juanito ends his relationship with Fortunata and he does so by giving her a piece of advice which brings us closer still, as we shall see, to Feijoo's «curso»: she should return to Maxi, her husband, because «Las conveniencias sociales, nena mía, son más fuertes que nosotros, y no puede uno estar riéndose de ellas por mucho tiempo, porque a lo mejor viene el garrotazo, y hay que bajar la cabeza» (III, iii, 1; 104); «educación» (i.e. good behaviour), «policía», «garrotazo»: these are the different but complementary ways of making the nation submit.

The second part of the chapter relates the attempt of Fortunata, now furious, jealous, wild, to confront La Delfina: «Ya verán, ya verán», she exclaims, and after deep meditation «A eso de las nueve, la dolorida se levantó con resolución del sofá... Pañuelo a la cabeza, mantón bien recogido sobre los hombros, y a la calle» (III, iii, 2; 107). The succession of nouns gives us the exact impressionistic image of popular feminine fury as Fortunata, dressed as she was on her first appearance in the novel (that is like «las madrileñas del pueblo» [I, iii, 4; 98]), rushes out into the street, as Madrid women did so often in political crises in those years. The image, of course, will remind us also of Mauricia's departure from Las Micaelas.

However, when Fortunata reaches the front door of the Santa Cruz house, she becomes afraid: «la contenía un cierto respeto que no acertaba a explicarse» (III, iii, 2; 109-10). She crosses to the other side of the street where a little later she sees the ladies of the house leave:

> Fortunata vió primero a una de pelo blanco, después a Jacinta, después a una pollita que debía de ser su hermana...; vió terciopelo, pieles blancas, sedas, joyas, todo rápidamente y como por magia. Las tres entraron en el coche, y el lacayo cerró la portezuela. ¡Pero qué cosas! Lo mismo fue ver a las tres damas, que a Fortunata le entró un fuerte miedo. ¡Y ella que pensaba clavarles las puntas de sus dedos como garfias de acero! (III, iii, 2; 112)

To cap everything, the coach almost knocks her down. Then Fortunata runs away now obsessed with the idea of her own respectability, which is really an obsession with her own worth, with her equality with Jacinta, although she does not have white furs, silks or jewels. This idea, which is hatched inside her (for in the external world the differences are obvious and for this reason the bourgeois ideology insists on inner liberty) will later be objectified in the present of her son to these same ladies.

But meanwhile she runs into Feijoo and we are now ready for the «curso de filosofía práctica», that is to say, we are ready to see if Fortunata achieves her wishes without any direct confrontations with the authorities or powers that be, or at least to see if she learns to survive with the appearance of dignity as her best teacher is going to instruct her, like Maxi tried to do.

We already know who Feijoo is: a retired soldier with many years' service overseas; an inveterate bachelor with a number of sexual experiences; an intelligent, friendly, kind man who still seems attractive despite his sixty-nine years: «progresista desengañado» («También él había sido loco» [III, i, 1; 13]). He is also a sceptic and a realist who, although a petty bourgeois, has some special contacts with the high bourgeoisie. He may not know the Santa Cruzs too well, but he is friendly enough with Villalonga, for example, for the latter to return some of his favours by recommending Juan Pablo and Nicolás Rubín for certain positions.

Logically, therefore, his «curso de filosofía práctica» will be based on a complete submission to what he calls the law of reality, which in this particular case, has two dimensions: the importance of social relationships, of what he, like the others, calls the social forms, and secondly, a clear view of nature's limitations. On the one hand he can see that at sixty-nine his relationship with Fortunata will soon have to go beyond the erotic level, and on the other, he can see that Fortunata will never be able to overcome her passion for Juanito. Insofar as his lessons propose hypocrisy as a defence mechanism against the ruling class, they do not differ substantially from the ideas of Juanito, Don Baldomero or even Maxi on the social behaviour required to avoid conflicts. His «curso», however, is more akin to Maxi's in that it is based on a deep respect not only for Fortunata (or for the «pueblo» in general), but for all individual liberties. The only problem is that, unfortunately, these liberties have to have a brake to control them. However, for Feijoo it is not a question of submission, but of doing things with style, by which it is understood that the basic point is never to lose one's temper; this is the direct opposite, then, of dashing out into the street.

The contradiction for liberal Feijoo, though, is clear enough: this concept of liberty is relegated to a secret interior, or its purity is betrayed by deceitful external behaviour. He knows full well, on the other hand, that there should not be deceit, only freedom and frankness between them both, companions in a new life style:

> Mira, yo te dejo en absoluta libertad. Puedes salir y entrar a la hora que quieras, y hacer lo que te dé tu real gana. Quiero que seas leal conmigo, como yo lo soy contigo. En cuanto te canses avisas... Aquí no me entres a ningún hombre, porque si algún día descubro gatuperio, me marcho tan calladito y no me vuelves a ver... Lo mismo haré si lo descubro fuera. (III, iv, 3; 137)

Furthermore, Feijoo's love for Fortunata and his nostalgia for lost causes («¡qué española es, y qué chocho me estoy volviendo!» [III, iv, 4; 145]) are such that the «curso» ends with two fundamentally important practical decisions. Now the sick father of his good friend, Feijoo leaves her a good supply of money and convinces her that she should return to Maxi. The decisive part of the «curso», then, is undoubtedly the apparent submission to the established norms of social behaviour. But there are enough subversive elements (rejection of marriage, companionship, mutual respect, *plus the possibility of economic independence*) for us to entertain some hopes for the future freedom of Fortunata.

The remarkable thing is that, without losing one iota of her sense of respectability, Fortunata learns the lesson to perfection and carries out old Feijoo's plan almost without an error. When she returns to Maxi, she handles the question of Doña Lupe and the money wonderfully well: she keeps her distance and then starts out on her third affair with Juanito with the greatest of discretion. She even submits quietly to what we could call the lessons of Doña Lupe who, like most of the other characters in the novel, insists on giving advice to her neighbour. Only later will the two women clash: precisely when Doña Lupe accuses Fortunata of nothing less, in fact, than «cantonalismo» and warns her that still «no han tocado a emanciparse» (IV, iii, 3; 176).

The failure of Fortunata's third affair with Juanito can not be blamed on her inability to learn the necessary formulae to survive in Restoration society. She fails simply because Juanito abandons her once again after his fight with Maxi, for whose great perspicacity Fortunata is not responsible either. We should note here that when Juanito abandons her for what will be the last time, the narrator gives us two reasons. The first is his «hastío de la revolución» (III, ii, 2; 66); the second is his «profundísimo hastío de Fortunata» (III, iii, 1; 96). Once again, at this decisive moment in the novel, the analogy, private life/history, on which the novel rests is directly established.

Then later when she is pregnant and alone after Feijoo's physical and mental collapse, Fortunata really and truly breaks the rules of the «curso de filosofía práctica» by leaving Maxi to return to her original home, No 11, Cava de San Miguel. This is a pure act of respectability, her true gesture of emancipation, which is only made possible, let us not forget, by the bonds which the army veteran had made out in her name. Inevitably, like all acts of emancipation, it is also a gesture of rebellion and perhaps of pride.

This is the subject matter of the last chapter whose division into two parts has not been given sufficient attention, probably because of the impressive ending when Fortunata puts her «idea» into practice just as she is sadly about to die. In fact, as critics have emphasized, throughout the sixteen sub-chapters or sections that make up the last chapter of the novel the dominant theme is Fortunata's obsession with her «idea». Only now it is not a question of one idea but of *two contradictory* ideas, which is the reason for the division of the chapter into two almost equal parts. In the first, in the second section, the first of her two «ideas» appears: it is nothing less than: «las leyes son unos disparates muy gordos» and that she, Fortunata, has nothing to do with them because she is the mother of the only heir of the Santa Cruz family. This idea makes her believe that Jacinta is now beneath her. Naturally, Fortunata does not stupidly try to erase class differences, but she knows only too well what an heir means in that society, especially for the ruling class. So she tells herself:

> Yo bien sé que nunca podré alternar con esa familia, porque soy muy ordinaria y ellos requetefinos; yo lo que quiero es que conste, que conste, sí, que una servidora es la madre del heredero, y que sin una servidora no tendrían nieto... Sí, señora doña Bárbara, es usted mi suegra por encima de la cabeza de Cristo Nuestro Padre, y usted salte por donde quiera, pero soy la mamá de su nieto, de su único nieto. (IV, vi, 2; 300-01)

We should not be surprised that these words, with which Fortunata, amongst other things, now laughs at the advice of «la idea blanca» and its threatening «cuidadito», are now termed «arrogantes afirmaciones» by the narrator. The fact is that, arrogant or not, Fortunata is right: the family wastes no time in sending Guillermina Pacheco to visit her. She too, of course, has her «idea»: «No es usted sola quien tiene ideas» (IV, vi, 5; 328). But although Guillermina confidently declares that God has made her «tutora de este hijo» (IV, vi, 5; 329), it is obvious that at this moment the mother is the one who holds the advantage.

However, «cuidadito»! Soon after giving birth to her son and still in delicate health, Fortunata leaves the house to get revenge on Aurora, Juanito's new girl friend. The sequence is important for several reasons. First, because it means that she loses her composure («se descompone») thereby straying from what she learned in Feijoo's lesson. She not only goes outside into the street to look for her new rival, but she also confronts her physically and gives her a drubbing. Another reason is that as a result of this fight the police show up and Fortunata is almost arrested. Finally, when she gets back to No 11, Cava de San Miguel, she falls ill because of an unexpected and unexplained disintegration. All of this is enough to bring Fortunata's pride down a peg or two. Now at home (this is just half-way through the chapter) she tells herself that she is as good as Jacinta: «por lo menos... Como no sea más. Pero pongamos que soy lo mismo» (IV, vi, 8; 353). The fact is that, now weakened and confronted by a new rival, Fortunata begins to seriously identify with Jacinta insofar as both women have now been deceived by Juanito. This leads Fortunata to think that her child can have three mothers: «yo, que soy la mamá primera», Jacinta, as the second and Guillermina as the third (IV, vi, 8; 353).

So the sign of the «idea» is now beginning to change until, with poor Pitusa on the edge of death and delirious, the «idea» finally acquires its opposite form, to the full satisfaction of Guillermina and the Santa Cruzs. Fortunata (and she herself remarks that it is a «bendita idea») gives away the child to Jacinta, and *the bonds that Feijoo had left her, to La Santa*. It is not necessary to recall here the details of the servile

31

meekness with which she makes her presents.[6] Perhaps it is not out of place to remember that this noble servant of the Church, its convents and charities to whom Fortunata leaves the old liberal's money, is now, as Peter Bly has emphasized,[7] the owner of the building in which the mother of the Santa Cruzs' heir dies. The narrator underlines this point by calling the Pacheco woman in this chapter not only a saint and founder but also a landlady and general. So, everything returns to order and calm (which the country had lost for some years) because of what the representative of the triumphant ruling class, Guillermina Pacheco, calls a «rasgo feliz y cristiano» (IV, vi, 14; 414).

This is a novel in which several characters have, in addition to various «ideas», various «rasgos». Especially notable are the «rasgos» of the «pueblo»: for example, there is the «rasgo» of Fortunata (which even Guillermina and Jacinta admire) when she rushes out of the house to give Aurora a beating. Feijoo, of course, had warned his friend against these «rasgos»; but there are «rasgos» and «rasgos». For the saints, generals, founders and landlords of the Restoration, «rasgos cristianos» are especially valuable, more so if they come from the lower classes who humbly recognize that their children will live better lives as a result of these «rasgos». We should not forget the last words of Fortunata to the heir Juan Evaristo Segismundo: «Me estoy muriendo... Hijo mío, Dios me quiere separar de ti; y ello será por tu bien» (IV, vi, 13; 404).

Between her education in Las Micaelas and the beating she gives Aurora, Fortunata, now on her deathbed, has finally learnt the major lesson. In short, she has joined the flock. Not only has she internalized the essential features of the ruling ideology, but she has also been the producer of a new Dauphin (Juan Evaristo Segismundo is now called «El Delfinito») to maintain the class order. The «pueblo» is alright as a quarry but, as Doña Lupe would say, let us have no talk of emancipation. So, «cuidadito»!

No less pitiful is our final picture of Izquierdo, Fortunata's uncle, the half-rebel, half-comic Federalista who blames the Moderados for the failure of the First Republic. Following the wise advice of La Santa in Part II, he will become during the Restoration an artist's model: a quarry then for traditional paintings. Here, then, is another of the traces left of this «pueblo» which has been so talked about in over two thousand pages of text.

In this return to order, in this débâcle of the desire for liberty, we can not forget Maxi either. He is the one character to opt, much more

---

[6] Unlike the conscious resistance of Torquemada to both his wife's family and the Church, to which he bequeaths his money *just in case* his salvation is at stake.

[7] Cf. his «Fortunata and No 11, Cava de San Miguel», *Hispanófila*, no. 59 (1977), 31-48.

radically than Feijoo, for absolute inner freedom. But that, of course, is called madness and is socially unacceptable, so he will spend the rest of his life in Leganés.

At the end of the novel with the restoration of order, we are left with: three dead characters (Mauricia, Fortunata and the old liberal Feijoo), a future schoolteacher, a mad petty bourgeois and a painter's model, as a reminder of the story which started La Noche de San Daniel. Indeed it is a tragedy, as Zahareas observed some time ago.[8] A tremendous subject which can only be understood in all its textual reality if we pay attention to the historical specificity of the text, to the precision and care with which in it the writer raises and solves the question of class relationships at a particular historical moment in a particular historical society.

Furthermore, the historical perspective of Fortunata y Jacinta goes well beyond 1876, since what the Spring Cortes of that year established was the structure of social relationships and thus of an ideology whose partial disintegration would not become evident until forty or fifty years later. That is exactly what the Restoration meant in Spain and we would be wrong to suppose, therefore, that the historicity of Fortunata y Jacinta is limited to presenting, symbolically or allegorically, the events of the years 1865-76. I would also dare to propose that the enthusiastic sensitivity shown by so many readers to the novel, to Fortunata's tragedy, to Feijoo's nostalgia or to Maxi's madness, is due precisely to their intuition that the whole novel is a vibrant story about the very sad but not definitive failure of some individual destinies as historical and social representatives. The interpretations of Casalduero, Zahareas, Rodríguez Puértolas and Bly, for example, seem to point in that direction. And when Stephen Gilman, like a new «quixoticized» Sancho, suggests that Fortunata does not die, but wins and is saved, that is to say, that she does not die for us, is it not perhaps a profound historical sensitivity that is operating unconsciously on his antihistorical analysis?[9] There in the text, whether we see them or not, are found the dialectical relations which make this reading possible. Insofar as they are its true structure, how can we believe that they do not function effectively?

In this sense the very special role of the narrator in Fortunata y Jacinta is fundamental. Who narrates this double/single story? The narrator introduces himself in the first lines of the novel as a friend of those who, as we have seen, will be the winners. He is a friend of Villalonga who is an intimate both of Juanito Santa Cruz and of the deputies supporting General Pavía's coup, which will lead to «La Restauración, vencedora».

---

[8] ANTHONY ZAHAREAS, «El sentido de la tragedia en Fortunata y Jacinta», Anales Galdosianos, III (1968), 25-34.

[9] I refer to his «The Birth of Fortunata», Anales Galdosianos, I (1966), 71-83.

This narrator can not, therefore, but share the attitudes held by his social friends. The result is that on more than one occasion we can not distinguish between his thoughts and judgments, and those of Don Baldomero or La Santa, for example.

So it is he and not one of his more conservative characters who, for example, calls the Restoration a «restablecimiento de la vida legal» (III, v, 2; 233). It is he, and not La Santa, who categorically labels as arrogant the undoubtedly tall but rigorously truthful claims of Fortunata that «una servidora es la madre del heredero, y que sin una servidora no tendrían nieto... es usted mi suegra por encima de la cabeza de Cristo Nuestro Padre, y usted salte por donde quiera, pero soy la mamá de su nieto, de su único nieto» (IV, vi, 2; 300-01). It is also the narrator who declares: «Quien manda, manda» (I, xi, 1; 457), who calmly pronounces, like the anglophile Moreno-Isla, that «El español es el ser más charlatán que existe sobre la tierra» (III, i, 3; 20). It is the narrator who begins the chapter called in fact «La Restauración, vencedora» by reaffirming his direct relationship with the ruling class: «Me ha contado Jacinta...» (III, ii, 1; 58). And it is the narrator, not any of his characters, who, as he builds this story in which the class conflict is so obvious, declares that in that Spain (Madrid) there was «una dichosa confusión de todas las clases», a «concordia y reconciliación de todas ellas» due in great part to the «temple democrático de los españoles» (I, vi, 1; 180). In the same way, later on and more deceptively still, it is the narrator who, when describing the Christmas Eve dinner in the house of the «opulentos señores de Santa Cruz», writes: «el conjunto de los convidados ofrecía perfecto muestrario de todas las clases sociales» (I, x, 5; 417). This is followed by a list of the dinner guests that clearly does not contain any representative of the «pueblo». This list does reveal very clearly that what the narrator understands by «todas las clases sociales» is in fact the grande fin-de-siècle union of petty bourgeoisie, commercial bourgeoisie and aristocracy. In other words, the new ruling class which is created and forged, not without contradictions, of course, by the Restoration.

A person who reflects the ideology of the new ruling class to the point of reckoning that the factions and classes which compose it are *all* of society's orders, must logically regard the death of Moreno-Isla as a leaf which falls from the great tree of Humanity in which we are all somehow equal. Since it will not be long before that other leaf of the great tree, Fortunata, falls, the notion is advanced that there is *in death,* in the best orthodox Western religious tradition, *an equality of life* between the owner of the house in which we first see Fortunata and in which she shall die, and the poor tenant who is deceived and abandoned by the same family of the Anglo-Spaniard. To ideologize the most obvious reality in this way is a self-deception practised by the narrator on himself and directed to the reader. It is also the final and concentrated version of

what the narrator expressed in Chapter VI of Part I («Más y más por-
menores referentes a esta ilustre familia») when, in addition to the words
already quoted above about the concord and reconciliation of all social
classes, he tells us that «el nacimiento no significa nada entre nosotros»
since «no hay más diferencias que las esenciales, las que se fundan en la
buena o mala educación, en ser tonto o discreto, en las *desigualdades del
espíritu, eternas* como los atributos del espíritu mismo» (my italics). We
should also add, of course, (and the parallel is accurate) that «La otra
determinación positiva de clase, el dinero, está fundada en *principios
económicos* tan *inmutables* como las leyes físicas, y querer impedirla viene
a ser lo mismo que intentar beberse la mar» (I, vi, 1; 181; my italics).

It is all a question of the well-studied ideological conjuring of the
bourgeoisie: all human beings are really equal (Liberty, Equality, Frater-
nity, leaves on the tree of Humanity). The differences that do obviously
exist are due to eternal inequalities of the spirit, and although it is true,
evident that there are differences of wealth, that also is inevitable because
they are the result of immutable, eternal economic principles. We should
not expect from the bourgeois mentality a logic without contradictions
to dismantle the contradictions of the system. What we should see in these
statements by the narrator is an attempt to resolve in a purely ideological
way the insoluble contradictions of the system. For two long and detailed
chapters we are given the *historical* vicissitudes of the rise to power of
the Spanish (Madrid) commercial bourgeoisie; but the existing social
order is explained not in terms of historical determinism but as a natural
phenomenon, a physical law which is eternal, immutable. At the same
time, and carried along by that mysterious internal logic of the bourgeois
mind which shies away from the truth, the narrator, who announces in
passing the central importance of our theme, puts all the responsibility
for social relationships on education which, however, is not education
in the strict sense of the word, but good or bad upbringing, that is to say,
social behaviour and manners, which, moreover, can not be separated
from one being, not stupid or smart, but stupid or prudent. There is
much emphasis, then, on all the vicissitudes of Fortunata who is not
stupid, or prudent; she has no social education and is, therefore, inevitably unequal in spirit. At the same time, of course, she is inevitably
unequal with regard to the positive class determinism of wealth.

We must just go over now, although briefly, the subject of education
as it is described in Part I of the novel. We will recall that the novel
begins with a picture of Juanito as a university undergraduate. Juanito will
reappear, again in a university context («entraba en la cátedra de Sal-
merón» [I, ii, 4; 54]), two thirds of the way through the long history of
Chapter II. The narrator uses the occasion to give a brief dissertation
on the relationship between education and social environment. Juanito

35

appears once more at the end of Chapter III in his famous encounter with Fortunata who, as we know, stands out in this scene not only because of her beauty and charm but also because of her uncultured language and behaviour. Chapter IV opens with the narrator commenting on certain changes in the customs and language of Juanito which «Barba-rita no dudaba de calificar de encanallamiento» (I, iv, 1; 104). In Chap-ter V, on the honeymoon of Juanito and Jacinta, the subject is once more broached when in describing his former lover, Juanito tells Jacinta: «Fortunata no tenía educación» (I, v, 5; 162). This is followed almost at the beginning of the next chapter by the passage which we quoted above about social classes and education. In Chapter VII («Guillermina, virgen y fundadora») we hear La Santa explaining (and it agrees perfectly with what we know the narrator has already said) that «La falta de educación es para el pobre una desventaja mayor que la pobreza» (I, vii, 2; 227). In the «Visita al cuarto estado» of Chapter IX, amongst other things, the poor education of the destitute is highlighted: the uncouth language and barbarisms of Izquierdo, for example, are caught in the comments of Ido on the words he sees painted on a wall («*No se premite tender rropa, y ni clabar clabos*»): «¡Vaya una barbaridad!... ¡Ignoran-tes!... ¡emplear dos conjunciones copulativas!» (I, ix, 4; 319). At the end of Chapter X it is decided that the false Pituso will go to Guiller-mina's boys' home where he will be given «educación y una crianza con-veniente» (I, x, 8; 454). Chapter XI at the end of Part I («Final, que viene a ser principio») ends with the reappearance of Fortunata who, ac-cording to Villalonga's description of her to Juanito, has experienced a great change: she is now very pretty, elegant and even wears a hat although «por supuesto, hablando, de fijo que mete la pata» (I, xi, 1; 464).

It is not surprising then that, as we have seen, the theme of the education of Fortunata-«Pueblo» is crucial to the novel. The only problem is that one of the revelations made during this long, difficult and unsuc-cessful process of education is that the narrator's thesis about existing class relationships in Spanish society towards the end of the nineteenth century is only a trick, since in fact at this point in history when the process of Fortunata's education is narrated, if indeed a class fusion (and confusion) between sectors of the old aristocracy and the new bour-geoisie has been achieved, the *new class* is radically different from the uneducated Fourth Estate to which Fortunata belongs.

The interesting point about our novel is that all this is also revealed to us by the narrator, just as he is responsible for conveying a sense of Fortunata's greatness and failure, or the sarcastic introduction of «fils à papa» Juanito Santa Cruz, or the contradictory image of Guillermina Pacheco.

I do not think that we can doubt that, like the characters of the ruling class whose lives are related, like the naive Máximo Manso,[10] the narrator also accepts, if not without ambiguities, the pragmatic and vulgar bourgeois version of the law of reality to which people try to subject Fortunata. The formal process which produces these ambiguities is analagous to that governing the construction of the novel as a whole, since what is established is a dialectical relationship between the *omniscient* author who is outside the novel (Galdós) and the behaviour, ideas and language of the *narrator* who appears in the first person as a *fictional character in the text.*

This distinction, also established by Kronik, helps the learned critic to show without a shadow of doubt that the play between reality and fiction, history or life and literature, what he calls the autoreferentiality of the text, his constant emphasizing of the fact that this history is literature, is central to the novel.

But at the same time it is also clear that this text which calls itself fiction is constantly referring to the history outside it, as I have tried to show. The result is that the fictional story is built on the base of real history. It is this duplication, which in fact is a dialectical confrontation, that, from an inevitably bourgeois perspective, of course, allows Galdós (or rather, the text) to critically transcend the limitations of his own class, that class which in its difficult rise to power, still precarious towards the end of the century, concluded, per force, by accepting the premises of its more conservative factions. It is not surprising, then, that years later, as Casalduero stressed some time ago, Galdós tried to resolve this contradiction by becoming a socialist.

At several levels then, the intensely vital experience offered us by *Fortunata y Jacinta* is the indestructible dialectical unity of the human being as a private or individual person and his socio-historical representativeness, which in the last resort determines his social class. It is recognized that this determinism is not mechanical nor does it exclude, therefore, contradictions. Insofar as this relationship occurs in a literary text and we are students of literature, the most important aspect of this relationship and its contradictions has to be, for us, what it tells us about every literary text, every object of art: that although it is not a reality and refuses to be one, to use Lukács's illuminating phrase, it is completely determined by the reality of the time in which it is produced. Hence, in a conscious literary work (Galdós's novels, for example; not Ido del Sagrario's concoctions), the person/history/class dialectic corresponds exactly to the fiction/non-fiction dialectic.

Perhaps we should point out in conclusion that nothing of what I have said above excludes the many very sensible interpretations of *Fortu-*

---

[10] Cf. my article on *El amigo Manso*, «*El amigo Manso* y 'el ciclo céntrico de la sociedad'», *Nueva Revista de Filología Hispánica,* XXIV (1975), 419-37.

nata y Jacinta that we have all read, including John Kronik's intelligent version. All I have tried to do is, simply, to fill out a little, in my own way, the considerable knowledge we already have of this extraordinary novel. But the interpretations of each one of us depend on our respective vision of the world, and the scientific validity of any critical reading has to lie in its rejection or acceptance when compared with other obligatory readings of the same text. That is to say: *there are correct readings* of a text and, insomuch as all of them are only approximations (because we have not exhausted all the text's possibilities, not because the text is inexhaustible), not only are they not mutually exclusive, they are also complementary. This does not mean (and here I reject the theoretical proposal of Kronik and the authorities he cites: Barthes, Kristeva, etc.) that the plurality of meanings of any text and the equal validity of all of them should be accepted, or that, as was suggested in the public discussion of these papers at the meeting for which they were written, every text permits a multiplicity of readings, all equally valid. *There are incorrect readings,* that is to say: just as we find interpretations of a text which not only are not mutually exclusive but even complementary, so we find readings which are mutually exclusive. With regard to *Fortunata y Jacinta,* to go no further, it is clear for example, that all the interpretations based on its triangular structures have to be incorrect, for the simple reason that although in Hispanic language and culture the relationship Fortunata/Juanito/Jacinta is called a triangle, in fact what functions in the novel is not any triangle, but pairs of opposites.

The liberal-bourgeois notion of pluralism, intrinsically confusing, causes havoc when applied to any task that is scientific or tries to be scientific. Applied to the reading of a novel with eclectic, sceptical, subjectivistic glibness, it only tells us that literary criticism is not (nor should it try to be) a science. Here, then, is one reality of life which for some mysterious reason we are not to try to approach in a scientific way!

It will be clear that the writer of this article thinks otherwise and therefore such an opinion is valid only if its converse is false. In this sense, the simple proposal of these pages, which could be profitably fused with the readings of Casalduero, Bly, Rodríguez Puértolas, Kronik and others, seems inevitable, not only for the proper understanding of *Fortunata y Jacinta* but also for any interpretation or study of the dialectical relationships between literary fiction and life.

The fact that realist writers in the Galdós tradition have so clearly perceived this relationship signifies, amongst other things, that they should still be the centre of our reflections on the subject.

University of California at San Diego.

Translated by Peter A. Bly.

JOHN W. KRONIK

Feijoo and the Fabrication of Fortunata

fabricate *vb.*

«to form by art and labor»
«invent, formulate, create»
«to make up for the purpose of deception»

fabrication *n.*

«the assembly of materials into a
structure»
«a making of many parts into a whole»
«an ingenious inventing of elaborate
falsehood»
«*Syn.* see FICTION»

THE PRETEXT

A recent and well-articulated line of thought has it that all literature is self-reflexive.[1] Structuralist critics in particular hold to the view that the work of art invariably reveals itself in its own making. Be that as it may, the fact is that twentieth-century literature has exhibited an unprecedented self-consciousness and therefore has devoted itself with special intensity to a scrutiny of its own nature and its structures. Robert Alter, who has examined this subject in all its sweep, rightly deplores that «with few exceptions, there has been a lamentable lack of critical appreciation for the kind of novel that expresses its seriousness through playfulness, that is acutely aware of itself as a mere structure of words even as it tries to discover ways of going beyond words to the experiences words seek to indicate». He goes on to furnish an explanation:

[1] This essay was read in rudimentary form at the Galdós Seminar that Peter B. Goldman organized for the 1977 Modern Language Association Convention in Chicago, Illinois. It has been published under the title, «Galdosian Reflections: Feijoo and the Fabrication of Fortunata», in *Modern Language Notes*, XCVII (1982), 272-310.

where explicitly Marxist and Marxist-influenced notions of the novel have continued to enjoy great currency, one still often encounters an insistence on the idea of the novel as «the epic of bourgeois life», its prime achievement conceived as the minutely circumstantial representation of changing social realities and how they impinge on individual existences.

One could scarcely deny that both moral and social realism have been at the heart of many major manifestations of the novel in its checkered history [but] in many important novelists from Renaissance Spain to contemporary France and America the realistic enterprise has been enormously complicated and qualified by the writer's awareness that fictions are never real things, that literary realism is a tantalizing contradiction in terms.[2]

Yet even so understanding an observer as Alter espies in the nineteenth century a waning of the self-conscious novel (see his Ch. 4). He offers good reason for this eclipse: the involvement with history, the external perspective that precludes the inner focus, the impulse to action that renders esthetic narcissism sinful. Evidently Alter is unfamiliar with Galdós, for anyone who can say that the realistic novelist avoids the paradoxes of the relationship between fiction and reality cannot be writing about Galdós. The line of demarcation between Galdós and the subjects of Alter's discourse, Dickens and Balzac, crosses precisely this terrain. Since Galdós is a child of the nineteenth century and modern-day readers are not given to discovering a self-reflexive dimension in the bourgeois novel, the insistent presence of that feature in Galdós's work has gone neglected, even among Hispanists. Not only in *El amigo Manso,* where the concern is obvious, but in all his writing he puts into play the dynamics of what the book is and what the book does. He is always conscious of the fictionality of his text and wants the reader to share that consciousness and to enjoy playing while taking positions before the realities portrayed. Writing later on, Ortega y Gasset may well have been unmindful of how applicable to Galdós's still humanized art was his perspicacious observation in *La deshumanización del arte* that a special sense of playfulness is what distinguishes the artist from the ordinary human being. The Latin origin of the word «illusion» (*ludus,* play, game) is not irrelevant in this respect. Galdós knew fully that art is forever a marvelous *trompe-l'oeil*. The chapter in *Fortunata y Jacinta* where Evaristo Feijoo takes Fortunata under his wing is one of the many sections of the novel that can be read as an internal mimesis of the fictional process.

Such a reading of this chapter, or of the rest of the novel, will carry the reader deeply into the constitution of *Fortunata y Jacinta* as a fiction. It will not disclose, except by analogy, the novel's social implications,

---

[2] *Partial Magic. The Novel as a Self-Conscious Genre* (Berkeley: Univ. of California Press, 1975), pp. ix, x.

and for that reason the approach may invite the charge that it denies history. It would be sheer foolishness not to recognize that a novel like *Fortunata y Jacinta* evolves against a specific and meaningful historical setting, that it is a product of a given social situation, and that Galdós uses it to comment on that social order. Self-consciousness in the novel stands as a subversive threat to the mimetic enterprise, but it does not proscribe history. The novel can hardly do without history. However, it is not a lesson in history, for it is history in a fiction, history turned story. Its relationship to its historical circumstance individualizes the work of literature, but, as Northrop Frye has observed, its connection with other literary works characterizes it.[3] Art is a stylization even when it purports to make a sociological statement. Harry Levin phrases that idea pithily: literature, instead of reflecting life, refracts it;[4] and Geoffrey Hartman marks the distinction in yet stronger terms: «Art is not reality; the relation of the one to the other is essentially liminal; between art and its translation into immediate relevance a threshold intervenes which cannot be crossed without destroying art's very place in society.»[5] That is the lesson that strikes me more than it does Carlos Blanco Aguinaga in his companion piece in this volume. Where his phonemes are historical data, mine are novelistic structures.

Both here and elsewhere,[6] Blanco maintains that history determines, governs the Galdosian text and, consequently, the reader's comprehension of it. But just as I am prepared to concede at least the shaping effect of the class system that dominates *Fortunata y Jacinta,* so does he grant that historical data in the novel are not extra-literary context, but language. Therefore, even the historically uninformed reader confronted with the ambiguous sign «Leganés» at the end of the novel cannot take it to be the monastery into which Maxi had hoped to escape: the linguistic context forestalls that possible misinterpretation. A history, the chronological record of human events, exists out there, beyond the novel; another history exists within the text: the illusion of history that narrative spins. Neither Blanco nor I wishes to squelch the dialectical relationship that operates between history and fiction. In *Fortunata y Jacinta* the distance between «nivelar» and «novelar» is minute. Our divergent critical pleas stem from our respective emphasis on differing textual components. Galdós's text prompts me to discern its illusionist complexion and to examine the metaphor that it has caused history to

---

[3] *Anatomy of Criticism* (Princeton: Princeton Univ. Press, 1957).
[4] *The Gates of Horn* (New York: Oxford, 1963), p. 20.
[5] «History Writing as Answerable Style», *The Fate of Reading and Other Essays* (Chicago: Univ. of Chicago Press, 1975), p. 109.
[6] «Historia, reflejo literario y estructura de la novela: el ejemplo de Torquemada», *Ideologies and Literature*, I, No. 2 (1977), 23-39.

become. In my order of priorities, knowledge of how a work works is essential to an apprehension of what the work is, all the more so when it insists internally on recognition of its constitutive nature as fiction.

Carlos Blanco's analysis is as convincing as it is illuminating, and I believe that his insights and mine can comfortably share the critical platform. What I am constrained to reject is the notion of «la lectura correcta», the exclusive supremacy of any single reading. One might well ask: is *Fortunata y Jacinta* an elaborate structure of words, or is it an expression of Galdós's gargantuan will? The balanced components of that question can be thrown into polemical juxtaposition by reference to two important books in the current critical discourse. The one is E. D. Hirsch's *Validity in Interpretation* (New Haven: Yale Univ. Press, 1967); the other, Norman N. Holland's *5 Readers Reading* (New Haven: Yale Univ. Press, 1975). Hirsch argues for the author's meaning as normative for interpretation. He confesses that no meaning represented by a verbal sign is manifest, that all meanings must be construed, and that something conspicuous in the textual architecture may have escaped the author's notice (p. 61); but he defends the determining power of the authorial will and therefore believes that the hermeneutic exercise must be limited to what the author knew and wished. The only valid interpretation, claims Hirsch, is the one that gets closest to the author's intent. Holland, on the other hand, after a series of controlled psychological experiments, concludes that reading is an act of perception and that perception is colored by personality. «A literary text, after all, in an objective sense consists only of a certain configuration of specks of carbon black on dried wood pulp. When these marks become words, when those words become images or metaphors or characters or events, they do so because the reader plays the part of a prince to the sleeping beauty. He gives them life out of his own desires» (p. 12). Holland insists that a literary text is not a fixed stimulus and that every act of reading is a constructive undertaking.[7] He concludes that all readings are by constitu-

---

[7] GEORGES POULET, «Phenomenology of Reading», *New Literary History*, I (1969), 53-68, expresses the similar idea that books, rather than living presences, are objects: «they wait for someone to come and deliver them from their materiality, from their immobility» (p. 53). Poulet also asserts that while «every work of literature is impregnated with the mind of the one who wrote it», each work lives its own life in each new reader (p. 58). In Ch. 5 of his book, Holland specifies that the process of reading is a search for our individual lifestyle, a matching of our own defense mechanisms with those to be found in the text, a projection of our fantasies, and a formation —or transformation— of the text according to our characters. Holland builds his findings on the research of earlier psychologists. For example: «the reader will abstract from the work of art only what he is able to perceive and organize; what he experiences and feels will determine the nature of his perceptions and the meaning he attaches to them» (CAROLINE SHRODES, «The Dynamics of Reading: Implications for Bibliotherapy», *ETC.: A Review of General Semantics*, XVIII [1961], 22).

tion subjective, that the reader's and the author's dynamics cannot correspond, and that therefore «one cannot posit even for highly trained readers a "correct" response in any given reader's mind to something definitively "in" the text» (p. 13).

This pluralistic basis for interpretation finds support in thinkers —readers— of varying orientation and pedigree. Gadamer holds the view that textual interpretation must transcend the author because a reader's conception of a text is necessarily different from the author's.[8] The structuralist and post-structuralist critics argue compellingly for any text's plurality of significations and for the equal validity of each. Barthes, for example, regards today's reader as a producer, not a consumer, of a text: «To read is to find meanings.» «The more plural the text, the less it is written before I read it», he says. Jonathan Culler echoes that idea when he writes: «meaning should not be something that we simply recover but something that we produce or create; interpretation should transform the world, not merely attempt to recover a past».[9] Sartre offers a pithy summation in *Qu'est-ce que la littérature?:* «Reading is directed creation» (Ch. 2). Wayne Booth believes, along with Henry James, that the author creates an image of the reader, makes the reader.[10] This is the ideal reader, rhetorically stimulated. In contention with him exists the actual reader who produces the meaning of the text. The talented author can reduce the distance between the two, as can the wise and generous reader, but the gap can never be fully bridged, since the reader that opens the book is not the hypothetical reader that the author established for the text. The term «implied reader» has recently gained acceptance as a way to incorporate «both the prestructuring of the potential meaning by the text, and the reader's actualization of this potential through the reading process».[11] Iser argues that a likely role for the reader is built into the novel as a frame of possible decisions among which the reader chooses in accordance with his individual disposition. In an attempt to make difficult distinctions, Iser fuzzes the issues terminologically, but his point is well taken: the work is more than the text. Just as a play

[8] HANS-GEORG GADAMER, *Truth and Method,* trans. G. Barden and J. Cumming (New York: Seabury Press, 1975).

[9] ROLAND BARTHES, *S/Z,* trans. Richard Miller (New York: Hill and Wang, 1974) pp. 4, 10, 11. Elsewhere he admonishes: «The *I* of the one who writes *I* is not the same as the *I* which is read by *thou*» («To Write: An Intransitive Verb?», in Richard Macksey and Eugenio Donato, eds., *The Languages of Criticism and the Sciences of Man. The Structuralist Controversy* [Baltimore: Johns Hopkins Univ. Press, 1970], p. 141). The Culler quotation is from *Ferdinand de Saussure* (New York: Penguin Books, 1977), p. 120. Consult also JULIA KRISTEVA, *Le Texte du roman* (The Hague: Mouton, 1970).

[10] *The Rhetoric of Fiction* (Chicago: Univ. of Chicago Press, 1961), pp. 49, 138.

[11] WOLFGANG ISER, *The Implied Reader. Patterns of Communication in Prose Fiction from Bunyan to Beckett* (Baltimore: Johns Hopkins Univ. Press, 1974), p. xii. See also esp. pp. 55, 274.

is fully realized not in its script, but upon representation, so too does the novelistic text that the author created take on life only in the reader's hands. Long ago, *Don Quijote* and *Tristram Shandy* already showed that the work of fiction, in Iser's words, «is something like an arena in which reader and author participate in a game of the imagination» (p. 275). If the work of literature is a communication, then the actual reader is an accomplice or collaborator in that operation, all the more intensely so in the case of a writer like Galdós, whose narrator, given to addressing the reader directly, thereby fictionalizes the reader.[12] The problem of who it is that wields ultimate authority over the text is not easily solved and is one that has troubled contemporary critical theory. It is no simple feat to locate meaning in a literary text, and more difficult yet is the chore of assigning responsibility. Hartman eloquently cautions that, difficult as it is to pinpoint intent, the authorial voice cannot be disregarded: «though a text is discontinuously woven of many strands or codes, there is magic in the web. The sense of an informing spirit, however limited or conditioned, or outwitting those limits and conditions, is what holds us. To exorcise that spirit is to make the web inefficacious» («The Fate of Reading», p. 254).

It is not my aim to exorcise the spirit of author-ity, but that the act of reading presupposes this power structure is not tantamount to a confession of exclusive dependency on the author for the reader's appropriation of the text. The text in its words contains the code that allows the reader to seize its meaning, but the text's meaning can materialize only in the reading of it. While a code presupposes an encoder who in establishing his semantic system had a particular message in mind, the literary text also posits the assumption of a multiplicity of decoders who decipher the text according to their private perceptions. In the polarity of critical postures whose opposition Hirsch and Holland represent, I incline towards Holland. I would not go so far as to espouse unflinchingly the position that Hirsch labels as «semantic autonomism», namely, that the meaning of the literary text is independent of authorial will, but I do subscribe to the notion of a diversity of textual meanings rather than to Hirsch's insistence on one meaning that is uniquely valid. In so doing I confess that in the end even the critic's choice is subjectively conditioned so as to lead him or her to embrace one rather than another epistemological path. But that circumstantial subjectivity preys on every critic without excep-

---

[12] See LOWRIE NELSON, Jr., «The Fictive Reader and Literary Self-Consciousness», in Peter Demetz, Thomas Greene, and Lowrie Nelson, Jr., eds., *The Disciplines of Criticism* (New Haven: Yale Univ. Press, 1968), pp. 173-91. Cf. WALTER J. ONG, «The Writer's Audience Is Always a Fiction», *PMLA*, XC (1975), 9-21: «writing is itself an indirection. Direct communication by script is impossible. [...] For man lives largely by indirection, and only beneath the indirections that sustain him is his true nature to be found. Writing, alone, however, will never bring us truly beneath to the actuality» (p. 20).

tion, and so it is rankly dangerous to label another critic's interpretation as «a dangerously subjective kind of critical attitude».[13] We may do well to pause for a series of questions. In reading a novel by Galdós, are we reading Galdós and his time, or are we reading a particular fictional text? Are we trying to get back to what Galdós said, or are we absorbing what the text says? Are we listening to a hidden voice, or are we decoding the signs on a page? *Must* we sit in awe of the hand that wielded the pen? Can our awe not fasten on the richness of the word? And can the word not carry its own authority? Is a reading that purportedly reaches the author's intentions more privileged than any other? *Is* there such a thing as a privileged reading? A couple of verses by Blake that Holland quotes (p. ix) illustrate the dilemma aptly:

> Both read the Bible day and night,
> But thou read'st black where I read white.

THE CONTEXT OF THE TEXT

The very first sentence of *Fortunata y Jacinta* posits a game, a game of hide-and-seek, of now-you-see-me-now-you-don't. It establishes that the narrator, as friend of the characters, is not the author, but a creature within the framework of the fiction: unnamed but existent, distant but involved, limited but all-knowing.[14] The game continues as, a few sentences farther on, the narrator-turned-copyist says, tongue-in-Galdós's-cheek, that he will suppress some of the data so as not to prolong this account, which turns out to be Galdós's longest novel. As the reader ploughs on, consumed by the anecdote and by the characters that populate this world, it is all too easy for him to forget that the narrative was launched in this spirit of game-playing in which the fiction construed as real flaunts its fictionality all the while that its reality is certified. When a novel is read in this light, the historical context that exists beyond the text is

---

[13] As Carlos Blanco labeled Gilman's mythic interpretation of Fortunata («On 'The Birth of Fortunata'», *Anales Galdosianos,* III [1968], 13).

[14] JOSÉ F. MONTESINOS's unconsidered assumption that the first-person narrator is Galdós invites refutation (*Galdós,* II [Madrid: Castalia, 1968], 207). JAMES WHISTON, in «Language and Situation in Part I of *Fortunata y Jacinta*», *Anales Galdosianos,* VII (1972), 79, speaks more judiciously of a «non-omniscient narrator [who] is himself a character», but he does not mention the oscillation between omniscience and non-omniscience. GEOFFREY RIBBANS also broaches the problem in his critical guide to *Fortunata y Jacinta* (London: Grant and Cutler, 1977), pp. 37-42. ANTONIO SÁNCHEZ BARBUDO, «El estilo y la técnica de Galdós», *Estudios sobre Galdós, Unamuno y Machado,* 2nd ed. (Madrid: Guadarrama, 1968), pp. 21-45, points out that Galdós, in a fashion peculiar to his novelistic way, immersed himself in the lowly world of his characters to such an extent that later writers accused him of «vulgaridad». What causes this impression is Galdós's manipulation of the narrator, who, as Sánchez Barbudo observes, is a man, a jocular one at that, who narrates from the inside.

momentarily dislodged by structures and patterns within the novel that govern its reading. The text becomes its own context.

For my reading of the Feijoo-Fortunata relationship that I shall ultimately propose, it is important to begin by extracting from the novel the vacillating levels of narrative point of view, which some commentators have already discerned, both in *Fortunata y Jacinta* and in other Galdós works.[15] The rules of Galdós's game prescribe flux and reflux between omniscience and eye-witness observation to mediate the shuttling between the consciousness of fiction and the illusion of reality. Galdós belongs to that sophisticated strain of artists who, as Scholes and Kellogg put it, «continually strive to achieve the impossible — to have their empirical bread and to eat their fictional cake too».[16] While in the first paragraph of *Fortunata y Jacinta* the narrator is inhibited by the finiteness of his own existence, the novel's second paragraph already smacks of reporting by an all-knowing scribe enthroned above the action. Yet in the sixth paragraph that voice, assuming the first person, connects his acquaintance with Juanito Santa Cruz to a specific place and to a time whose specificity he has forgotten and therefore has to reconstruct with jogs to his memory. Two paragraphs later, when he reports that everyone calls the young man «Juanito», he ponders the reason for the diminutive but confesses: «Esto sí que no lo sé» (I, i, 1; 12).[17] However, once into the second section of Chapter I, the narrator dispenses information to which as mere

[15] STEPHEN GILMAN's «Narrative Presentation in 'Fortunata y Jacinta'», *Revista Hispánica Moderna*, XXXIV (1968), 288-301, does not examine the question of narrative point of view; he is concerned, rather, with the temporal status of the narrative recital that turns «then» into «now». MARIANO BAQUERO GOYANES, «Perspectivismo irónico en Galdós», *Cuadernos Hispanoamericanos*, no. 250-52 (1970-71), 143-60, and FRANCISCO AYALA, «Los narradores en las novelas de 'Torquemada'», *ibid.*, pp. 374-81, do discuss narrative posture, though both arrive at limited conclusions. Ayala also offers random but suggestive thoughts in «Galdós entre el lector y los personajes», *Anales Galdosianos*, V (1970), 5-13. KAY ENGLER, in an article directly pertinent to our subject, «Notes on the Narrative Structure of *Fortunata y Jacinta*», *Symposium*, XXIV (1970), 111-27, studies what she calls Galdós's «instability of vision». See also her book, *The Structure of Realism: The Novelas contemporáneas of Benito Pérez Galdós* (Chapel Hill: North Carolina Studies in the Romance Languages and Literatures, 1977). Two important theoretical considerations of narrative perspectivism, BOOTH's *The Rhetoric of Fiction* and NORMAN FRIEDMAN, «Point of View in Fiction: The Development of a Critical Concept», *PMLA*, LXX (1955), 1160-84, serve as starting points both for ENGLER and GERMÁN GULLÓN, *El narrador en la novela [española] del siglo XIX* (Madrid: Taurus, 1976), whose chapters on Galdós are of special interest.

[16] For a valuable discussion, in historical perspective, of the authority of the first-person versus the third-person narrator, see ROBERT SCHOLES and ROBERT KELLOGG, *The Nature of Narrative* (New York: Oxford, 1966), pp. 243 ff.

[17] References to *Fortunata y Jacinta* are to part, chapter, and section; the page indications after the semi-colon are taken from the first edition: Madrid: La Guirnalda, 1887. Each of the four volumes of this edition is paginated separately. I have modernized some punctuation and accentuation in accordance with recent editions.

observer he could not possibly have had access. He spends many pages on background details about the Santa Cruz and Arnaiz families that no casual bystander could have possessed and which would have had to be imparted to a younger intimate of theirs in exactly the same way that the narrator enlightens us. Not only data are provided, but also personal reactions from the characters' vantage points and with their private psychic vocabulary. Then suddenly (I, ii, 4; 50), the narrator says in reference to Baldomero and Barbarita: «Les conocí en 1870.» That is, he made his acquaintance with them, supposedly, when Baldomero was sixty years old and Barbarita fifty-two. The physical description of the pair into which he then launches corresponds appropriately to the observer's perspectives and capacities at that point in space and time. (We are dealing with an observer acute enough to notice whether or not Barbarita was wearing a corset.) But it includes the following sentence: «Su cabello se había puesto ya enteramente blanco, lo cual la favorecía más que cuando lo tenía entrecano.» If the narrator met Barbarita at a time when her hair was «enteramente blanco», he could not know how she looked with it «entrecano». That level of miraculous insight also allows him to go into thoughts on child rearing that Baldomero had some twenty years before 1870. The «now-I-know-it-now-I-don't» game continues in reference to Estupiñá. On the one hand, the narrator reports: «En 1871 conocí a este hombre» (I, iii, 1; 78). On the other hand, he deposes reams of historical and psychological evidence that no one meeting Estupiñá at the age of sixty-eight could have husbanded. How, for example, could that narrator who met him in 1871 know in detail what was done and said in Estupiñá's fabric shop decades earlier? The narrative instability dissolves at times into pure mischief, as when on the occasion of Estupiñá's visit to the ailing Juanito the narrator reports: «le contaba mil cosas divertidas, que siento no poder reproducir aquí» (I, viii, 5; 284), or when, speaking of José Izquierdo, the narrator appropriates his character's linguistic quirks: «De una manera y otra, casado y soltero, trabajando por su cuenta y por la ajena, siempre mal, siempre mal, ¡hostia!» (I, ix, 6; 330).

Some of those critics who have commented on the multitiered operation of Galdós's narrator have remarked that the narrative presence diminishes in the later stages of the text. While that observation is statistically accurate, the juggling of narrative levels never disappears from the novel.[18]

---

[18] It is hard to resist citing the following case late in the novel where the narrator, in a self-conjuring third-person reference, is still at his most playful: «A las doce de un hermoso día de octubre, D. Manuel Moreno-Isla regresaba a su casa, de vuelta de un paseíto por *Hide Park* [sic]... digo, por el Retiro. Responde la equivocación del narrador al *quid pro quo* del personaje, porque Moreno, en las perturbaciones superficiales que por aquel entonces tenía su espíritu, solía confundir las impresiones positivas con los recuerdos» (IV, ii, 1; 104).

Early in Part III, for instance, the narrator says of a participant in a «tertulia»: «No sé cómo se llamaba el viejo catarroso, porque todos allí le nombraban *Pater;* hasta el mozo que le servía dábale este apodo» (III, i, 4; 32). Often the reader identifies the narrator with the creator who christens his characters, and the reader grants him that right. At other times, as in this case, the narrator is distinct from the creator; he is a simple beholder who cannot learn a character's name if someone does not mention it. Curiously in this instance the narrator is not ostensibly a member of that particular «tertulia», for he dialogues with us rather than with the patrons, yet he has to be present in the café, regularly and within earshot of the group, to be able to make that statement. The reader registers the impression of a dual existence in the text: one being who has invented that scene fictively; another who has recreated it historically.[19] Emile Benveniste explains that a narrative «I» and «you» denote a presence, while the third person signals an absence.[20] Galdós's habits of narration produce a constant alternation between presence and absence. What in a flesh-and-blood creature is the illness of schizophrenia, in an immortal fiction is a constitutional gift of multiplex clairvoyance. There is no greater testimony to this meaningful split than the last sentence of the novel, where Maxi, both human being in this world and narrator of his cause, speaks of himself in the third person.

The sequence of four sentences that records Juanito's reaction to his mother's suggestion of a marriage to Jacinta illustrates to perfection the almost simultaneous projection of a narrator who functions pluralistically.

> Ya dije que el Delfín prometió pensarlo; mas esto significaba sin duda la necesidad que todos sentimos de no aparecer sin voluntad propia en los casos graves; en otros términos, su amor propio, que le gobernaba más que la conciencia, le exigía, ya que no una elección libre, el simulacro de ella. Por eso Juanito no sólo lo decía, sino que hacía como que pensaba, yéndose a pasear solo por aquellos peñascales, y se engañaba a sí mismo diciéndose: «¡qué pensativo estoy!» Porque estas cosas son muy serias, ¡vaya! y hay que revolverlas mucho en el magín. Lo que hacía el muy farsante era saborear de antemano lo que se le aproximaba [...] (I, iv, 2; 113)

The first sentence already has the narrator at three levels, marked by three separate clauses. 1) The narrator/historian openly enters as manip-

---

[19] Occasional sections of *Fortunata y Jacinta* are so removed narratively from the world of fiction to which they pertain that that pertinence is lost, and they read like essays. One case in point is the description of the custom of the «tertulia» (III, i, 3). Here no sense of game prevails, no illusion of multivalence or ambiguity, no play of levels. The narrator, easily identified with the author, discourses, from the posture of his personal opinions, on the situation at hand. The third-person references in these sections abstract the narrative context. Discourse gives way to history.

[20] *Problems in General Linguistics,* trans. Mary E. Meek (Coral Gables: Univ. of Miami Press, 1971), Ch. 19.

ulator of the account («Ya dije»). 2) The narrator/observer confesses his limitations as recorder of observable phenomena, beyond which everything else is conjecture («sin duda»). 3) The omniscient narrator reveals the psyche's inner motives not as one who concludes from the observable, but as one who is privileged to know all («su amor propio [...] le gobernaba más que la conciencia»). 4) In the second sentence all narrative limitations are abandoned as omniscience reigns supreme. The narrator is able not only to reclaim the character's thoughts; he actually knows the character better than the character knows himself («se engañaba a sí mismo»). 5) That supremacy is followed up quite logically in the third sentence with a shift in point of view that identifies character and narrator in indirect free discourse. 6) Finally, taking advantage of his sundry roles, the narrator passes judgment on the character («el muy farsante»).[21]

The omniscient narrator who sits at the creator's level of cognition and prescience can report thoughts, interpret glances, forecast actions, distinguish hidden meanings behind spoken phrases. How deeply and fully the narrator of *Fortunata y Jacinta* knows the characters is reflected in a sentence like «En el alma de Jacinta, no obstante, las alegrías no excluían un cierto miedo, que a veces era terror» (I, v, 1; 121). Yet that same narrator will quit the creative divinity's platform and sidle up to a character in order to extract information at the human level of confidant: «Me ha contado Jacinta que una noche llegó a tal grado su irritación por causa de los celos [...]» (III, ii, 1; 58). Or he may adopt the even less privileged posture of forgetful reporter: «Creo que fue el día de la Concepción cuando Rubín salió de su cuarto con un cuchillo en la mano detrás de Papitos, diciendo que la había de matar» (IV, iii, 5; 192).[22]

The reader who refuses to accept as a game the novel's shifting stances will reach the inevitable judgment that Galdós is guilty of inconsistency and carelessness. Such a reaction is unfortunate, for it misses the thrust of the game, which is the game of fiction itself. The invitation to the game has two stages. First, since *Fortunata y Jacinta* is not a novel with multiple narrators, as is *Wuthering Heights,* for example, but rather a novel with a single narrator who operates at multiple levels, the reader is drawn into a consciousness of the distinction between creator and narrator, or, as Lowrie Nelson defines the author's double role (p. 190),

---

[21] That habit of taking sides openly and of sitting in moral judgment is perhaps the most surprising of the various narrative postures and the one most vulnerable to censure. Among the more blatant instances is the following: «Hacía mal Barbarita, pero muy mal, en burlarse de la manía de su hija. ¡Como si ella no tuviera también su manía, y buena!» (I, vi, 5; 203).

[22] What LOWRIE NELSON says of *The Brothers Karamazov* applies also to Galdós's technique: «The first-person witness, then, is a latent resource whose usefulness is apparent and whose inconsistent presence is attenuated by the overwhelmingly vivid presentation of the omniscient narrator» (p. 180).

between contriver and communicator.[23] A fiction, the reader is admonished, has to be invented and it has to be told. The steps may be simultaneous or contiguous, but they are not the same. One can say that Galdós invented for the telling of his tale an omniscient narrator who in turn invents for himself the occasional role of eye-witness subnarrator. The omniscient narrator has recourse to his eye-witness subself whenever he wishes to shift to an illusion of a certain sort. And so he is perceived as a mummer in two guises, the one boundless, the other limiting. The reader whom the narrative engages in its shiftiness is brought to an awareness, not of the veracity of the account, but of the mechanism adduced to effect the illusion of verisimilitude, hence of its falseness. In other words, the result of the narrator's game at its various levels is to remind the reader that the novelist does not reproduce reality, but rather he creates it. If reality is one text and the novel another, then at best fiction is the rewriting of another text. The artist is caught between *Dichtung* and *Wahrheit*, but truth in art is always fable.

Once the creative act has been enunciated and implanted in the reader's consciousness, the narrative instability performs a second self-revealing function: the display of fiction as a volitional act of writing. Having established his reportorial presence in the opening lines of the novel, that narrator takes full control at the end of the second chapter in the first open demonstration (except for a parenthetical interjection regarding Estupiñá) of his power over the narrative: «Pero al llegar aquí, me veo precisado a cortar esta hebra, y paso a referir ciertas cosas que han de preceder a la boda de Jacinta» (I, ii, 6; 75).[24] If one individual had not imagined this story, it would not exist; neither would it exist if another had not deigned to tell it. The passive observer/recorder of events is also the almighty master of their presentation. He holds sway not over the creations but over their textuality, and he exercises that authority readily. At the very moment that he is creating Jacinta from the angle of an onlooker documenting her physical traits, her manner, her dress, he injects a frank reminder of his manipulative control over both narrative and reader: «Luego veremos» (I, iv, 2; 116-17). As (imag-

---

[23] Grappling with this problem in perceptive fashion, PETER A. BLY, in «The Use of Distance in Galdós's 'La de Bringas'», *Modern Language Review*, LXIX (1974), 87-99, points out that the author, not in any autobiographical sense, assumes a dual existence as narrator and actor (p. 94). Bly properly concludes that if Galdós is speaking here at all, it is through a literary persona.

[24] Other instances of this power: «Vamos ahora a otra cosa» (I, vi, 1; 180); «Dejemos sueltos estos cabos para tomarlos más adelante» (I, vi, 2; 185); Doña Lupe «bien merece toda la atención que le voy a consagrar más adelante» (II, i, 1; 9); «Volvió Jacinta al comedor. Si cumplió o no el encargo de Guillermina, lo veremos a su tiempo» (III, ii, 4; 94-95); «Conviene apuntar, antes de pasar adelante [...]» (IV, iii, 8; 216); «Algo más cotorrearon, pero no hace al caso» (IV, v, 3; 261).

ined) events become words to be preserved as a (fictional) record, the narrator assumes command of narrative time, hence of historical time within the fiction. Succession, order, logic or rupture, digression, concurrence are all determined by him. The reader's inevitably linear progress through the book is kept from corresponding to the diachronic progress of events in historical time by this intrusive manipulator. What the reader is drawn to realize is that this trickster cannot interfere with the flow of events; he has jurisdiction only over the word, that is, over the *reporting* of events. Each time that such a narrative shift or interruption takes place, the reader is reminded of the nature of the narrative object as a construct of words artificially manufactured and artfully deployed in the illusionist game.

The following passage from the Micaelas scenes permits a fitting synthesis of the effects of Galdós's narrative craft:

> Es cosa muy cargante para el historiador verse obligado a hacer mención de muchos pormenores y circunstancias enteramente pueriles, y que más bien han de excitar el desdén que la curiosidad del que lee, pues aunque luego resulte que estas nimiedades tienen su engranaje efectivo en la máquina de los acontecimientos, no por esto parecen dignas de que se las traiga a cuento en una relación verídica y grave. Ved, pues, por qué pienso que se han de reír los que lean aquí ahora que Sor Marcela tenía miedo a los ratones [...] (II, vi, 8; 306)

To begin with, the narrator is vested with the properties of a historian. Since he is an impartial investigator and reporter, it is presumably no untoward exaggeration or pretense to speak of this account as «una relación verídica». Yet the reader of the novel knows full well that this is pretense at an absence of pretense, and the narrator acknowledges that subterfuge in the same breath with which he claims historicity. He announces that the object before us is a book, and he makes explicit the presence of an implied reader. The here and now of the reading act is literally flashed onto the page. The written document takes precedence over its factual propellants, and the wording suggests invention as much as reporting. Returning to Benveniste's distinction: this narrative is not history but discourse. Accordingly, this historian of the created event, unlike the historian who is a social scientist, is free to exercise his power over the narrative, which he does here precisely at the moment when he purports to be enslaved by an insignificant detail. The truth is that this historian is not burdened by any obligation to events that existed before him, and the account is not nearly so «grave» as it claims. Unlike the «serious» historian, this one can luxuriate in the game of twitting his reader and the narrative itself. The lighthearted pair of sentences is a revelation on that narrator's part of his self-consciousness as manipulator of a complicated «máquina de acontecimientos».

51

The reader whose attention the text, with its tactics of narrative zig-zagging, has fixed on the act of narrating willy-nilly grasps many sections of the novel as exposés of the fictive process. Such a reading, without excluding other contexts, converts the identity of the text into its context. If, however, that ploy is regarded as too subtle a beckoning into the open arms of fiction to justify a reading that is self-referential at the same time as it is referential, then one can adduce as further and direct evidence several extraordinary statements in *Fortunata y Jacinta* that are flagrant proclamations of its constitution as a novel.[25]

When Juanito goes to pay his crucial call on the ailing Estupiñá in his house on the Plaza Mayor, the narrator makes the following comment: «Y sale a relucir aquí la visita del Delfín al anciano servidor y amigo de su casa, porque si Juanito Santa Cruz no hubiera hecho aquella visita, esta historia no se habría escrito. Se hubiera escrito otra, eso sí, porque por doquiera que el hombre vaya lleva consigo su novela; pero ésta no» (I, iii, 3; 96). This astonishing declaration, along with some of the others in this vein, has not escaped the critics' notice,[26] but its most remarkable dimension apparently has: the play of the fiction against itself, the wag-gish ostentation of reality that turns the camouflage of fictionality into fictional self-proclamation. The metafictional structure conjures Juanito's visit to No. 11 Cava de San Miguel as a real-life event that results in the telling of a story, a fictional account designated as «novel». But Juanito's subsequent active participation in that novel would appear to place him both inside and outside the fiction. Actually, the declaration of Juanito as a fictional character in the novel of Fortunata affirms his existence prior to their initial encounter as a fiction garbed as reality. The reader recognizes that while Juanito's reality outside the fiction is ironically cast in these two sentences, the narration's self-proclamation as fiction is unguarded and straight-forward. The act of writing is unfurled like a banner in the wind. And writing is equated with creation: it is the raw material all about us molded into substance. In the end, the statement, rather than making fiction seem real, fictionalizes life. The pretense at history confesses to be story; not an occurrence in time, but writing, language in space. History is replaced by the illusion of history as the text adroitly pinches the reader into awareness that the object in his hand is a novel.

In a stroke of perfect symmetry, the self-reflexive statement that pre-

---

[25] AGNES M. GULLÓN's statement that *Fortunata y Jacinta* is «a novel free of literary self-consciousness» is at first unsettling («The Bird Motif and the Intro-ductory Motif: Structure in *Fortunata y Jacinta*», *Anales Galdosianos*, IX [1974], 52). But one reads on with relief, for by the next page she has proved the op-posite.
[26] E.g., STEPHEN GILMAN, «The Birth of Fortunata», *Anales Galdosianos*, I (1966), 76.

cedes and announces Fortunata's entry into the novel is balanced by a similar one immediately after her exit. The scene is the funeral procession:

> En el largo trayecto de la Cava al cementerio, que era uno de los del Sur, Segismundo contó al buen Ponce todo lo que sabía de la historia de Fortunata, que no era poco, sin omitir lo último, que era sin duda lo mejor; a lo que dijo el eximio sentenciador de obras literarias que había allí elementos para un drama o novela, aunque, a su parecer, el tejido artístico no resultaría vistoso sino introduciendo ciertas urdimbres de todo punto necesarias para que la vulgaridad de la vida pudiese convertirse en materia estética. No toleraba él que la vida se llevase al arte tal como es, sino aderezada, sazonada con olorosas especias y después puesta al fuego hasta que cueza bien. (IV, vi, 16; 428-29)

Ironies notwithstanding, the self-revelation could not be more unabashed. Fortunata is recreated narratively after her death as the character is recreated in each reading. History again lives on in its transformed state as story, and life necessarily suffers a conversion in its transposition into esthetic matter. The process here described and debated is the process that has been undertaken and is about to be completed. The text is what it is: would-be life embellished, vulgarity turned showpiece in the magic of creation.

The novel inside the self-revealing frame finds opportunities to unfold itself as such, as when Guillermina says to Jacinta: «Si empezamos a hacer disparates y a portarnos como dos intrigantas que se meten donde no las llaman, mereceremos que nos tome Ido por tipos de sus novelas» (IV, vi, 10; 377). Statements like Guillermina's, which ostensibly stamp her with reality by registering her self-awareness as an entity outside the realm of fiction, ironically fan the reader's apprehension of the character's fictionality.

A fundamental mirroring agent in *Fortunata y Jacinta* is Ido del Sagrario himself, the writer of pulp novels. Ido has received so much critical attention that there is no need to review his function in *Fortunata y Jacinta;* but from the metanovelistic perspective, the conclusion at which Gullón arrives bears some correction. He writes: «Como siempre, la virtud de la duplicación consiste en hacernos sentir que lo inventado ocurre en otro plano; que lo imaginado está en la ficción discurrida por Ido, mientras los acontecimientos descritos por el narrador son vida, pura y simple. Conscientes de esta duplicidad reconocemos en el narrador y en los personajes de quienes habla, seres de nuestra especie; los imaginarios quedan más al fondo y están tejidos de otra fibra».[27] Gullón is of course right in his perception of a particular illusion that is created, but he perhaps enters too eagerly into the game of the text at its own level. A

---

[27] RICARDO GULLÓN, *Técnicas de Galdós* (Madrid: Taurus, 1970), pp. 199-200. Gullón's unequivocal assertion that Feijoo fails in the lesson he prepares for Fortunata should also be read with caution (pp. 157-59).

more distant view lets us recognize the game, and the recognition, which Gullón himself displays but then purposely denies in his approximation to the text, actually propels us in the opposite direction: an awareness of fiction's bag of tricks and of their deployment in this highly tricky fiction.[28] By the same token, one might well ask, playing Galdós's game: do the characters in *Fortunata y Jacinta* live in the historical circumstance of Valera, Camús, Mendizábal, and María Cristina; or are Valera, María Cristina, and the others characters in the fictional circumstance of this novel? When the narrator says defensively, «Como todo esto que cuento se refiere al año 74, natural es que en el café se hablara principalmente de la guerra civil» (III, i, 3; 22), the text evokes the historical context of the narrative action and appears to be history recounted by one who is living it. The technique, however, allows two approaches: 1) the fictional creatures are living in a real historical circumstance and therefore are —or seem— real; 2) the historical circumstance is replanted into a fictional context and therefore becomes itself part of that fiction. The reader knows that imagined beings cannot take on carnal historical substance (Don Romualdo notwithstanding), but only the illusion of historicity. On the other hand, the historical can readily become the stuff of fiction, at which point it no longer is history and cannot be treated as such. In *Fortunata y Jacinta* a group of café patrons talking about Sagasta is a group of characters talking about a character named Sagasta. What the narrator says of Juan Pablo's girl friend Refugio —a startling commentary when one stops to reflect on it— possibly applies to all: «personaje de historia, aunque no histórico» (III, iv, 8; 186).

THE TEXT WITHIN THE TEXT

The fourth chapter of Part III, «Un curso de filosofía práctica», like any other part of *Fortunata y Jacinta* and like the novel as a whole, is an

---

[28] GULLÓN's view ratifies GUSTAVO CORREA's in *Realidad, ficción y símbolo en las novelas de Pérez Galdós* (Bogotá: Instituto Caro y Cuervo, 1967). For Correa, whom Gullón cites, the contrast between fictional and real worlds in *Fortunata y Jacinta* accentuates the novel's sense of history. The idealistic nature of Ido's fiction, he says, gives Galdós's fiction its stamp of authenticity. Correa focuses, not unjustifiably, on the differing timbres of the outer and inner fictions and draws his conclusions from the contrast between them rather than descrying the reflexive process and its consequence of fictional self-revelation (pp. 137-38). In setting Ido's fictions against Galdós's purported «realities», he has simply unveiled a distinction between realistic and non-realistic fictions. He has not uncovered two worlds, one of fiction, the other of reality, because, sitting close by Galdós's side, he has not pondered the fact that in a fiction-within-a-fiction *all* is a fiction. The inner fiction, through its specular function, while appearing to invest the outer fiction with reality, actually corroborates its fictionality. In his comment on the paragraph in the funeral scene, Correa comes closer to recognizing this fact (pp. 142-44).

agglomerate of possible readings. It is certainly the portrait of a decadent society; and it is a picture of Madrid at that time: social classes, politics, language, customs, dress. In this regard it is a structure that functions as a microcosm of the novel. The chapter may be viewed as a lesson on the values of bourgeois domesticity and order. At the same time, it is an examination of the tension between social principles and social formulas, between absolute and relative moral values. It is an ideological exposition on a variety of subjects, from the theater to marriage. It depicts the pathetic plight of woman in that society. It is a sketch of the waning days of a «progresista desengañado» (III, i, 1; 11). Not the least of its features is the development of what is perhaps the warmest human relationship in the entire novel. And of course, there is the temptation to read Feijoo as an autobiographical projection of Galdós.[29] I am prepared to reject none of these readings or others, even though their levels of significance vary and their juxtaposition reveals some, probably resolvable, incompatibilities. By the same token, the pluralistic posture before the text that I take for granted must embrace the likely reading of the reader who by this stage of the novel has been fully sensitized to its self-referential dimension. «Un curso de filosofía práctica» is a chapter in a novel, a text within another text. The chapter is the text that we shall analyze. Its context is the larger text, the book. That context suggests a reading of Feijoo's «curso» as an act of artistic creation. In other words, the story of the special affiliation between Feijoo and Fortunata is the portrayal of the creation of Fortunata by Feijoo.

Fortunata's relationship throughout the novel to those who cross her path is ready justification for such a reading of the Feijoo chapter. «Será siempre lo que quieran hacer de ella los que la traten», Feijoo says to Maxi (III, iv, 9; 196), and at the close Maxi summarizes the scheme that had imprisoned Fortunata: «Ahora que no vive, la contemplo libre de las transformaciones que el mundo y el contacto del mal le imprimían» (IV, vi, 16; 438).[30] Fortunata herself, on a walk through Madrid in her new status as an honorable married woman, considers the changes that others had wrought on her person:

[29] MICHAEL NIMETZ, among others, insists that Feijoo is a Galdosian self-portrait. See his *Humor in Galdós* (New Haven: Yale Univ. Press, 1968), pp. 85, 189, n. 5, 195. MONTESINOS is of the same opinion (II, 266).

[30] STEPHEN GILMAN, in «The Consciousness of Fortunata», *Anales Galdosianos*, V (1970), 57, speculating on Fortunata's absence from the early part of the novel, reasons that Galdós «sep[a]rated his heroine from her wretched biography and amplified her as a creature of the consciousness of the newly married couple. The unsuspecting reader at the end of Part I is now ready to know her in terms of her extraordinary attraction *for* and presence *in* a whole gallery of other minds: Maxi, doña Lupe, Mauricia, Feijoo, Segismundo Ballester». Fortunata's nature as a fiction and what Gilman considers her superior and liberated consciousness run parallel courses.

> Había nacido para menestrala; no le importaba trabajar *como el obispo*
> con tal de poseer lo que por suyo tenía. Pero alguien la sacó de aquel su
> primer molde para lanzarla a vida distinta; después la trajeron y la llevaron
> diferentes manos. Y por fin, otras manos empeñáronse en convertirla en
> señora. La ponían en un convento para moldearla de nuevo, después la
> casaban... y tira y dale. Figurábase ser una muñeca viva, con la cual ju-
> gaba una entidad invisible, desconocida, y a la cual no sabía dar nombre.
> (II, vii, 5; 391)

At least a half dozen characters in the novel take an active part in
the fabrication of Fortunata, each according to his or her private creative
norms. The most avid among these is Maximiliano, who gives title to the
chapter, «Afanes y contratiempos de un redentor». Here Maxi initiates
his campaign to redeem, reform, reeducate, regenerate Fortunata. He out-
lines her first course in practical economics, proposes to uplift her morally,
to undertake her social salvation, to improve her personality, and to
imbue her with a cultural base, starting with her speech. «Sentíase Maximiliano poseedor de una fuerza redentora, hermana de las fuerzas creado-
ras de la Naturaleza» (II, ii, 2; 67). Maxi's Galatea, however, becomes
openly rebellious («¿Qué creías?, ¿que yo iba a sufrirte tus lecciones
y no te iba yo a dar las mías?» [IV, vi, 9; 366]) and teaches him the
impotency of his creative impulses. Finally he confesses that his Fortunata was a fabrication of his, an artistic construct emanating from his
imagination: «la veo, no como era, sino tal y como yo la soñaba y la
veía en mi alma; la veo adornada de los atributos más hermosos de la
divinidad» (IV, vi, 16; 438).

Maxi's brother Nicolás also takes it upon himself to exercise his «nue-
vas artes» of redemption (II, iv). He visits Fortunata in order to persuade
her to break with Maxi but at first contact apprehends her as matter for
him to mold. His pride and vanity operate in the terrain that befits his
priestly function, but the moral context of his inspiration notwithstanding, his designs correspond to an artist's visions of a triumphant creative
act. The priest and the artist alike have cause to gloat over the sublimity
of their role as reformers/re-formers of souls. Nicolás's participation in
the rebuilding of Fortunata is articulated through the verb «edificar»,
which he uses twice: the first time it is singled out for commentary and
the second time it is italicized (II, iv, 5; 198, 201). The dual meaning
that has developed from the Latin root should not be lost on the reader.
That Fortunata is to become spiritually superior, edified, is Nicolás's
intent; but Fortunata does not think and act according to an orthodox
moral code, and when «edificar» is divested of its moral connotations, it
simply points to Fortunata as an emerging structure, an object in the
process of being built.

Doña Lupe is next to join those in whom, one after the other, Fortunata awakens the creative spirit. From the moment that she comes face

to face with the beautiful raw material until long after Fortunata has abandoned her house, Lupe's authoritarian nature impels her to work on Fortunata as a sculptor or writer might, «desbastándola y puliéndola hasta tallarla en señora». The narrator steps in to explain that kindness is not the motive behind this impulse, as Maxi surmises: «en rigor provenía de esa imperiosa necesidad que sienten los humanos de ejercitar y poner en funciones toda facultad grande que poseen» (II, iv, 8; 225). It takes time for Doña Lupe to recognize that her creative faculties meet their match in Fortunata's stubborn constitution, in «esa independencia estúpida», as Lupe calls it (IV, iii, 3; 177).

Mauricia devises no such studied plans for Fortunata, but her influence on her friend —first as a diabolical voice in the Micaelas convent, then on her deathbed where she preaches remorse and forgiveness— is immediate and visible. Fortunata readily acknowledges her susceptibility to Mauricia's promptings. Guillermina, too, is one of the bevy of builders inside Galdós's novel that construct Fortunata as Galdós's novel as a whole constructs her. The sway that Guillermina holds over Fortunata is so intense that creator and creation literally fuse in Fortunata's perception of Guillermina. Even Segismundo Ballester assumes a position of superiority over Fortunata, gives her advice, proposes that he become her lover and guide, and later watches over her during her pregnancy and illness. Each of these characters steps in to fill the vacuum left by the narrator who in advancing remarkably little information about Fortunata has relegated to others the task of defining identity where apparent mystery prevails.

Only a second reading of the novel reveals the special importance, in this connection, of Juanito's words that Villalonga quotes back to him: «'El pueblo es la cantera. De él salen las grandes ideas y las grandes belle- zas. Viene luego la inteligencia, el arte, la mano de obra, saca el bloque, lo talla...'» (I, xi, 1; 464). Farther on, at one of those moments, rarer in Galdós's later novels, where the author's opinion is so blatantly stated that author and narrator become virtually indistinguishable, the comment is repeated almost verbatim: «el pueblo, en nuestras sociedades, conserva las ideas y los sentimientos elementales en su tosca plenitud, como la cantera contiene el mármol, materia de la forma. El pueblo posee las verdades grandes y en bloque, y a él acude la civilización conforme se le van gastando las menudas, de que vive» (III, vii, 3; 377). Whatever the other implications of these reduplicating comments,[31] they describe in all-embracing terms, and notably by way of a metaphor that invokes the artistic process, the task that each of Fortunata's fabricators undertakes.

[31] Among the more interesting interpretations is that of PETER A. BLY, «Fortunata and No. 11, Cava de San Miguel», *Hispanófila*, no. 59 (1977), 31-48.

Fortunata is the quarry, source of great beauty and ideas; Feijoo is the artist, intelligent and laboring. Of all her fashioners, he is the most significant. The importance of the segment of the novel in which he and Fortunata interact is announced earlier on by the sovereign narrator who decides how much space Feijoo is to receive: «Don Evaristo González Feijoo merece algo más que una mención en este relato» (III, i, 2; 12). This character in a tale, here declared as such, subsequently turns maker of a character. But the act of literary creation, like a course or educational program, requires preparation, and in two of the three chapters that precede the one in question, that groundwork is laid.[32]

The first textual link between Feijoo and Fortunata occurs in a café conversation that Feijoo holds with Juan Pablo: «Pero Rubín se puso a hablar con Feijoo, que le preguntaba por aquel inexplicable casamiento de su hermano con una mujer maleada» (III, i, 3; 28). (Feijoo had been mentioned twice earlier in Part II as a friend and former suitor of Doña Lupe.) The future inventor of the internal fiction here appears to be in a position of ignorance; that is, the «idea» has taken root but is unspecified, unadorned, undeveloped. With that brief glimpse the matter is dropped until three sections later, where the subject comes up again when a friend of Maxi's stumbles into the new café into which Feijoo and Juan Pablo had moved their «tertulia». The coincidence leads in natural fashion to a discussion of Maxi's wedding, and Juan Pablo comments that his sister-in-law is «una buena pieza» (III, i, 6; 45). Feijoo again asks how Juan Pablo could have consented to that marriage and adds his opinion that Fortunata is indeed «guapa». He reveals that he saw her the day before in her house, in fact had seen her several times. The flashing idea or observation is established as recurrent, has taken firmer hold, and has begun to crystallize in a minimal snatch of description. No interior creation is yet undertaken, and Fortunata is still offstage, so to speak. The outside narrator is in exclusive dominance over the inside creator's absorption of his raw material. At that juncture the potential interior creation is again broken off, with Feijoo saying: «Es largo de contar... dejémoslo para otra noche», and the outside narrator adding in a conjectural tone: «Era sin duda cosa delicada para dicha delante de testigos» (III, i, 6; 46). Here the potential inside narrator, better informed than the observing outside narrator, rejects that role so as to reserve for himself the role of creator. The word withheld now is an indication that the script stored away for later has been outlined. The reader, like Jacinta in Part I of the novel, has been made the victim of an ironic situation that stimulates his interest because an inside narrator has been contrived

---

[32] For a different but convincing justification of the leisurely introduction of Feijoo, see AGNES GULLÓN, «The Bird Motif», pp. 63-64.

and then silenced, temporarily it would seem. There are no other references to the subject in Chapter I.

Not until the third chapter, in fact, is the Feijoo-Fortunata connection again broached, this time more concretely as Juanito, arriving at Fortunata's house, meets Feijoo leaving it. The several visits that Feijoo had paid her are now specified as three, and Fortunata's respect for the old gentleman —«Es un señor muy bueno y muy fino» (III, iii, 1; 99)— as well as her lack of amorous interest in him are immediately communicated. With the space between Fortunata and Feijoo so narrowed, it is logical that a textual encounter between the two should now take place, as it does in the next section (III, iii, 2). While the linear chronology of events is rigorously maintained, Fortunata's initial ingress into Feijoo's life occurs twice. She first entered Feijoo's worldly existence when Juan Pablo introduced them on the street one day, as we learn later on (III, iv, 3; 135), and that led, as we already know, to a series of courtesy calls. That much is recounted as having happened, that is, it takes place outside the novel's stage-action. Fortunata's second initial entry into Feijoo's existence ensues also by chance, on the street near the Puerta del Sol, but it is a face-to-face encounter within the text and thus with Feijoo in his fictional existence. The transition from indirectly reported to directly witnessed event is emphasized in the second instance by the facts that Feijoo recognizes Fortunata even though her face is covered against the cold with her shawl and that their friendship is stamped as established, though on a formal basis. The reader cannot help noticing that Feijoo was introduced into the book earlier in order to be kept in reserve for the moment he was needed, which is now. Occasional reminders of his presence had maintained the reader alert to a likely function on his part in the novelistic structure. The nature of that function becomes clear at this point. Feijoo's concerned, paternal attitude towards Fortunata emerges as he tries to calm her in her incoherence and takes her home in a coach, reassuring her all the while. The narrator is extremely careful to portray Feijoo in the best possible light through epithets that display the narrator's own positive feelings towards him («el buen don Evaristo», «el simpático coronel retirado»), by uncovering the depths of Feijoo's distress from within him («Feijoo la siguió, afligidísimo de verla en tan lastimoso estado»), and by attributing to him solicitous words and actions, as befits the part he is to take. In the same instant Feijoo is struck for the first time with a sense of exaltation at Fortunata's beauty. The scene is set for his further visits and for the action of Chapter iv. For Feijoo, Fortunata passes from idea to incarnation. She is at first a seed planted in his consciousness by his powers of observation. For a time the idea brews and develops in his mind; he questions and observes further, both within himself and externally. Finally, in miraculous fashion, the chance observation, the idea, is displaced from remoteness to immediacy, it is wedded to inspiration, and the creative powers are kindled. The artist is ready to act and to bring his idea to life in his terms. The evidence that the text provides of an incipient extratextual relationship between Feijoo and Fortunata, followed by their contact within the text at the end of Chapter iii and then by the textual expansion of that association in Chapter iv traces a program of imaginative creation.

The initial conversation between Fortunata and Feijoo in Chapter iv contains the creator's declaration of intent: he plans to mold a new character: «yo me he propuesto sacarla a usted del terreno de la tontería y ponerla sólidamente sobre el terreno práctico» (III, iv, 1; 119).[33] The two terrains are, first, that of the character as amorphous material in need of shaping, and then that of the idea concretized as fiction. The paradox contained in this transition, as so often happens in Galdós, is that the created object is to be more concrete and palpable than its living prototype.[34] That fictional object is created in two stages, as Feijoo's proposal and the experience of the text up to this juncture insinuate: the character first penetrates the creator's imagination, and when the idea is translated into a word on a page, it materializes for the reader as an existent possibility; the character's ultimate materialization occurs with the close of the narrative, where the creative process of portrayal comes to an end and the idea as projected may or may not be realized, depending on whether control is affirmed or the illusion of autonomy is effected.[35] By that token, Feijoo's words are also an announcement of the possibility of failure or success on the part of the creator and of the options that the creator may exercise in the casting of illusion. Feijoo's statement of

[33] Evidently advised of the theory that repetition is the secret to education, Feijoo restates his creative scheme: «Yo te enseñaré a ser práctica, y cuando pruebes el ser práctica, te ha de parecer mentira que hayas hecho en tu vida tantísimas tonterías contrarias a la ley de la realidad» (III, iv, 3; 135). The juxtaposition of lie and reality in this formula cannot be overlooked. On the other hand, once fired by inspiration, the creator is consumed by his vision: «Mas no por esto desistió de llevar adelante un plan que había llegado a ser casi una manía, absorbiendo todos sus pensamientos» (III, iv, 7; 173); «Su proyecto llegó a dominarle de tal modo, que no sabía pensar en otra cosa, y de la mañana a la noche estaba dando vueltas al tema» (III, iv, 8; 182). The use of the word «tema» should not escape the reader.

[34] When dream first becomes one of this novel's important dimensions (significantly, in an artistic context: at the opera), the narrator assigns to dream, as to fiction, an extraordinary, magical creative capacity: «cayó la dama en sueño profundísimo, uno de esos sueños intensos y breves en que el cerebro finge la realidad con un relieve y un histrionismo admirables. La impresión que estos letargos dejan suele ser más honda que la que nos queda de muchos fenómenos externos y apreciados por los sentidos» (I, viii, 2; 251).

[35] That is why it is potentially misleading to speak of the «birth» of a literary character, as Gilman does (see n. 26). From a perspective inside the novel, where the character is a human being, he is born —enters the world— like anyone else in the particular circumstances described. From the reader's perspective, the character's birth is not his appearance in the novel, but the consummation of his creation, which is effected only when the character exits from the anecdote.

purpose unveils this portion of the novel as a fiction-within-a-fiction. Since in this case there is a projection towards the future rather than a retrospective view, as when Juanito summarizes for Jacinta his experiences with Fortunata, no structure of irony obtains, and the reader of one fiction is simultaneously the reader of the other. What Feijoo has in mind, the civilizing of the beautiful savage, here transliterated into the bourgeois circumstance, connects on a transcendental plane with a mythic structure. Literary invention is myth creation in the first place, and that harmonizes with the mythic overtones of Feijoo's intent. Finally, at the lowly level of Fortunata's condition, Feijoo's plan for his friend and mistress echoes the pattern, now fully bared, to which she has been subjected throughout the novel: an orphan from the «cuarto estado», Fortunata has no background of her own and is ever the creation of others. Feijoo wishes to inject into Fortunata a state of equilibrium. But if Fortunata is unfamiliar with that word, she is also unfamiliar with the state that it signifies. She displays her inner disharmony not only in the inconstant ways of her past, but in her perception of them in the present. From that vantage point she judges herself evil at one moment, clean and free of guilt the next. She resorts in fear to religion one day, and another day she goes about with an unruffled conscience. She is in this regard the child of caprice, a barometer of circumstance, and of course pliable matter for those who wish to cement her nature in accordance with their conceptions, needs, or desires. Rather than a text to be read, she is a text to be written; or perhaps more accurately, she is meant to be read as a text to be written. Juanito is referred to as the «maldito autor de sus desgracias» (III, iv, 3; 139), and if it is not Juan, then it is someone else who invents and forms her, as we have shown. Now it is Feijoo's turn. Of course, we know that behind Feijoo there is another intelligent and artistic hand constantly at work, shaping, developing, and determining Fortunata, but that knowledge does not dispel the illusion.

Feijoo, wise and enlightened revival of his eighteenth-century namesake, by virtue of his age, experience, and personality fits the role better than any other of Fortunata's authors. In fact, as Ribbans points out (p. 76), he is less developed than the other important secondary characters precisely because his exclusive role is to influence Fortunata. His sexual interest in her does not diminish his function as a figure with whom she can place her trust and her burdens. It is natural that he should be for her both a father-confessor («He visto mucho mundo —afirmó Feijoo con tolerancia de sacerdote hecho al confesonario—» [III, iv, 1; 121]) and a father substitute. As such, he dispenses consolation and advice and determines her next steps. The expression «Hija mía», with which he addresses Fortunata several times, takes on special significance for the reader when it is used to introduce precisely the paragraph where Feijoo decides to make her into his creation. She is to become, literally, a child of his.

A purely disinterested party he is not. On the contrary, he maps a course where a bargain is struck between creator and creation. He is giver of life, benefactor; but like any author, he receives his pleasure and his due from his creation.

With the very breath with which he issues it, Feijoo himself places his profession of his intended (re)creation of Fortunata into a literary framework. As happens often in Galdós, the theater is the preferred metaphor: «Eso de devolver dinero es un romanticismo impropio de estos tiempos. [...] Conque déjese usted de *rasgos* si no quiere que la silbe, porque esas simplezas no se ven ya más que en las comedias malas» (III, iv, 1; 119). Ironically, Feijoo's project itself has the overtones of a romantic gesture. But the point is that Fortunata in her identity as Feijoo's idea is saturated with literature, and literary she is to remain. In a curious inversion, the reader, who has just been told, «Look! These people are real because only real people go to the theater», is alerted through this technique to his own status as a reader of literature. The subject again is raised early in Feijoo's educational campaign when he queries Fortunata about her tastes in the theater (III, iv, 1; 124). The following observations can be made concerning their exchange: 1) Literature once more fosters literature and develops in its own context. 2) The game of the reality of characters who attend plays is again entertained. 3) The presence of the dramatic art, particularly in a dialogue, fans the reader's consciousness of his bearing witness to literature. 4) Feijoo and Fortunata have very different tastes in the theater, which demonstrates that artistic matter is refractory: to create Fortunata in his image will be no easy task for Feijoo. 5) There is ironic mirroring in the fact that the type of drama that moves Fortunata to tears and whose rhetoric Feijoo deplores might well describe the drama in which the characters of this fiction are enmeshed. That confusion of planes is suggestively punctuated by the elliptical sentence with which Feijoo brings this brief discussion to a close: «Para dramas, hija, los de la realidad...»[36]

Another conversion into literature of the literary characters involved in this chapter occurs when the two tell each other stories of their past (III, iv, 4; 145-47). When Feijoo recounts to a fascinated Fortunata his adventures in Cuba and elsewhere, he is twice referred to as «el narrador». And then: «Lo mismo hacía Fortunata cuando le tocaba a ella ser narradora, incitada por su protector a mostrar algún capítulo de la historia de su vida, que en corto tiempo ofrecía lances dignos de ser contados y aun escritos.» Again, several implications pertinent to our angle of view can be gleaned from this sentence. 1) It affirms the important principle,

---

[36] The theater's function in *Fortunata y Jacinta* is many-sided and complex. ROBERTO SÁNCHEZ studies one aspect in his *El teatro en la novela: Galdós y Clarín* (Madrid: Insula, 1974).

reiterated near the end of the work, that a novel lies within each one of us. 2) Everyone is shown to have a dual capacity: as narrator and as subject of a fiction. That is, the lived reality of a person is of a fettle to be made into fiction; and, conversely, every being has the capacity for creating/narrating a fiction. 3) If a life, like a book, is divided into chapters, the distinction between the two may not be superficially discernible. Also, Feijoo may be writing one more chapter in the life of Fortunata. 4) The final phrase invests the act of writing with special prestige and places on the writer a burden of responsibility for quality in the choice of his contents. 5) The sentence under scrutiny and the two that precede and follow it stress that both Feijoo's and Fortunata's «narrations» are true. The outside narrator steps in personally to give that assurance. The reaction of Fortunata then charges that truth with the air of fictionality: «Si eso se dice, no se cree... Y si lo escriben, pensarán que es fábula mal inventada.» Writing, with the higher stature and the permanence that accrue to it from the heralded word, is not so easily denied as speech is. On the other hand, the act of narration is shown to fictionalize fact. There is no way to untangle the contradictory notions that writing embodies supreme authority and that fiction is a written lie. This submersion in the morass of literature, however, should give pause to the reader as he speculates on the relationship between Feijoo and Fortunata.

In the realm of literature, the Word is king, and the self-reflexive text inevitably turns to review the key to its constitution. «Perdone usted si hablo mal. Soy muy ordinaria. Es mi ser natural», says Fortunata (III, iv, 1; 120); and later: «yo apenas sé leer y no le saco sentido a ningún libro...» (III, iv, 2; 129). Constantly self-effacing, displaying herself as devoid of the talents that the bourgeoisie prizes in its women —painting, embroidery, piano playing— Fortunata suggests that the conquest of the word might have elevated her in social status and made her other than she is. When Fortunata says over and over, whether in a semi-delirious or in a tranquil condition, «Yo quiero ser honrada», she has no grasp of the meaning of those words that echo the lesson of her earlier teacher/creator, Maxi. The phrase uttered from her perspective is empty and perverted in the eyes of the bourgeois society; measured by that group's hypocritical standards, it is just as vacuous and, quite naturally, incomprehensible to Fortunata. An uneducated creature like Fortunata who is baffled to start with by the complex ambiguity of language is doomed to remain unattuned to the subtleties with which society invests the word. When Fortunata's proclamation of her honor has assumed the tones of a litany, the text itself finally comments on it: «Lo de la honradez, que ella anhelaba ignorando el valor exacto de las palabras, no tenía sentido» (III, iv, 3; 138). But what is the exact value of these words, of any words? The reader at this point is forced to take notice of the nature of language and to relate it to social values. Of course words are meaningless; they must be imbued with meaning; for that reason they are artificial constructs. Fortunata cannot understand words in whose construction, because of her origins in a lower estate, she has not participated. She can be brought to that level (raised? lowered?) with the acquisition of a bourgeois veneer: «ya que no fuese honrada, al menos pareciéralo». Marriage can be the artifice that gives honor meaning; so can discretion.

The subtleties and ironies that language encases transcend and subvert its surface functions. Fortunata's linguistic deficiency is a siren call to those bent on her reeducation, but contradictory evidence puts into question the outcome of such a campaign. Her own conviction is that her level of linguistic accomplishment signals her essence. In that light, if past attempts to reshape her have failed, Feijoo is not certain to fare better. On the other hand, at least on one occasion she shows herself able to manipulate language and by extension is also capable of manipulating her aspiring creator. When Feijoo tells her that the first order of the day is that she become practical, she pretends not to know the word: «—Pues nos haremos *pléiticas* —dijo la señora de Rubín, ridiculizando la palabra para ridiculizar la idea» (III, iv, 1; 122). Deface the sign and you disparage its signification. This reductive tactic attacks, however gently, the word, the lesson it is designed to convey, and the individual who mouths it unceasingly, all in the very first session. Fortunata may not be quite so needy of reform as Feijoo believes and therefore may not be as malleable as he hopes. Whatever the likely result, the creation of Fortunata begins at the linguistic level, as the literary art demands. The reader, for his part, assesses the power of the word in the creation of a fiction. The fiction in this instance is multilateral. First, the word is basic to the fiction that Feijoo carves out of Fortunata. As she learns to verbalize new concepts, she becomes another, or that at least is the plan.[37] Secondly, the word is basic to the fiction that the decayed bourgeois society creates for itself and lives out. The humbug that characterizes this class is an elaborate construction that depends on the pliancy of language. Thirdly, the word is basic to the novel —the fiction— in the reader's hands. Unbeknownst to Fortunata, deluded fictional creature who believes herself real, the word, in fact, is what renders her superior: no matter what her mastery over language, language is master over her. As a literary being, she is created of language, and it is in a book that she acquires meaning.

---

[37] The creator puts words into his character's mouth: «Apréndete de memoria mis palabras, y repítelas todas las mañanas a renglón seguido del Padrenuestro. / Como un dómine que repite la declinación a sus discípulos, [...] iba incrustando en el caletre de su alumna estas palabras» (III, iv, 6; 167-68). A student learning a lesson, an actress absorbing her part, a creation in the becoming: that is Fortunata in this situation.

The recurrence of motifs dealing with literature is one feature of this chapter that a reading of it as a self-reflexive structure elicits. Another is the power that is attributed to the creative impulse, regardless of its ultimate achievements. Feijoo harps on his intention to make of Fortunata his personal creation from the inside out and expresses his confidence in his creative talents: «Y yo he de poder poco o le he de recortar a usted el corazón para que haya equilibrio. [...] ¡Oh! Se necesitan muchas lecciones [...] Usted no sabe de la misa la media. Parece que acaba de nacer, y que la han puesto de patitas en el mundo. [...] Yo le voy a enseñar a usted una cosa que no sabe. [...] Vivir [...] Conque prepararse, que empiezo mis lecciones» (III, iv, 1; 121-22). In his thoughts, Feijoo gives metaphoric expression to his sense of superiority as artistic creator. «Es un diamante en bruto esa mujer. Si hubiera caído en mis manos en vez de caer en las de ese simplín, ¡qué facetas, Dios mío, qué facetas le habría tallado yo!...» (III, iv, 2; 128).[38] Indeed, a polished literary creation is as many-faceted as a diamond. For its production, it requires an artisan like Feijoo, and he needs the convergence of the proper raw material, inspiration, and the right opportunity. In possession of these ingredients, Feijoo, as the writer of this script, has complete jurisdiction over the narrative events, which obey his pen: «Como lo que debe suceder sucede, y no hay bromas con la realidad, las cosas vinieron y ocurrieron conforme a los deseos de D. Evaristo González Feijoo. Bien sabía él que no podía ser de otro modo» (III, iv, 3; 134).

One of the early steps that the complicated design of a fiction requires is the tracing of an appropriate scenario for the action. Feijoo first lays down certain ground rules that determine Fortunata's movements, then situates her spatially in a section of Madrid that is new for Fortunata and new to the novel. One might say, playing the game according to its rules, that the setting is no longer Galdós's but Feijoo's. The more important change, though, is the developing personality of his creation. It is evident that Feijoo's views have their effect on Fortunata, for example after his disquisition on the morality of illicit love. With the plot sketched out in his mind and the narrative fully his, he maps her future life: there is to be a reconciliation between Maxi and Fortunata, and they are to

---

[38] This chapter persists in defining Fortunata as putty in the hands of others, the creation of those that chanced across her path. Feijoo twice says that had she fallen to him earlier, she would have been spared much ignominy and been different, «una configuración admirable». Nicolás, when it was his turn to fashion Fortunata, had expressed the same thought: «Ya tengo las manos en la masa... no es mala masa; pero hay que trabajarla a pulso...» (II, iv, 6; 206). Also Doña Lupe: «Sentía la señora de Jáuregui el goce inefable del escultor eminente a quien entregan un pedazo de cera y le dicen que modele lo mejor que sepa. Sus aptitudes educativas tenían ya materia blanda en quien emplearse» (II, vii, 1; 347). In other words, a character is its creator's handiwork and takes on distinct shapes according to its creator's ethos and talent.

live at Doña Lupe's. Feijoo's powers are such that the secondary characters in the story of Fortunata also become his puppets. A creator like
Doña Lupe's creator and therefore on an equal footing with him, he sees
through Doña Lupe's façade and into her motivations as easily as he unrid-
dles his own creation. That is why he can say to Fortunata (and the choice
of words is significant): «¡Ah!... leo en ella como leo en ti» (III, iv, 8;
183). Nicolás Rubín, when he initiated his re-formation of Fortunata, had
used similar phrasing: «lo que yo necesito ahora es leer en su interior» (II,
iv, 4; 191). And Fortunata's last admirer, the pharmacist Ballester, also
says to her: «Su cara de usted es para mí un libro, el más hermoso de los
libros. Leo en él todo lo que a usted le pasa» (IV, iii, 1; 160). Much in
the vein of Galdós's comment that his creatures always accompany him,
Feijoo gloats: «¡Oh!, entiendo bien a mi gente»; and the following boast
could well apply to both in their creative moments: «Conozco las calle-
juelas de la naturaleza humana mejor que los rincones de mi casa» (III,
iv, 8; 182). Similarly, that he hardly knows Maxi, he says, will be no
deterrent in swinging Maxi to his plan. When the plot he is weaving
goes well, Feijoo can claim with satisfaction: «En fin, chica, que esto
marcha» (III, iv, 8; 183). It is no wonder that Fortunata becomes filled
with admiration for his special gifts, and in the context of a self-referential
reading, her awed respect for him becomes a paean to the creative artist:
«¡Cuidado qué sabía el tal! Toda la ciencia del mundo la poseía al de-
dillo, y la naturaleza humana, *el aquel de la vida,* que para otros es tan
difícil de conocer, para él era como un catecismo que se sabe de memoria.
¡Qué hombre!» (III, iv, 7; 169-70).

The Pygmalion myth comes to mind, but unlike the Cypriot sculptor,
this artist first falls in love not with his creation, but with its raw
material, with the idea he has discovered rather than with what he has
made of it. (Maxi's earlier campaign fits the Pygmalion relationship more
directly.) After some time, however, the parallel becomes more apt: «Y
la verdad era que con aquella vida tranquila y sosegada, eminentemente
práctica, se iba poniendo [Fortunata] tan lucida de carnes, tan guapa y
hermosota que daba gloria verla» (III, iv, 4; 142). Since Feijoo is responsible for Fortunata's flowering and his love for his handiwork intensifies,
it is not surprising that the narrator should select and then call to our
attention with uncommon insistence an image that conjures the worship
of an art object: «Por la solitaria calle de las Aguas se comunicaba brevemente Feijoo con su ídolo. No me vuelvo atrás de lo que esta expresión
indica, pues el buen señor llegó a sentir por su protegida un amor entrañable, no todo compuesto de fiebre de amante, sino también de un
cierto cariño paternal, que cada día se determinaba más» (III, iv, 4;
144-45).

The above quotation, with its narrator recounting the creation of a

66

fiction by a fictional character, flaunts, as so many passages in this section do, the dual level of this fiction-within-a-fiction. That self-revelation as fiction intensifies as the consummation of Feijoo's enterprise draws nearer. A key scene is the conversation between Feijoo and Juan Pablo (III, iv, 7; 175-80). As he drafts an outline for reconciling Fortunata with Maxi, Feijoo, the artist ruminating his next pages, mentally composes the phrases he plans to use in approaching Juan Pablo about the matter. Dissatisfied, recognizing that his story is not consistent with the situation as he has developed it to this point, he looks for a way to recompose the lines. The very pressure to continue provides its own solution. In the ensuing exchange with Juan Pablo, Feijoo, now creator and narrator at once, parades his inventive gifts and, along with them, the process of fiction. Building on the reality of Fortunata's present condition and her relationship to him, he twists the facts to suit his new needs. A triple level of mirroring is produced: Feijoo creates a fiction within the fiction that he has been creating inside Galdós's narrator's fiction. For a moment, Juan Pablo, disbelieving Feijoo's tale, suspects the truth; but Feijoo, the adroit manipulator, converts that statement of truth into a fiction and returns his fiction to the status of truth. Or if not truth, then apparent truth, for the outside narrator, ostensibly confused himself, doffs his omniscience at this point and pretends to be unable to make a distinction: «Rubín creyó o aparentó creer [...]» The levels of fiction and truth and their dividing lines are in utter disarray here in a game whose delight rests with all those levels and in their confusion. The final round in this playful compilation of hoaxes is the narrator's ironic revelation of Juan Pablo's imposture. Juan Pablo had received money from Feijoo, and he knows, we are told, that one must always believe and agree with a benefactor: «Allá en su interior pensaría Rubín lo que quisiese; pero de dientes afuera se mantuvo en el papel que le correspondía.» So, we have Juan Pablo acting out a role, weaving his own fiction in response to Feijoo's fiction about his fiction-within-a-fiction.

The questions that remain concern the fate of Feijoo himself and of his creation. As Fortunata staged a dual entry into Feijoo's text, so does Feijoo leave the scene in two steps. The reader of Part III might well wonder why Galdós keeps Feijoo ailing for so long and might even suspect that Feijoo is simply to drop from the anecdote. But the timing of his death could not be more appropriate. Exactly a week after Fortunata's death, and in the same final section of the book, Feijoo is laid to rest in the same cemetery. Little narrative to-do is made of the event: two brief sentences: «Cuando salían del cementerio, entraba un entierro con bastante acompañamiento. Era el de D. Evaristo Feijoo» (IV, vi, 16; 436-37). As the creation passes into memory, so does the mortal creator, who cannot predecease his creation if that invention is to live its full novelistic cycle.

It is a necessary technicality that Feijoo, the man, who helped to invent Fortunata, must survive her at least briefly. Cervantes dies after Don Quijote, Flaubert after Emma Bovary, Galdós after Feijoo; Molly Bloom's textual existence reaches its final word before James Joyce utters his. This inevitable sequence has no bearing on the longevity of the fictional creation. The homage paid to the creative artist may be substantial, as Feijoo's impressive funeral cortege testifies, but the glory that accrues to the fiction that acquires life with every reading is even greater. Maxi and Ballester, the two who shed tears over the Fortunata that Feijoo helped to mold, pay no attention to his funeral. So unobtrusive, in fact, is the final demise of Feijoo that a critic as acute as Nimetz (p. 207) mistakenly believes him dead by this time. In the long run the fiction outlives its creator and allows the creator to live on in memory through the creation. To the extent that Feijoo is in the unusual category of a fictional creator of a fiction, he survives as a literary creation himself, but the creator of Fortunata disappears while she is privileged, or destined, to suffer immortality. The creative act presupposes the sacrifice of the creator to his creation. Like Ballester after Fortunata's burial, the reader «llevaba fresca en su mente la imagen de la que ya no era nada» (IV, vi, 16; 429), who never was any palpable thing. Her acquaintances among Madrid's society and Church who provide her with a first-class funeral cannot grant this creature of the «pueblo» their unhesitating final blessing. But can any reader-acquaintance of Fortunata's who has lived through her fictional fabrication deny her her rightful place among the angels? Can it escape any reader's notice that «la vulgaridad de la vida» has become «materia estética»? An angel, a fiction: both are pure and everlasting spirit.

So it is that while he dies later, Feijoo exits corporeally from Fortunata's existence well before his death. Fortunata's return to Maxi and Lupe is the final act of the script as he had composed it, and when the task according to his blueprint is accomplished, he can «die» in the sense that the creator gives way to his creation the moment that he writes «The End». «Todo acabó...», says Feijoo, and the paternal relationship so often mentioned is now reconfirmed in phrases that can be read as the projection of the fiction beyond its maker: «Fortunata, no soy para ti más que un padre... Aquel que te quiso como quiere el hombre a la mujer, no existe ya... Eres mi hija. Y no es que hagamos un papel aprendido, no; es que tú serás verdaderamente para mí, de aquí en adelante, como una hijita, y yo seré para ti un verdadero papaíto» (III, iv, 9; 198).

Fortunata frets (in indirect discourse) over a problem that is a logical one for a character conscious of herself as a fabrication: «¿Qué iba a ser de ella, privada de la dirección y consejo de tan excelente hombre?» (III, iv, 7; 169). What becomes of any literary creation once out of its creator's dominion? Does it then become the plaything of its readers' caprice? Has it been forever programmed by its inventor, or is there a possibility of options? Galdós's text raises these questions that inhere to fiction and perhaps have no answers.

From the moment the 69-year-old Feijoo's health begins to fail, he labors to assure Fortunata's existence beyond his disappearance. «La aventura del viejo Feijoo ha pasado a la historia...» (III, iv, 9; 197), he concludes; and indeed, his involvement in the creative act has produced a story to be read. The creator is responsible for implanting his creation on the path of a continuing life to be given it by future readers and interpreters. Exercising authorial control, he can place limits on the possible interpretations. He can put the brake on a reader's unbridled imagination. «Necesita mi niña un freno», says Feijoo (III, iv, 6; 164), and he casts her to evolve within prescribed parameters. He has no guarantees, though, because he can influence but not determine another's perceptions; and so, since fiction involves three parties, the complexion with which the creation emerges from the narration is not a measure of its subjection to its creator's full, authoritarian command.

The fact that this chapter is a text-within-a-text converts it into a metaphor for the relationship between the textual space and the space beyond the text. This internal structure permits the dramatic and concrete representation of the abstract and irresolvable ambiguities that a fictional text projects. On leaving Feijoo's tutelage, Fortunata acts out the fiction's potential for freeing itself from its creator. Actually, Feijoo foresees two possible endings for his story of Fortunata, and he provides a script for both. The one presupposes adjustment, conformity, fidelity: that is, allegiance to his norms. The other anticipates inconformity but decorously camouflaged: that is, a step towards rebellion but still under authorial suzerainty. A third possibility —inconformity engaged in without decorum, that is, full autonomy— does not fall within Feijoo's venue. But has Feijoo managed to hew his character physically and morally, spiritually and practically in such fail-safe manner that she will not seek her autonomy once he is done with her? The unexplained terror that the old man feels overtaking him on his way home in the last section of the chapter may well be a premonition of failure. The title of the chapter, «Un curso de filosofía práctica», already harbors a threat with its subversive paradox of the practical and the abstract. Unaccustomed to formal training, Fortunata is unlikely to take well to a pedagogical experiment of which she is the subject. She has already failed Juanito's and Maxi's «cursos», as Manolo and Irene had failed Máximo Manso's. One might even wonder if Feijoo was not misguided in his expectation of success when he was working against the innate characteristics of his material. Neither the text nor Fortunata ever allow us to forget that she is matter difficult to mold, most significantly in these early admonishing words where she recalls Juanito's exasperation with her: «El se empeñaba en que yo fuera de otro modo; pero la cabra siempre tira al monte. Pueblo nací y pueblo soy; quiero decir, ordinariota y salvaje...» (III, iv, 1; 125). Feijoo is perhaps doomed to failure in his campaign because what he really is attempting to do is to recast the «pueblo» as bourgeoisie. That is tantamount to perverting and betraying nature. If not impossible, the effort is immoral: it is not meant to be. The alliances between the old aristocracy and the new merchant class leave no room at the top for the «pueblo». Perhaps a creature like Fortunata is not built to exist in the rarefied air of Madrid's higher ground. Then again, perhaps it is that no fiction is controllable. In that self-defining utterance of Fortunata's, the literary, mythic, and social dimensions of the novel coalesce.

But *does* Fortunata rebel or forget? *Does* Feijoo fail? Or has she passed Feijoo's course despite first appearances? It is important to remember that when Feijoo is ready to die, die he does —but not until Fortunata is gone. At a given point, the creator-creation scheme is always reversed, as Cervantes proved before Galdós and Unamuno after him. The fiction's conferral of immortality upon the creator is literally dramatized later in *Fortunata y Jacinta* when Fortunata returns to call on Feijoo, thus reviving him into the text, just as, in parallel fashion, José Ido del Sagrario goes to Galdós's Madrid home to pay him a visit.[39] A psychological reading affords easy explanations for her action, but we see that she returns for advice when the mold into which she had been poured has broken apart and her script has run out. The price she has to pay for her strike towards independence is the discovery that, though born of her creator, she now belongs to others, if not to herself, and that his active power is a thing of the past: «Salió, pues, Fortunata de la triste visita con la impresión de haber perdido para siempre aquel grande y útil amigo, el hombre mejor que ella tratara en su vida y seguramente también el más práctico, el más sabio y el que mejores consejos daba. Verdad que ella hizo tanto caso de estos consejos como de las coplas de Calaínos; pero no dejaba de conocer que eran excelentes, y que debió al pie de la letra seguirlos» (IV, iii, 6; 206-07). Only now is she truly an orphan, ready to act on her own, to give birth to a new life, and to give flesh to her own fiction, «la pícara idea».

The answer as to whether Fortunata stands in bondage to Feijoo or is free from his prescriptions for her is not simple. After her reestablishment as an «honest woman», Fortunata sees little of Feijoo. With his

---

[39] So Galdós reports in his *Memorias de un desmemoriado (Obras completas,* 2nd ed., VI [Madrid: Aguilar, 1951], 1663). A game along this order earlier on brought *Lo prohibido* to a close. Augusto Pérez's later visit to Unamuno also comes to mind.

lesson fresh in her mind, she is, in fact, living in a state of equilibrium, and Feijoo is pleased to notice that his advice and teachings have not been lost on her. His presence in her husband's home understandably makes Fortunata uncomfortable, and outside forces conspire to assure the separation of creator and creation. Maxi looks on Feijoo with disfavor; and on one occasion the narrator cuts short a conversation between Feijoo and his former mistress by having Doña Lupe enter just as Fortunata is about to consult her mentor about her most recent problems. Feijoo's rare visits to the house cease altogether when he becomes too ill to go out.

After their personal contacts end, Feijoo continues in the text as a constant presence in Fortunata's mind, and her behavior in relation to her experience of him is an unbroken seesawing between obeisance and deliverance. She is in any case not quite the same being she was before he created her, for she now carries a dimension in her psyche that is Feijoo's responsibility. When during Mauricia's illness she loses her composure and identifies herself to Jacinta in a fit of emotion, she immediately thinks of Feijoo and of his recommendation that she should always maintain her self-control. The incident is an early slip from the creator's design, and it does not occur without a guilty feeling of betrayal on the creation's part. Soon thereafter comes the first expression of open rebellion when a resurgence of her dislike for Maxi overwhelms her and replaces the affection that Feijoo had predicted would in time take root in her. She says to herself: «Ni sé yo en qué estaba pensando Feijoo... Tonto él, y yo más tonta en hacerle caso» (III, vi, 6; 312). The next moment, when she considers fleeing from her home, the specter of Feijoo and of his disapproval brings her back to her senses. Feijoo's warnings again keep flashing across her mind as she embarks on her third liaison with Juanito and cause her to heed appearances, at least for the moment. Later, in a confrontation with Doña Lupe concerning this last escapade with Juanito, Fortunata formulates her reasoned response in the shadow of Feijoo's recommendations. Again and again, she thinks the thoughts and speaks the words that he had made her rehearse; under the influence of his wisdom, she never shakes the desire to consult him. Once her final plans crystallize in her mind, a sense of her autonomy takes possession of her, and she rejects the creative schemes of which she was the subject in all her days: «Tenía *su idea* y para nada necesitaba de consejos ni de la protección de nadie. Se las componía sola mucho mejor» (IV, i, 6; 52). She does write the end of her own story as she steals a march on Guillermina's behind-the-scenes machinations and determines the disposition of her son herself. Yet on her deathbed Fortunata still has a final recollection of Feijoo and of the prohibitions he imposed on her. At the same time she feels no remorse at having just flouted them.

71

Her relationship to her creator ends with the irresolvable duality of dependency and independence in coexistence.

Fortunata has not, as she confesses and as is obvious, heeded the word —«al pie de la letra»— but on the other hand, the return to Feijoo's house, the need for his guidance, the sorrow at his figurative passing, the indelible memory of his lesson, even the conscious rejection of his power, all betoken his continuing presence in her. She appears to have broken her shackles, but the autonomy of the literary creation is never more than an illusion. There is no better testimony to the persistence of Fortunata's raw nature alongside the forming impact of Feijoo's recreation of her than the first two given names that her son bears: Juan Evaristo: the fusion of passion and reason, of rebellion and submission, of the failure and the success of creation. The order of the two names perhaps signals the continuing primacy of the biological person in Fortunata, of the indestructibility of the myth of the «pueblo», but her disposal of the child is surely her most practical act.

Cornell University.

72

PETER A. BLY

Ripples on the Pond:
Interdependent Approaches to the Galdós Chapter

The immediate problem facing a critic asked to comment upon a single chapter chosen at random from a very long novel is one of methodology: does he simply limit his remarks to the chapter in question or does he extend them to the rest of the novel?[1] In their brilliantly fluent analyses of Part III, Chapter IV of *Fortunata y Jacinta* both Carlos Blanco Aguinaga and John Kronik chose the latter course. However, in so doing, they created two further methodological problems. First, both scholars started from the general confines of the novel before approaching the individual chapter in question. Secondly, both argued cogently for the priority of their own particular critical approach (which can be loosely labelled Marxist [Blanco] and Semiotic [Kronik]) despite a genuine acknowledgement of the validity and complementariness of the other.[2] However, if we choose to examine Part III, Chapter IV, first as a self-contained unit, we discover that the pre-eminence claimed for the Marxist or Semiotic perspective is unfounded; that instead an interdependence of both perspectives is the only possible approach and that this is suggested by the internal structure and thematic nature of the chapter, just as the chapter itself, despite its hermetic appearance, has later to be linked with its companions in the rest of the novel.[3] Like ripples on a pond, the

---

[1] As critic of the critics, I am presented with the same problem: do I limit my remarks to a discussion of the approaches they have taken, or do I stray far and wide to cover other, vastly different perspectives. Rightly or wrongly, I have chosen the former path.

[2] «Self-consciousness in the novel stands as a subversive threat to the mimetic enterprise, but it does not proscribe history» (KRONIK, p. 41); «but at the same time it is also clear that this text which calls itself fiction is constantly referring to the history outside it... The result is that the fictional story is built on the base of real history» (BLANCO AGUINAGA, p. 37).

[3] Unexplained references to non-appearing characters (the Santa Cruzs, Doña Lupe), to past events (Fortunata's infidelity to Maxi) are small reminders of this interdependence.

chapters in a novel and the methodological perspectives applied to their analysis are, perforce, interdependent creations.

The first substantial ripple that our reading of the text generates is constituted by the principal subject of the chapter: Feijoo's creation of a new, more socially acceptable Fortunata. As Kronik has so persuasively demonstrated, the many allusions to analogous acts of artistic creation serve to reinforce the fictionality of that mental creation which, in turn, is an internal self-referential mirror of the narrator's verbal creation of the written text. However, of greater importance in my opinion, is the special manner in which Galdós structures these analogous motifs around Feijoo's fabrication and presents the interdependence of history and fiction, projecting upon that creation a decidedly ironic and disparaging light, and bringing into serious doubt the efficacy and wisdom of the whole enterprise.

The first analogy has to be to the creation of a human being: a child is born, reared and then at the chapter's close is launched into the adult world. But for this to happen, the old Adam or the old Fortunata must die. It is thus not accidental that our first vision of her in the chapter is of a sick, bedridden woman: «Estaba Fortunata en su gabinete, tendida en el sofá, la cabeza reclinada sobre un almohadón de raso azul. Tenía puesta la bata de seda y un pañuelo blanco finísimo a la cabeza, tan ajustado, que no se le veía más que el óvalo del rostro. Estaba ojerosa, pálida y muy abatida» (III, iv, 1; 117-18).[4] Indeed the very first sentence of the chapter refers us to the unusually serious state of Fortunata's health: «Dos o tres veces fue D. Evaristo al siguiente día a enterarse de la salud de Fortunata» (III, iv, 1; 117). Her illness, though, is not primarily due to physical fatigue or accident but to anxiety about her social status: «de tanto pensar que era honrada, le dolía horriblemente la cabeza» (III, iv, 1; 117). Fortunata recovers and «al otro día... estaba un poco mejor, se había levantado y apetecido un sopicaldo» (III, iv, 1; 117). Feijoo then describes her mental state in pertinent terms: «parece que acaba de nacer, y que la han puesto de patitas en el mundo» (III, iv, 1; 121) and announces the synopsis of the course of instruction he will give her throughout the chapter as: «Yo le voy a enseñar a usted una cosa que no sabe. —¿Qué? —Vivir... Vivir es nuestra primera obligación en este valle de lágrimas» (III, iv, 1; 122). Subsequent allusions to Fortunata's recuperation and indeed unprecedented physical development thus continue to remind us of the corresponding progression of the philosophical course upon which Feijoo is engaged: «Y la verdad era que con aquella vida tranquila y sosegada, *eminentemente práctica,* se iba ponien-

---

[4] All textual references are taken from the first edition (Madrid: La Guirnalda, 1887), and are accompanied by the appropriate volume, chapter, section and page number. Italics are mine unless otherwise stated.

do tan lucida de carnes, tan guapa y hermosota que daba gloria verla. Siempre tuvo la de Rubín buena salud; *pero nunca, como en aquella temporada,* vio desarrollarse la existencia material con tanta plenitud y lozanía» (III, iv, 4; 142). Feijoo encourages this physical expansion as an appropriate stimulant, aid, for his philosophical instruction, but without realizing the dangerous competition it might present for the latter's efficacy:

> Pero en su frugal colación [Feijoo] gozaba viendo comer a su protegida, cuyo apetito era una bendición de Dios.
> —Hija, tienes un apetito modelo. Te estoy mirando, y al paso que te envidio, *me felicito de verte tan bien agarrada* a la vida. Así, así me gusta... No te dé vergüenza de comer bien, y puesto que lo hay, aplícate todo lo que puedas, que día vendrá... ¡ojalá que no!... Cuando digo que *tienes lo mejor de la vida por delante!*... Y buena tonta serás si no engordas todo lo que puedas, y te pones las carnes aun más duras y apretadas si es posible. *Figúrate si con esas tragaderas estarás bien dispuesta para el amor.*
> Después de esto y mientras Fortunata se *comía una cantidad inapreciable de pasas y almendras,* cogiéndolas del plato una a una y llevándoselas a la boca sin mirarlas, *el bondadoso anciano siguió sus habladurías con cierto desconcierto, y como desvariando.* (III, iv, 5; 157-58)

If Fortunata balks initially at the projected course work, she is appropriately characterized as a little child: «Quiero ser honrada —repitió Fortunata sin mirarle, como *los niños mimosos que insisten en decir la cosa fea por que les reprenden*» (III, iv, 2; 13).

References later in the chapter to a father-daughter relationship between the two reinforce the notion that the new, reborn and matured Fortunata is a creation of Feijoo: «el buen señor llegó a sentir por su protegida un amor entrañable, no todo compuesto de fiebre de amante, sino también de un cierto cariño paternal, que cada día se determinaba más» (III, iv, 4; 144-45). Later Fortunata will overwhelm him with «los cariños y cuidados de una hija amantísima con el mejor de los padres» (III, iv, 5; 160). However, it is quite obvious that this parental relationship is only an imposed role, a dramatic, theatrical part to play: «Desde que tomara con tanto cariño *las funciones paternales,* se había dejado toda la barba, usaba hongo y una gran bufanda alrededor del cuello» (III, iv, 8; 182). This role-playing emerges quite emphatically, despite the negation, from later reminders by Feijoo: «Todo acabó... Fortunata, no soy para ti más que un padre... Aquel que te quiso como quiere el hombre a la mujer, no existe ya... Eres mi hija. *Y no es que hagamos un papel aprendido, no;* es que tú serás verdaderamente para mí, de aquí en adelante, como una hijita, y yo seré para ti un verdadero papaíto (III, iv, 9; 198)... Repito lo de antes. Aquello se acabó... y ahora soy tu padre, tú, mi hija... trátame de usted... *ocupemos nuestros puestos... aprendamos a vivir vida práctica*» (III, iv, 10; 206).

This father-daughter outline replaces the initial mould of two lovers[5] and is necessitated by Feijoo's sudden physical decline resulting from his sexual endeavours. Herein lies a further layer of irony in this series of alternating allusions to and images of physical creation and health: Feijoo consistently maintains to Fortunata that people are attracted to each other, fall in love, because of Nature's procreative urge:

> El amor es la reclamación de la especie que quiere perpetuarse, y al estímulo de esta necesidad tan conservadora como el comer, los sexos se buscan y las uniones se verifican por elección fatal, superior y extraña a todos los artificios de la Sociedad. Míranse un hombre y una mujer. ¿Qué es? *La exigencia de la especie que pide un nuevo ser, y este nuevo ser reclama de sus probables padres que le den vida.* Todo lo demás es música, fatuidad y palabrería de los que han querido hacer una Sociedad en sus gabinetes, fuera de las bases inmortales de la Naturaleza. ¡Si esto es claro como el agua! Por eso me río yo de ciertas leyes y de todo el código penal social del amor, que es un fárrago de tonterías inventadas por los feos, los mamarrachos, y los sabios estúpidos que jamás han obtenido de una hembra el más ligero favorcito. (III, iv, 5; 158-59)

The grotesque language of the last sentence alerts us to the unconscious irony of these remarks: the laugh is really on Feijoo who is incapable of living up to his prescription which he condenses in the slogan: «ande el mundo y crezca la especie, que para eso estamos» (III, iv, 3; 140): because of his age, he cannot produce that object which he claims is the raison d'être of any love affair. So he has to make do with second best: a surrogate spiritual creation in Fortunata's mind.[6]

Moreover, this act of creation and growth is balanced by a series of allusions and images of physical death. When the chapter opens, Feijoo is the picture of good health, in contrast to his pupil: «Sonrisa de alegría y esperanza contraía sus labios, mostrando su dentadura intachable. Su cara, que era siempre sonrosada, poníasele encendida, con verdaderos

---

[5] In retrospect, he now sees his love-making as a role: «Yo he sido en esto poco práctico, siéndolo tanto en otras cosas; pero *ya que se me olvidaron los papeles en el caso este de hacer el pollo a los sesenta y nueve años,* voy a recogerlos para prevenir las malas consecuencias» (III, iv, 5; 152).

[6] A comic inversion of the father-daughter relationship is achieved when Fortunata pointedly addresses Feijoo as «hijo» (III, iv, 5; 156). The equivocal relationship of Fortunata's neighbours, the two seamstresses, to their male guardian («Las del tercero, que eran las amas o sobrinas del ecónomo de San Andrés, que allí vivía» [III, iv, 5; 154]), could well be another ironic parallel to the principal relationship of Fortunata and don Evaristo. Having been originally told that Feijoo has no «familia próxima» (III, iv, 6; 165), we are surprised when told at the end of the chapter that he does have some relatives; significantly «eran dos sobrinas, residentes la una en Astorga, la otra en Ponferrada» (III, iv, 10; 210). In an aptly entitled short story he wrote in 1871, «La mujer del filósofo», Galdós had humorously noted the contrasting health of the married couple: «y sigue él adelgazándose y consumiéndose, y ella echando carnes y reventando de salud y lozanía... Está escrito que el filósofo no ha de reproducirse», *Obras completas,* ed. F. C. Sainz de Robles (Madrid: Aguilar, 1968), VI, 1668.

ardores de juventud en las mejillas. Era, en suma, *el viejo más guapo, simpático y frescachón que se podía imaginar... Pues de cuerpo, ya quisieran parecérsele la mayor parte de los muchachos de hoy.* Otro más derecho y bien plantado no había» (III, iv, 1; 126-27). But his sexual exertions take their toll and his health suffers a rapid decline which he cannot but contrast with Fortunata's radiance: «Cada día más guapa... y yo cada día más viejo» (III, iv, 4; 142).[7] The course of Feijoo's decline may not be so uniform as that of Fortunata's ascent to healthy plenitude (a temporary recuperation is followed by a relapse into senility and then a further recovery and survival into 1876 [III, iv, 10; 207-13]), but the contrast is strong enough to cast an ironic shadow upon the healthiness or fitness of the chapter's purported spiritual creation.

Other ironic imagery includes the respective ministers of life and death: the doctor and the priest. On his first visit to Fortunata, Feijoo acts the doctor: «Como D. Evaristo *se preciaba de saber algo de medicina,* tomóle el pulso» (III, iv, 1; 118). Later the same evening he repeats the act but with different intentions: «*Echábaselas de médico;* pero examinaba la cara por lo bonita que le parecía, no por buscar en ella síntomas hipocráticos» (III, iv, 1; 123). The realistic counterpoint is sounded when Feijoo's own health deteriorates and requires the attention of doctors and medicines: «¡Quién me había de decir a mí que llegaría a ocuparme de que existen boticas en el mundo! Yo, que jamás caté píldora, ni pastilla, ni glóbulo, tengo mi alcoba llena de potingues; y si fuera a hacer todo lo que el médico me dice, no duraría tres días» (III, iv, 5; 153-54). In a further ironic twist, medicine is shown to be unable to give a correct prognostication of Feijoo's health as he confounds the doctor by surviving the year's end and living into 1876 (III, iv, 10; 209).[8] Galdós takes up the

---

[7] The ironic contrast is summed up in a pair of self-referential plastic images; Fortunata looks at herself in her mirror: «Y ella, cuando se miraba al espejo, no se resistía a la admiración de su propia imagen» (III, iv, 4; 142). The mirror of Feijoo's decline is appropriately a convent door: «Pasando junto a la carcomida puerta del convento de la Latina, no pudo menos de mirarse en ella como en un espejo. Se vio allí bien claro, cual vestigio honroso conservado sólo por indulgencia del tiempo» (III, iv, 5; 150).

[8] Time is also presented by Feijoo as a great doctor, perhaps the best: «El tiempo es un médico que se pinta solo para curar estas cosas» (III, iv, 1; 124). The passage of time in the chapter, and during the Feijoo-Fortunata relationship, is stressed during an exchange between Feijoo and Maxi in the cafe: «Cinco meses lleva mi estómago de indisciplina —replicó el ladino viejo, que quería sin duda meterle a Maxi en la cabeza aquello de los cinco meses» (III, iv, 8; 187). Feijoo is obviously alluding to Fortunata's abandonment of the matrimonial home (at the end of Part II) which must have occurred soon after their wedding during the hot summer of 1874 (II, vii, 12; 447). The eventual return of Fortunata to the Rubín household takes place in March of 1875 (III, v, 1; 216). The time elapsed between the dates would then be roughly a symbolic nine months. Feijoo's association with Fortunata does not cover this period, however. He first asks about her when talking with Juan Pablo (III, i, 6; 45) towards the end of 1874, when the return of the Bourbons is a solid expectation (III, i, 5; 42). (GEOFFREY RIBBANS,

77

motif again in the cafe sequence.[9] Maxi, the linchpin in any successful implementation of Feijoo's plan, is also another recuperated individual, according to Feijoo: «Anoche le vi, y no me ha parecido tan raquítico. Ha engordado; ha echado carnes, y hasta me pareció que tiene un aire más arrogantillo» (III, iv, 9; 199-200) and would also seem capable of producing children, a possibility that Fortunata with greater realism than Feijoo flatly rejects (III, iv, 9; 201). It must also be remembered that Maxi is now a druggist's assistant who, in an ironic echo of the chapter's opening sequence, asks Feijoo about his health: «¿Pero qué es lo que usted tiene? —preguntó Maximiliano con presunción de médico novel o de boticario incipiente, que unos y otros se desviven por ser útiles a la humanidad. —¿Que qué tengo? ¡Ah! una cosa muy mala. La peor de las enfermedades. ¡Setenta años!» (III, iv, 8; 187). Juan Pablo's empty «vulgaridades hipocráticas» (III, iv, 7; 176) add another layer of irony.

Religious allusions and imagery complement these earthly preoccupations with life and death, but again in an ironic manner. In many respects the dramatic climax of the chapter is reached when Feijoo almost dies. At this point, to the great surprise of all who know him, he accepts the Last Sacraments: «Creyeron los más que D. Evaristo se alborotaría con esto, pues siempre hizo alarde de libre pensador; mas con gran sorpresa de todos, oyó la indicación del modo más sereno y amable, diciendo que él tenía sus creencias, pero que al mismo tiempo gustaba de cumplir toda obligación consagrada por el asentimiento del mayor número» (III, iv, 10; 208-09). The act is clearly one of social conformism devoid of all true religious meaning, even for the clergy who later are concerned that the Church be included in Feijoo's will: «Indicáronle los clérigos de la parroquia si no dejaba algo para sufragios por su alma, y él, con bondadosa sonrisa, *replicó que no había olvidado ninguno de los deberes de la cortesía social,* y que, para no desafinar en nada, también quedaba puesto el rengloncito de las misas» (III, iv, 10; 211). The grotesque distortion is added when Feijoo recalls to Villalonga at the end

---

«Contemporary History in the Structure and Characterization of *Fortunata y Jacinta*», in *Galdós Studies,* ed. J. E. Varey [London: Tamesis, 1970], p. 102, says that the relationship between Maxi and Fortunata in Part II is not plotted against concrete political developments.) Feijoo's «baby» (the recreated Fortunata) is a child of stunted growth (3 months at the most), hardly likely to survive entry into the real word.

[9] As will be demonstrated later, the second half of the chapter, dealing mostly with Feijoo's cafe talks, appears to have the function of providing a grotesque, comic inversion of the Feijoo-Fortunata course of instruction. This function can be glimpsed in such minor details as the emaciated figure of Villaamil («momia animada por arte de brujería» [III, iv, 8; 185] or the preposterous hypothesis momentarily advanced by Feijoo that Lupe's lost breast will be miraculously reborn (III, iv, 8; 183). Fortunata's splendid development has its own ironic parallels, then. WALTER T. PATTISON, *Benito Pérez Galdós* (Boston: Twayne, 1975), p. 103, has noted a similar pattern of contrasting gradations for the whole novel.

of the chapter: «La noche que me dieron el Viático, en el momento aquel, miré para este lado y lo primero que vi fue a *Ramsés II* [i.e. Villaamil; Galdós's italics] con una vela en la mano. ¡Cómo me miraba el infeliz!… Creo que no me morí de tanto como rezó Villaamil, pidiendo a Dios que viviera» (III, iv, 10; 213).

Fortunata, whose gait had earned Juanito's disapproval («Tú cuando vas por ahí con tu velito y ese pasito reposado, sin mirar a nadie, parece que vas de casa en casa pidiendo para una misa» [III, iv, 1; 126]) goes to church at the beginning of her liaison with Don Evaristo, but clearly only under the pressure of an extremely guilty conscience so that, as the narrator indicates, these observances have more to do with an obsessive impulse or mania rather than true faith: «Con estos diferentes estados de su espíritu se relacionaban ciertas intermitencias de manía religiosa» (III, iv, 3; 136). At other more tranquil moments, she avoids church, content to mumble a few «Our Fathers» as she goes about the house. At the end of the paragraph Galdós deflates this religious attendance or the conscience that gives rise to it with a series of absurdly mundane allusions: «Entre creerse un monstruo de maldad o un ser inocente y desgraciado, mediaban a veces el lapso de tiempo más breve o el accidente más sencillo; que se desprendiese una hoja del tallo ya marchito de una planta cayendo sin ruido sobre la alfombra; que cantase el canario del vecino o que pasara un coche cualquiera por la calle, haciendo mucho ruido» (III, iv, 3; 136-37). Clearly Fortunata's faith is as deficient as Feijoo's. In a serious course of social philosophy this shortcoming would not be considered of importance were it not that it is presented by Galdós in a disparaging light. The philosophy of life is still opposed by the philosophy of the after-life, but in a rather hilarious manner, as a series of religious images emphasizes.[10] If the sick Fortunata «parece una hermana de la Caridad» (III, iv, 1; 118), «doctor» Feijoo whose house «tenía algo de convento» (III, iv, 4; 144) listens to her recollections of past times with Juanito Santa Cruz «con tolerancia de sacerdote hecho al confesonario» (III, iv, 1; 121).[11]

[10] Even simple words and phrases achieve this purpose. Feijoo describes their tryst as Paradise (III, iv, 3; 129); Fortunata regards Feijoo's experience of life as «un catecismo que se sabe de memoria» (III, iv, 7; 170). The narrator unabashedly indicates that Fortunata is Feijoo's idol: «no me vuelvo atrás de lo que esta expresión indica» (III, iv, 4; 144). The material the two seamstresses have left over is used to make ridiculous «trajes para Niños Jesús y para Vírgenes» (III, iv, 5; 155).

[11] The contrasting roles of doctor and cleric are of course derived from the life history of Colonel Feijoo's historical namesake, the monk-cum-philosopher-cum-commentator of life's attractions, Benito Jerónimo Feijoo. We know that Galdós had in his library the monk's *Obras escogidas,* 6th ed. (Madrid, 1881-88), Biblioteca Universal, vol. 115; see H. CHONON BERKOWITZ, *La biblioteca de Benito Pérez Galdós* (Las Palmas: El Museo Canario, 1951), p. 137. I. L. McCLELLAND'S *Benito Jerónimo Feijoo* (Boston: Twayne, 1969) is a useful guide to the life and

Kronik has ably highlighted the images of artistic creation in the chapter (see pp. 64-67). However, it is also to be noted that these images refer to a distanced hypothesis: Feijoo wistfully dreams of what he *could have done* had Fortunata fallen into his hands earlier, not what he can do in the present. The obvious corollary is that Feijoo's spiritual creation of Fortunata can only be, at best, something inferior to the ideal. Moreover, these self-referential plastic images receive their own ironic reprise (again in the second half of the chapter) when the narrator describes Fortunata's nightmarish recreations of her in-laws, the Rubíns:

> Así como en las mutaciones de cuadros disolventes, a medida que unas figuras se borran van apareciendo las líneas de otras, primero una vaguedad o presentimiento de las nuevas formas, después contornos, luego masas de color, y, por fin, las actitudes completas, así en la mente de Fortunata empezaron a esbozarse desde aquella noche, cual apariencias que brotan de la nebulosa del sueño, las personas de Maxi, de doña Lupe, de Nicolás Rubín y hasta de la misma *Papitos* [Galdós's italics]. Eran ellos que salían nuevamente a luz, primero como espectros, después como seres reales, con cuerpo, vida y voz. Al amanecer, inquieta y rebelde al sueño, oíales hablar y reconocía hasta los gestos más insignificantes que modelaban la personalidad de cada uno. (III, iv, 7; 170)

Other images and allusions to cultural activities sprinkled throughout the chapter again cast an ironic shadow on Feijoo's fabrication of Fortunata. In the initial exchange between the two lovers, Fortunata's taste for Romantic melodramas is dismissed by the realistic Feijoo as out of fashion like her idea of returning Juanito's money («un romanticismo impropio de estos tiempos» (III, iv, 1; 119):

> —¿Le gusta a usted el teatro?
> —Eso sí, sobre todo los dramas en que hay cosas que la hacen llorar a una.
> —¡Ave María Purísima!... Esas obras en que sale aquello de «¡hijo mío!... ¡padre mío!...».
> —Esas, y otras en que hay pasos de mucha aflicción, y sacan las espadas, y se desmaya una actriz porque le quitan el hijo.
> —¡Alabado sea el Santísimo! —dijo Feijoo con socarronería—. En eso sí que son contrarios nuestros gustos, porque yo, en cuanto veo que los actores pegan gritos y las actrices principian a hacerme pucheritos, ya

works of the historical figure, reflections of which can be seen perhaps in our chapter in such minor details as the blessing of Feijoo's regiment by Pope Pius IX (Pope Benedict XIV was a great admirer of Fray Benito Jerónimo), the interest of Colonel Feijoo in women (the monk's appropriately entitled *Teatro crítico universal* (1740) contains discussions on sexual love and the attractions of women); and don Evaristo's two nieces live in Galicia and Asturias (reflecting the area of the historical figure's birth and residence; see note 6 above). Galdós's use of the eighteenth-century historical figure as a source is ironic: his nineteenth-century fictional counterpart is trying to apply an out-of-date philosophy, inappropriate to the contemporary reality of Fortunata's problems. Thus even Feijoo's surname is an immediate signal that alerts us to the lack of wisdom of his plan.

estoy bufando en mi butaca y mirando para la puerta... Nada de lágrimas. Lo que le conviene a usted ahora es reírse con las piececitas de Lara y Variedades. Para dramas, hija, los de la realidad.[12] (III, iv, 1; 124-25)

In the context of our previous discussion on the imagined father/ daughter relationship and its theatrical role-playing by the two, the inversion of that dialectic in the above extract when now the Romantic dramas recreate a father-son relationship contributes to the deflation of Feijoo's act of creation. It is highly ironic that he is urging his lover to forsake these tastes when, later, after his sexual exertions, he will want to establish a parental role. One could also say that Fortunata in her taste for melodrama is creating something as a spectator, identifying herself emotionally with the events of the drama, empathizing under the dramatic catharsis, just as she creates an emotional and physical state of abstraction with her preference for «todas aquellas flores que *ilusionan el sentido* en cuanto uno se acerca a ellas» (III, iv, 1; 123; Galdós's italics). She may not be able to play «tresillo» under Juan's direction, but she can play «tute». So there is a base of creativity in Fortunata that can be used and developed. The tragedy of this chapter and the rest of the novel is that her emotional creativity, her ability for loving and creating friendships and producing children is eventually re-directed by Feijoo, re-channelled into more domestic, more socially acceptable, bourgeois creations. When the street barrel-organ tempts all the females in the apartment house to improvise dances, Fortunata remains surprisingly quiet, smiling at Feijoo (III, iv, 5; 154) (the cafe scene again offers the inversion: Feijoo now can hardly withstand the din of the piano and violin trying to be heard above the chatter and shouts of people [III, iv, 9; 190]). Fortunata becomes more domesticated, now improving her skill in native Spanish cooking: «No era glotona; pero sí *inteligente en víveres y en todo lo que concierne a la bien provista plaza de Madrid*» (III, iv, 4; 142). «Muchos días comían o almorzaban juntos, y *como ambos amantes habían convenido en enaltecer y restaurar prácticamente la hispana cocina,* hacía *la individua* [Galdós's italics] unos guisotes y fritangas, cuyo olor llegaba más allá de San Francisco el Grande» (III, iv, 4; 145). The joint effort is important: Feijoo's guidance even in these normally female matters reveals the extent to which he controls his creation; but we already know that: «D. Evaristo, que tan práctico quería ser en la vida social, debía de serlo más en la doméstica, y, conforme a sus ideas, lo primero que tiene que hacer el hombre en este valle de inquietudes es *buscarse un buen agujero donde morar, y labrar en él un perfecto molde de su carácter*» (III, iv, 6; 165). The words of the last sentence are im-

---

[12] Feijoo has similar words of reprobation for Maxi's former desire for marital revenge: «¿A qué vienen esos odios y esas venganzas de melodrama? —dijo gozoso don Evaristo—. Para perderse nada más» (III, iv, 9; 193).

portant for it is the individual who has to create his own mould to suit his character. By trying to domesticate Fortunata, collaborating with and guiding her in this culinary development, Feijoo is imposing what he feels should be Fortunata's role in society: that of a domesticated wife. It is certainly not Fortunata's real «molde» or one that suits her for long. Fortunata is not really free to shape her own mould. This becomes even more apparent when Feijoo one day purchases for her a Singer sewing machine: «con lo que ella se entretenía mucho» (III, iv, 3; 138). She is now asked by her seamstress neighbours to help them to «pespuntar y dobladillar unas tiras para tableado de vestidos» (III, iv, 5; 155).

Fortunata's literary creations (albeit in the oral tradition) must not be overlooked either. For Feijoo's instruction and amusement and (again significantly) under his guidance, she narrates episodes from her past life. Despite the unadorned style, by the selection of material and through sheer dramatic intensity she is able to captivate her one-man audience: «Lo mismo hacía Fortunata, cuando le tocaba a ella ser narradora, *incitada por su protector a mostrar algún capítulo de la historia de su vida,* que en corto tiempo ofrecía lances *dignos de ser contados y aun escritos.* No se hacía ella de rogar, y como tenía la virtud de la franqueza, y no apreciaba bien, por rudeza de paladar moral, la significación buena o mala de ciertos hechos, todo lo desembuchaba. *A veces sentía D. Evaristo gran regocijo oyéndola, a veces verdadero terror; pero de todas estas sesiones* salía al fin con impresiones de tristeza» (III, iv, 4; 147). On other occasions it is some daily event in the neighbourhood (most are never presented directly) that she recreates for Feijoo: «Pero ¿no sabes, *hijo* [Galdós's italics], lo que me han dicho hoy? —prosiguió Fortunata conteniendo la risa—. ¡Ay qué gracia!... Te lo contaré para que te rías» (III, iv, 5; 156). Another development, though in the opposite direction, is Fortunata's recovery of old behavioural patterns like placing her hands on her hips all the time or «el hablar arrastrado, dejoso y prolongando ciertas vocales» (III, iv, 5; 156). All of these practical developments in Fortunata's way of life are real and meaningful and certainly counter her initial contention that «Pueblo nací y pueblo soy; quiero decir, ordinariota y salvaje... Yo no sé ninguna labor delicada; no sé coser en fino; no bordo ni toco el piano. Tampoco pinto platos como esa Antonia, amiga de Villalonga, la cual está siempre de pinceles; yo apenas sé leer y no le saco sentido a ningún libro... ¿Qué he de hacer? Fregar y limpiar» (III, iv, 1; 125-29). Feijoo shows her during the chapter that she can do something more than that, that she can in fact create, but the areas in which he gives her direction are those activities that he likes to see a young woman do: they suit his purpose of keeping Fortunata secluded for his own sexual gratification. Moreover, these domestic virtues do not really fit the real context of Fortunata's abilities and needs: her creative outlets are so patently emotional and physical that all else becomes, however well she progresses in the coursework from Feijoo, a poor and inauthentic substitute.

Fortunata's storytelling is patterned on her tutor's eloquent, more polished literary performances in the same autobiographical field («Hablando de esto, se animaba llegando hasta la elocuencia» [III, iv, 3; 139-40]) which rivet her admiring attention: «Fortunata le oía embelesada, puestos los codos sobre la mesa, la cara sostenida en las manos, los ojos clavados en el narrador, quien bajo la influencia de la atención ingenua de su amada, se sentía más elocuente, con la memoria más fresca y las ideas más claras» (III, iv, 4; 145; see also 147). In fact Feijoo's performances become so literary, fictionalized, that Fortunata can hardly believe them: «Si eso se dice, no se cree... Y si lo escriben, pensarán que es fábula mal inventada» (III, iv, 4; 147). When Feijoo delivers his moral instruction, Fortunata receives it in the same «meal-table» posture: «Fortunata le miraba con sorpresa mezclada de temor, el codo en la mesa, derecho el busto, en una actitud airosa y elegante, llevando pausadamente del plato a la boca, ahora una pasita, ahora una almendrita» (III, iv, 5; 159). Fortunata's attention is now not so enraptured. The ironic reverberations between the two sessions undermine the seriousness of the latter one. So does the theatrical description of the pedagogical instruction:

> Como un dómine que repite la declinación a sus discípulos, machacando sílaba tras sílaba, cual si se las claveteara en el cerebro a golpes de maza, D. Evaristo, la mano derecha en el aire, actuando a compás como un martillo, iba incrustando en el caletre de su alumna estas palabras:
> —Guardando... las... apariencias, observando... las reglas... del respeto que nos debemos los unos a los otros... y... sobre todo, esto es lo principal... no descomponiéndose nunca, oye lo que te digo... no descomponiéndose nunca... (*A la segunda repetición del concepto, la mano del dómine quedábase suspendida en el aire; y sus cejas arqueadas en mitad de la frente, sus ojos extraordinariamente iluminados, denotaban la importancia que daba a este punto de la lección*)... no descomponiéndose nunca, se puede hacer todo lo que se quiere. (III, iv, 6; 167-68)

Feijoo's arched eyebrows are almost a facial cipher of exaggeration and theatricality (see the same hand gestures in a repeat performance [III, iv, 10; 203]). When illness intervenes, Feijoo continues his lessons through written notes (III, iv, 10; 209).[13] In fact their relationship is initiated on

---

[13] In an ironic anticipation of this methodology (gravely ignored by Feijoo), Juanito's break with Fortunata had been effected on similar lines: by a letter of advice and money: «No la [la carta] he leído hasta esta mañana. Aquí se despide otra vez, dándome consejos y echándoselas de santo varón. Me manda dentro de la carta cuatro mil reales» (III, iv, 1; 119). During their liaison Juanito «me *sermoneaba* porque no tengo ese aire de francesa que tiene la Antoñita» (III, iv, 1; 126).

a pedagogical note: «El primer día le leyó la cartilla, que era muy breve» (III, iv, 3; 137).

Equally suspect is the disinterestedness of Feijoo's relationship and plans for Fortunata, a suspicion that is again borne out by textual evidence. In the first stage when he is healthy and can only think of sexual gratification,[14] he is overly anxious to present himself as the only solution for Fortunata's immediate maintenance problem:

> Usted, compañera, no tiene ahora más remedio que aceptar el amparo de un hombre. Sólo falta que la suerte le depare un buen hombre. ¿Se echará usted a buscarlo por ahí entre sus relaciones, o saldrá a pescar un desconocido por calles, teatros y paseos? A ver... Dígolo porque si quiere usted ahorrarse este trabajo, *figúrese* que aburrida ha salido por esos mundos, que ha echado el anzuelo, que le han picado, que tira para arriba, y que ¡oh, sorpresa! me ha pescado a mí. *Aquí me tiene usted fuera del agua dando coletazos de gusto por verme tan bien pescado.* (III, iv, 2; 133)

In a chapter replete with self-referential images of creation, Feijoo persuades Fortunata to believe that she has gone through the action of searching for male support («figúrese») but this counterfeit, unreal creation imposed by Feijoo really reveals his personal concern that he be the chosen support. Despite accompanying disclaimers, Feijoo shows considerable pride in his suitability as the only candidate: «*sin vanidad, creo que sirvo para todo...* Conque a decidirse. *Modestia a un lado,* dígole a usted, que dificilillo le sería, en su situación, encontrar acomodo mejor... Y no vacilo en decirlo —agregó *alzando la voz, como si se incomodara—. Le ha caído a usted la lotería, y no así un premio cualquiera, sino el gordo de Navidad»* (III, iv, 2; 133). Their secret ménage is such a success that Feijoo's vanity is again consolidated: «Con este sistema de cautela y recato, les iba tan bien que D. *Evaristo no cesaba de congratularse»* (III, iv, 3; 139). In his anxiousness to occupy the position as quickly as possible, Feijoo removes the possibility of Fortunata choosing another man, and presents himself as a windfall of good luck. Fortunata really has no choice at all in the matter; but again the most disturbing feature is Feijoo's excessive belief in his own merits. This superiority continues when, forced by sexual over-exertions to think of a social solution for Fortunata's future, he elaborates his philosophical scheme: «¿Verdad, chulita, que tengo razón? ¿Verdad que sí?... Verás qué plan. Al principio puede que te escueza un poco; pero... no hay otro remedio, no hay otro remedio» (III, iv, 5; 159-61). His concern in securing Fortunata's physical and social future after his death soon becomes an ominously unhealthy

---

[14] He resolutely rejects the written or spoken instruction at this stage as he feasts his eyes on Fortunata hard at work: «Yo no tengo aquí *álbunes* ni libros para que se entretenga. — Maldita la falta que me hacen a mí los *álbunes»* (III, iv, 2; 129; Galdós's italics).

obsession: «Mas no por eso desistió de llevar adelante un plan que había llegado a ser casi una manía, absorbiendo todos sus pensamientos» (III, iv, 7; 173)... «Su proyecto llegó a dominarle de tal modo, que no sabía pensar en otra cosa, y de la mañana a la noche estaba dando vueltas al tema» (III, iv, 8; 182). It is fitting, then, that our last picture of Feijoo in this chapter should be one of an extremely self-satisfied old man: «Y D. Evaristo se quedó solo, pensativo y dulcemente ensimismado, saboreando en su conciencia el goce puro de hacer a sus semejantes todo el bien posible, o de haber evitado el mal en la medida que la Providencia ha concedido a la iniciativa humana» (III, iv, 10; 213). It would seem that Feijoo has once more succeeded in getting his own wishes realized: «Soltero y con fortuna suficiente *para quien no tiene mujer ni chiquillos ni familia próxima,* Feijoo vivía en dichosa soledad, bien servido por criados fieles, *dueño absoluto de su casa y de su tiempo, no privándose de nada que le gustase, y teniendo todos los deseos cumplidos en el filo mismo de su santísima voluntad»* (III, iv, 6; 165). The reference to wife and children is important for now Feijoo has a wife and child, in the single person of Fortunata, but he is still able to have his own way and ignore the reality of her claims and needs.

Even if Fortunata were the most ideal pupil (and she does make progress in understanding Feijoo's abstruse concepts [15]), Feijoo's system of natural and social philosophy possesses its own internal contradictions. Having defined heterosexual love as the «reclamación imperiosa de la Naturaleza...; la Naturaleza diciendo *auméntame...* No hay medio de oponerse... la especie humana que grita *quiero creer...* ¿Me entiendes?» (III, iv, 10; 204; Galdós's italics), he rigorously enjoins Fortunata not to give in to her feelings completely: «Ojo al corazón es lo primero que te digo. No permitas que te domine» (III, iv, 6; 164). Having said that love is uncontainable he now reckons that it is in part controllable if social appearances are carefully maintained. That is a very difficult and dangerous division to maintain; but what makes it even more untenable in the concrete example of Fortunata's life is that Feijoo dismisses any notion of Juanito (the only man Fortunata truly loves, as Feijoo has had

---

[15] At first Fortunata cannot understand her teacher «sin duda por el lenguaje que empleaba su amigo» (III, iv, 5; 157). However, with time «algo y aun algos se le iba clareando en el entendimiento» (III, iv, 7; 172), until at the end she is nodding agreement —surely too mechanically to be true— at Feijoo's instruction: «Fortunata había comprendido. Hacía signos afirmativos con la cabeza, y cruzadas las manos sobre una de sus rodillas, imprimía a su cuerpo movimientos de balancín o remadera... Fortunata entendía, y seguía balanceándose de atrás adelante, acentuando las afirmaciones con su cabeza despeinada» (III, iv, 10; 203-04). However, the danger signals are sounded very early on: «La gratitud que hacia Feijoo sentía, era más viva aún que antes, y habría deseado que la vida que con él llevaba continuase, pues aunque algo tediosa, *era tan pacífica que no debía ambicionar otra mejor: 'Si dura mucho esto, ¿llegaré a cansarme, y a no poder sufrir esta sosería? Puede que sí'»* (III, iv, 7; 170-71).

ample chance to realize) being her lover anymore: «Lo segundo es que tengas mucho cuidado en elegir... porque si caes en la tentación de querer a un hombre indigno, adiós mi dinero, adiós decoro» (III, iv, 10; 205-06). In the final analysis, Feijoo is trying to achieve the impossible, a reconciliation of opposites, or to square the circle, in his own words (III, iv, 2; 134). Thus his course of instruction is clearly not a product or creation of a man «con un gran sentido de la realidad» (III, iv, 9; 200). He does not practise what he preaches: «Las cosas son como son, no como deseamos que sean» (III, iv, 2; 132). But by the chapter's end, he has, as usual, achieved his wishes and pre-ordained the future life of Fortunata to his own satisfaction.

The Rubín family provides the ironic counterpoint to Feijoo's careful scheming disguised as social philosophy. Doña Lupe has her «filosofías pardas» (III, iv, 8; 182) whilst Maxi and Juan Pablo have become serious students of philosophy engaging in heated debates in the incongruous surroundings of a Madrid cafe. Galdós's ridicule emerges very clearly:

> ¡Y estas cosas se decían en el rincón de un café, al lado de un parroquiano que leía *La Correspondencia* y de otro que hablaba del precio de la carne! En una de las mesas próximas había un grupo de individuos que tenían facha de matuteros o cosa tal. A la derecha veíanse dos cursis acompañadas de una buscona y obsequiadas por un señor que les decía mil tonterías empalagosas; enfrente una trinca en que se disputaba acerca de Lagartijo y Frascuelo, con voces destempladas y manotazos. Y por la escalera de caracol subían y bajaban constantemente parroquianos, dando patadas que más bien parecían coces; y por aquella espiral venían rumores de disputa, el chasquido de las bolas de billar, y el canto del mozo que apuntaba. (III, iv, 8; 189-90; Galdós's italics)

If Juan Pablo pays «la atención más filosófica del mundo» (III, iv, 7; 178) to all that Feijoo discusses, the latter does not reciprocate: patently bored by the empty debate of the two brothers, he prefers to gaze at Refugio: «Don Evaristo, en tanto, miraba a Refugio, examinándole el rostro, la boca, el diente menos. La muchacha sentía vergüenza de verse tan observada, y no sabía cómo ponerse, ni qué dengues hacer con los labios al llevarse a ellos la cucharilla con leche merengada» (III, iv, 8; 188). Do we not have in this scene the chapter's own ironic reprise in miniature? The philosophical talk of the two brothers is a grotesque commentary on Feijoo's philosophizing and sermonizing, whilst his staring at Refugio reveals the real motivation behind his interest in Fortunata. Though he may laugh at the two brothers («¡Buen par de chiflados estáis los dos! —dijo para sí D. Evaristo mirando con curiosidad el portillo que en la dentadura tenía Refugio» [III, iv, 8; 189]), the laugh is really directed towards his own unrealistic philosophy and its implementation.

In the gallery of self-referential images of creation that we have been examining, the narrator's role has been particularly important, for it has been he who through his selection of language and manipulation of detail has allowed the reader to construct the pattern of ironic references to the major creation of Fortunata's new social attitude. However, the narrator would be acting untrue to the nature of his creation if he were to present himself as the omniscient unidentified narrator unaffected by the inconsistencies of his chapter, for in so doing, he would be giving an unambiguous frame to his chapter. Instead, that frame, consistent with the texture of the creation within it, is suitably perplexing and enigmatic, thanks chiefly to his, the narrator's, own insertion into the story he is creating. He may speak with authority confirming the truth of Feijoo's recollections retold to Fortunata («Debo advertir que nada refería Feijoo que no fuese verdad» [III, iv, 4; 147]) or anticipating Feijoo's remarkable survival into 1876 (III, iv, 10; 209), but on other occasions, when giving some kind of value judgment on Feijoo's actions and motives he shows a surprising absence of criticism. He seems to have an unqualified admiration for his main subject calling him «mi hombre» (III, iv, 1; 117; III, iv, 10; 204) or, more emphatically, «el buen señor» (III, iv, 1; 126), «este excelente hombre» (III, iv, 7; 178) or «el bonda-doso anciano» (III, iv, 5; 158). This admiration blinds the narrator to the inherent contradictions of his words at times: having praised Feijoo's gifts to needy friends as «estas caridades discretas... aquello no era pres-tar, sino hacer limosna, *quizás la más evangélica, la más aceptable a los ojos de Dios*» (III, iv, 7; 178-79), in the next breath almost, when referring to the concrete example of Juan Pablo, he talks about these gifts as «tales favores» which demand some form of repayment. Equally discon-certing for the reader is the narrator's stated acceptance of the provisions Feijoo makes in his will: «hizo la distribución de todo con un acierto que declaraba su gran delicadeza y el aprecio que hacía de las amistades consecuentes. Respecto a Fortunata *lo dispuso tan bien que no cabía más*» (III, iv, 10; 210). The effect of his ironic parallels prior to this conclusion has, however, been to place grave doubts on this sort of materialistic solution.

Ultimately, any narrative voice in any novel will be somewhat enigma-tic, for the narrator has, perforce, to straddle the two worlds of fiction and reality. It is in fact *his* narrative voice which defines and establishes the essential polarity of every novel: the fictional recreation of material taken from an extra-literary reality. This polarity is, of course, comple-mentary and co-equal. The pre-eminence that Kronik claims for the text and Blanco for the determinant of social reality is simply not valid: pre-eminence can only be applied to the order of analysis: the text was our unavoidable first ripple, the socio-historical reality of 1875-76 which provides the raw material must be the subject of our second analytical ripple. Galdós's inclusion of references to that reality does serve as a reminder of its determinism within the chapter, but if that were their only function, the length and nature of those socio-historical references would hardly be justified. Instead, Galdós integrates them fully into the chapter's structure and theme so that the two polarities, fiction and history, become equally interdependent and enriching; they become interchangeable.

There are two important «blocks» of political history in the chapter: each covers a different part of recent Spanish history. The first concerns Feijoo's military exploits overseas in Cuba, the Philippines and Italy in the 1840s, and the second «block» deals with the political events of 1875-76, the period of the fictional action. In addition the two blocks are presented at different points in the chapter so that certain comparisons can be made: Feijoo's adventures are related in section iv, the 1875 developments in sections vii, viii, x. There is an undoubted thematic relation between the two in much the same way that the other self-referential images have an ironic counterpoint. Feijoo's heroic exploits in far-away places in the past are presented, actualized, to the reader in an exaggerated Romanticized fashion:

> Tú no puedes hacerte cargo de aquellas noches de luna en Cuba, *de aquella bóveda de plata resplandeciente,* de aquellos manglares que son jardines en medio *de los espejos de la mar*... Pues aquella noche *de que te hablo, estábamos acechando* junto a un río, porque sabíamos que por allí habían de pasar los insurgentes. Oímos un chapoteo en el agua; creímos que era un caimán que se escurría entre las cañas bravas. De repente, pim, ... un tiro. ¡Ellos!... Al instante toda nuestra gente *se echa* los fusiles a la cara. Tata-ra-trap... Un negrazo *salta* sobre mí y, zas le *meto* el machete por el ombligo y se lo *saco* por el lomo... No me he visto en otra, hija.
>
> También había estado en la expedición a Roma el 48. ¡Oh, Roma! Aquello sí que era cosa grande. ¡*Qué bonito aquel paso* de Pío IX bendiciendo a las tropas! (III, iv, 4; 145-46)

The events of history seem to have a peculiarly individualistic slant from Feijoo in order to magnify his own bravery. The same individual perspective is dominant in the account of contemporary Restoration details when national politics seem to be arranged for the profit of the individual with continuous manipulation of government jobs and the electoral system. The links between these two «blocks» of historical relation are made closer by the common factor of Feijoo's participation: he is an expert manipulator of the patronage system as he obtains positions for the Rubín brothers (Nicolás and Juan Pablo) and promises something for Villaamil: indeed the chapter concludes with a picture of Feijoo harassing Villalonga with the latter's recommendation (III, iv, 10; 211-12). Feijoo, the political pedlar, is a far cry from the swashbuckling Colonel Feijoo of Cuban days.

The inverted values of contemporary politics (exploitation for personal self-profit) are further criticized by their association with such a mundane place of leisure as the cafes, so clearly ridiculed for their animal noises and bustle. Galdós declares: «De aquellas célebres mesas habían salido ya un ministro, dos subsecretarios y varios gobernadores» (III, iv, 8; 184). It is also from these same tables, in another cafe, and from the same group of people almost (Villalonga, Feijoo, Juan Pablo and Maxi) that the future social salvation of Fortunata will emerge; the correspondence with the political appointments joins in equal union the two spheres, with a consequent interchange of ironic meaning.

The personal exploitation of politics is best illustrated in the presentation of Don Basilio Andrés de la Caña re-appointed to the Civil Service after the restoration of the Bourbons. His new position of affluence, like that of others, is reflected in the change of clothes he wears «digna de pasar a la historia» (III, iv, 7; 173). This inversion of the true significance of politics reaches its highest point of comic exaggeration when Galdós observes that changes of government are almost brought about by slackness of trade in the clothes industry: «cuando pasa mucho tiempo sin cambio político, cogen el cielo con las manos los sastres y mercaderes de trapos, y con sus quejas acaloran a los descontentos y azuzan a los revolucionarios. "Están los negocios muy parados", dicen los tenderos; y otro resuella también por la herida diciendo: "No se protege al comercio ni a la industria"» (III, iv, 7; 174). In light of the foregoing, Don Andrés's «ademanes gubernamentales» when ordering his coffee to be delivered to his office is a farcical display of power «por el cual los circunstantes podrían comprender, sin necesidad de más explicaciones, el cataclismo que iba a ocurrir en la Hacienda si D. Basilio se retrasaba un minuto más» (III, iv, 7; 175). The important point, however, to notice here is that this sartorial/political change parallels that of Fortunata's life. The restoration of the Bourbons marks a new era in Spanish politics, just as Feijoo's relationship is a new development for Fortunata. Politics and Fortunata are going through a new phase in their lives. It is important to note the extent to which the political change affects Don Basilio's appearance: «el estreno de levita de paño fino... *transformó* a don Basilio». Like Fortunata, he has put on weight and changed physical appearance: «Hasta parecía que había engordado, que tenía más pelo en la cabeza, que era menos miope y que se le habían quitado diez años de encima. Se afeitaba ya todos los días, lo que en realidad *le quitaba el parecido consigo mismo*» (III, iv, 7; 173-74). If the parallel between the political material and Fortunata's re-education is correct, then, the success of Feijoo's plan is put considerably in doubt: it will only be a cosmetic, superficial change like that in Caña's clothes. That Galdós was thinking of this parallelism is shown by his next scene: after Caña has saluted Feijoo on his way out of the cafe to the office the old man's thoughts return to his plan for Fortunata: «Al quedarse otra vez solo, D. Evaristo arrugó el ceño. Ocurriósele una contrariedad que entorpecería su plan» (III, iv, 7; 175). Nor should it be overlooked that Feijoo's adventures in far-away places had not been all martial: his amorous exploits are equally important and are also somewhat fancifully exaggerated: «Y la conversación rodaba, sin saber cómo, de la bendición papal a los amoríos del narrador. En esto era la de no acabar, *y de la cuenta total salían a siete aventuras por año, con la particularidad de que eran en las cinco partes del mundo»* (III, iv, 4; 146). His liaison with Fortunata is the last of a long series, also associated with political developments.[16]

Furthermore, Galdós transfers the vocabulary of politics to his fiction: warning Fortunata to control her emotions, Feijoo notes: «Si el corazón se te conserva en el tamaño que ahora tiene, si no hay medio de recortarlo, *si se te pronuncia,* ¿qué le vamos a hacer?» (III, iv, 9; 202). «Lo primero que tienes que hacer es sostener el *orden público,* quiero decir, la paz del matrimonio» (III, iv, 10; 205 [Galdós's italics]); «Lo que llaman infidelidad no es más que el fuero de la naturaleza que quiere imponerse contra *el despotismo social,* y por eso verás que soy tan indulgente *con los y las que se pronuncian»* (III, iv, 5; 157), all of which could be the colourful vocabulary of any army veteran, but more likely it is Galdós joining history and fiction in heavy embrace. When Feijoo decides because of failing health to terminate his sexual role with Fortunata, he declares: «La aventura del viejo Feijoo ha pasado a la historia» (III, iv, 9; 197)... «Hay algo en mí que ha hecho dimisión; pero dimisión irrevocable; efectividad concluida, funciones que pasaron a la historia» (III, iv, 5; 160). Speaking with Maxi, he likens his physical decline to a «cesantía»: «me he rendido, y espero tranquilo el *cese»* (III, iv, 8; 187; [Galdós's italics]); again, not an inappropriate simile in a cafe where he will shortly be harassed for a recommendation by the «cesante» Villaamil (III, iv, 8; 191). The overall result is that if fiction is upgraded, history is downgraded. Fortunata's affair with Feijoo becomes an «episodio nacional», whilst the historical material takes on an air of unreality, fiction.[17] In this context, the Spanish word «historia» wonderfully combines the duality that Galdós feels, finding paradoxical expression in his description of Refugio as «personaje de historia, aunque no histórico» (III, iv, 8; 186).[18]

---

[16] Significantly, Maxi's newly-discovered interest in philosophy is the result of Fortunata's desertion: «La desgracia me ha hecho a mí volver los ojos a las cosas que no se ven ni se tocan. Si no lo hubiera hecho así, me habría muerto ya cien veces» (III, iv, 9; 192-93).

[17] *La de Bringas* is perhaps the *novela contemporánea* of Galdós which best illustrates this process of equalization.

[18] This vision of the co-existence, co-equalness, of history and fiction in *Fortunata y Jacinta* finds an important formulation in Galdós's notes on the novel in his autobiography, *Memorias de un desmemoriado*:

One final socio-historical ripple on the pond of this chapter's analysis has to be considered. As befits a so-called Naturalist writer, Galdós supplies many details about the location of Fortunata's hideaway apartment in the Calle de Tabernillas and Feijoo's residence in the calle de Don Pedro (III, iv, 4; 143-44). This second location is significantly secluded, undisturbed by the hustle and bustle of central Madrid: «En toda la casa no se oía ni el ruido de una mosca, pues el Ministro Plenipotenciario del principal era hombre solo, y fuera de las noches de recepción, que eran muy contadas, creeríase que allí no vivía nada» (III, iv, 4; 144). The neighbouring embassy provides an international political dimension to the chapter, consonant with Feijoo's international adventures, but it is also an appropriate echo for the later mission or negotiations that Feijoo will conduct with the Rubín brothers to effect the return of Fortunata to the family: when at one point Juan Pablo accuses the colonel of having an affair with Fortunata «la diplomacia de Feijoo se alarmó, creyendo llegada la ocasión de sacar, si no todo el Cristo, la cabeza de él» (III, iv, 7; 177). Thus Galdós's choice of neighbour for Feijoo —such a minor point— is not without its later reverberation: after all he could have chosen some other profession, but he preferred one that would contribute to the chapter's central theme.

The allusion to Christ in the previous quotation reminds us that

Expirando el verano, volví a Madrid, y apenas llegué a mi casa, recibí la grata visita de mi amigo el insigne varón don José Ido del Sagrario, el cual me dio noticia de Juanito Santa Cruz y su esposa Jacinta, de doña Lupe, la de los Pavos, de Barbarita, Mauricia la *Dura* [Galdós's italics], la linda Fortunata y, por último, del famoso Estupiñá.

Todas estas figuras pertenecientes al mundo imaginario, y abandonadas por mí en las correrías veraniegas, se adueñaron nuevamente de mi voluntad. Visité a doña Lupe en su casa de la calle de Cuchilleros y platiqué con el usurero Torquemada y la criada Papitos. Pasaba largas horas en el café del Gallo, donde me entretenía oyendo las conversaciones de los trajinantes y abastecedores de los mercados de aves. Por la escalerilla subía y bajaba veinte veces al día, y en Puerta Cerrada tenía el cuartel general de mis observaciones. En la Plaza Mayor pasaba buenos ratos charlando con el tendero José Luengo, a quien yo había bautizado con el nombre de Estupiñá. *Ved aquí un tipo fielmente tomado de la realidad. No lo describo porque ya lo habréis visto en su natural traza y colorido.*

El viaje de boda de Juanito Santa Cruz y su regreso a Madrid, así como la intriga del bárbaro Izquierdo, traficante en niños, *son hechos imaginarios aunque parezcan reales. Lo verdaderamente auténtico y real es la* figura de la santa Guillermina Pacheco. Tan sólo me he tomado la licencia de variar el nombre. La santa dama fundadora se llamó en el siglo doña Ernestina. Recaudando cuantiosas limosnas, así en los palacios como en las cabañas, creó un asilo en cuya iglesia reposan sus cenizas. Esta gloriosa personalidad merece a todas luces la canonización» (*Obras completas,* VI, 1679).

The baffling contradictions in the last two paragraphs can thus be explained by Galdós's belief in this interdependence and interchangeability of history and fiction.

Fortunata's apartment is in an area of Madrid «*donde Cristo dio las tres voces y no le oyeron*» (III, iv, 4; 143; Galdós's italics); it is so far out of Madrid that it seems like a country village. Surely all of this distancing from Madrid is suitable for Feijoo's purpose: it is undiscovered by his «amigos más sagaces» (III, iv, 3; 139). But it is hardly the right environment in which to prepare Fortunata for social rehabilitation: after a month's seclusion, Fortunata ventures back into the city one day, as far as Puerta Cerrada, but «al sentir el mugido de la respiración de la capital en sus senos centrales, volvióse asustada a su pacífica y silenciosa calle de Tabernillas» (III, iv, 4; 144). In other words, the chapter's topography is another meaningful guide or warning about the efficacy or suitability of Feijoo's «curso de filosofía práctica».[19]

The inhabitants of the neighbourhood also constitute a reflection on the position of Fortunata: in the immediate area of the Calle de Tabernillas, the people are «modestamente acomodado» (III, iv, 4; 143) just as Fortunata is now fairly affluent, thanks to Feijoo. However, in the more distant area of the calle de la Solana «habita tanta pobretería», a warning for Fortunata of the alternative to her liaison with Feijoo. Of greater significance is Galdós's description of the taludes del Rosario where «la vecindad no es muy distinguida, ni las vistas muy buenas, por caer contra aquella parte las prisiones militares y encontrarse a cada paso mujeres sueltas y soldados que se quieren soltar. Al fin de la calle del Aguila también desmerece mucho el vecindario, pues en la explanada de Gilimón, inundada de sol a todas las horas del día, suelen verse cuadros dignos del Potro de Córdoba y del Albaicín de Granada» (III, iv, 4; 143). Is this just a typically detailed Naturalist description or is it rather an artist's careful selection of appropriate material to fit the theme of his chapter, for after all, what are Fortunata and Feijoo but «una mujer suelta» and a «soldado que se quiere soltar»? The point surely is that Galdós is able to use his Madrid topography to underline the real nature (and ultimate chances of success) of the Feijoo/Fortunata relationship.[20]

---

[19] The important topography of the novel has been partially and unevenly studied by the following critics: CARLOS BLANCO AGUINAGA, «On 'The Birth of Fortunata'», *Anales Galdosianos*, III (1968), 13-24; PETER A. BLY, «Fortunata and No 11, Cava de San Miguel», *Hispanófila*, no. 59 (1976-77), 31-48; PHYLLIS ZATLIN BORING, «The Streets of Madrid as a Structuring Device in *Fortunata y Jacinta*», *Anales Galdosianos*, XIII (1978), 13-22; JOSÉ GAVIRA, «Algo sobre Galdós y su topografía madrileña», *Revista de la Biblioteca, Archivo y Museo del Ayuntamiento de Madrid*, X (1933), 63-74.

[20] Feijoo regards legalized marriage as a prison and married couples as «prisioneros el uno del otro, y darían algo por soltar el grillete» (III, iv, 5; 157). However, the irony is that Feijoo has managed to confine Fortunata to a limited, restricted area of Madrid in a kind of open-door prison: the narrator's remark «vivían retiradamente» (III, iv, 3; 139) comes immediately after Feijoo's assurance that Juanito, if he shows up in the area «a Segura llevan preso».

This topography motif also receives its ironic reprise in the chapter's cafe sequences: Juan Pablo and other habitués change their favourite cafe from time to time for no good reason: Villaamil informs Feijoo: «¡Ah! ¿buscaba usted a Juan Pablo? Pues *del salto se ha ido* al café de Zaragoza. Dice que le cargan los ingenieros» (III, iv, 8; 185). In the internal arrangement of the different cafe «tertulias» we can see a microcosm of the different groups that make up Spanish society (Galdós had already developed this idea in the first chapter of Part III, «Costumbres turcas»). These cafe tertulias concern themselves, absurdly, with topics not within their domain of expertise: «los ingenieros de Caminos hablaban de política europea, y más acá los de Minas disputaban sobre literatura dramática. No lejos de éstos, un grupo de empleados en la Contaduría central se ocupaba con gran calor de pozos artesianos, y dos jueces de primera instancia, unidos a un actor retirado, a un empresario de caballos para la Plaza de Toros y a un oficial de la Armada, discutían si eran más bonitas las mujeres con *polisón* o sin él» (III, iv, 8; 184). Again, Galdós's selection of illustrative examples is not accidental: by showing at this inconsequential and mundane level, how people interfere absurdly in topics beyond their capabilities or unsuited to their training, Galdós is really constructing a fictional commentary on the unwarranted meddling of Feijoo in Fortunata's life: like the «tertulianos», Feijoo is interested in his subject, but given his training and experience, is he the right person to undertake this social regeneration of Fortunata or are his methods correct? One final small point commands attention: Feijoo has some difficulty in making his way around the tables in the café de Zaragoza to get to the Rubíns' corner: «Desembozándose, avanzó el anciano por *la tortuosa calle que dejaran libre* las mesas del centro, y miraba a un lado y otro buscando a su amigo. Ya tropezaba con un mozo cargado de *servicio* [Galdós's italics], ya su capa se llevaba la toquilla de una cursi; *aquí se le interponía* el brazo del vendedor de *Correspondencias* que alargaba ejemplares a los parroquianos, *y allá le hacían barricada dos individuos gordos que salían o cuatro flacos que entraban*» (III, iv, 8; 186). Again the selection of this series of obstacles is not insignificant: Feijoo is stopped by a hilarious succession of parts of bodies or material objects; the climax is the oxymoronic last phrase. Can we not see in this obstacle race an ironic echo of the much easier passage Feijoo has when communicating with his idol in the Calle de Tabernillas? («Por la solitaria calle de las Aguas se comunicaba brevemente Feijoo con su ídolo» [III, iv, 4; 144])?

In short, the historical material is closely integrated into the structure and theme of the chapter: it is the necessary interdependent corrective that Feijoo's re-education of Fortunata has to have: without it, the criticism of the philosophical plan would lack authenticity; it is a plan which is trying to prepare Fortunata for re-immersion in society, so the socio-political material shows us to what sort of society Fortunata will be returning and also allows us to assess the chances of her success. But the socio-political structure is presented in such an absurd fashion that it comes to constitute an ironic counterpoint to that plan. Furthermore, like the images of self-referential creation which constitute an internal ironic counterpoint to the creation of Fortunata, the political material is so structured to have its own internal arrangement of point and counterpoint.

This marvellously structured chapter that is Part III, Chapter IV of *Fortunata y Jacinta,* is really a self-contained unit full of contrasting patterns. If it has generated a series of ripples and minor ripples on our surface of literary criticism, we must not forget that it is only part of a much larger whole and that all its ironic echoes may not appear so ironic when viewed against the ripples produced by later and earlier chapters. The apparently futile and misguided attempt by Feijoo to recreate Fortunata may well turn out to be not so unsuccessful as it portends here; certainly the nature of the ironic statement is not to preclude alternative interpretations. If it has been possible to talk of ripples, or contrasting presentations, in this paper, due recognition must be given to the hands that threw this chapter into our pond: Carlos Blanco Aguinaga and John Kronik (and Peter Goldman, for his enthusiastic incitement) are to be congratulated for giving such a weighty chapter a dynamic propulsion that is still producing ripples over the aqueous surface of our minds.

Queen's University,
Kingston, Canada.

PETER B. GOLDMAN

Feijoo and the Failed Revolution: A Dialectical Inquiry into «Fortunata y Jacinta» and the Poetics of Ambiguity

I. INTRODUCTION. DISCIPLINE AND SUBVERSION: THE FAILURE OF FEIJOO

There are two important lessons which Feijoo tries to teach Fortunata in Part III, Chapter IV, «Un curso de filosofía práctica»: discipline and subversion: [1]

> Hay que guardar en todo caso las santas apariencias, y tributar a la sociedad ese culto externo sin el cual volveríamos al estado salvaje. En nuestras relaciones tienes un ejemplo de que cuando se quiere el secreto se consigue. Es cuestión de estilo y habilidad. Si yo tuviera tiempo ahora, te contaría infinitos casos de pecadillos cometidos con una reserva absoluta, sin el menor escándalo, sin la menor ofensa del decoro que todos nos debemos... Te pasmarías. Oye bien lo que te digo, y apréndetelo de memoria. Lo primero que tienes que hacer es sostener el *orden público,* quiero decir, la paz del matrimonio, respetar a tu marido y no consentir que pierda su dignidad de tal... Dirás que es difícil; pero ahí está el talento, compañera, ... Hay que discurrir, y sobre todo, penetrarse bien del propio decoro para saber mirar por el ajeno... (III, iv, 10; 204-05; Galdós's italics)

Feijoo encourages her to be revolutionary, but Fortunata ends her days irredeemably bourgeois. She fails to maintain her self-discipline, violates decorum, and finally also does herself physical violence. Successful revolutionaries have always observed that the most effective rebel is the one who knows when to blend decorously with the scenery and

---

[1] BENITO PÉREZ GALDÓS, *Fortunata y Jacinta (Dos historias de casadas)* (Madrid: La Guirnalda, 1887), 4 vols. Each volume is paginated separately. All references to this novel are from the first edition. To facilitate identification in other editions, each reference in this essay indicates part or volume, chapter, and section followed by page number in the first edition. The accentuation is modernized; Galdós's punctuation is retained.

when to do battle. The effective insurgent is the one who understands and appreciates the necessity of subverting by preserving appearances: by seeming to be if not counterrevolutionary, then intractably conservative; by using, in other words, the «system» for the purposes of its own destruction. Fortunata, on the other hand, does not maintain this essential self-control.

If she does consummate one revolutionary act by giving birth to the new «Delfín», she also destroys herself; her destruction furthermore reverses her revolution and inaugurates the definitive consolidation of the middle classes in power. Symbolic of this strengthening of midde-class hegemony is the delivery of the child, the product of her sacrifice, to Church and established Society incarnated in Guillermina and Jacinta. Yet it must be emphasized that Feijoo did not want this to be the destiny of his lover and pupil.[2] On the contrary, it was his hope that Fortunata would reestablish «el orden público» in her life, so that she might create and benefit from a greater *dis*order: double adultery, equivalent to the subversion of two bourgeois families, Rubín and Santa Cruz. In this Fortunata was a student of limited vocation and Feijoo less of a preceptor than has been thought.

Carlos Blanco, for instance, makes the point that Feijoo, as a representative of the bourgeois world of Madrid, recaptures Fortunata for that society in order that subsequently she may be destroyed by it. In contrast to Blanco's social definition of Fortunata's *restauración,* Geoffrey Ribbans sees Feijoo's work on and with Fortunata in aesthetic terms: «His practical philosophy, his relativist morality, his regard for forms typify the moral climate which leads to the *Restauración,* while at the same time his primary structural function in the novel is to bring about the second domestic restoration between Fortunata and Maxi — in the chapter entitled "Otra restauración"» (pp. 108-09). These essays are provocative and interesting, yet I will dispute both categories of conclusions. First because I believe Feijoo less shallow and hypocritical; it is Juanito, Moreno

---

[2] Until she storms out of her apartment in search of Aurora, thereby creating a scandal which cannot be hidden from the public, and also doing herself irreversible bodily harm, Fortunata is well on the way to achieving her goals as we will see. She is the architect of her own destruction physically and effacement socially. Fortunata's is a deviance akin to that described by HOWARD S. BECKER, *Outsiders. Studies in the Sociology of Deviance* (New York: The Free Press, 1963). On p. 11 Becker cites an early (1926) work by Bronislaw Malinowski on the matter of sexual behavior: «public opinion is lenient, though decidedly hypocritical. If the affair is carried on *sub rosa* with a certain amount of decorum, and if no one in particular stirs up trouble —public opinion will gossip, but not demand any harsh punishment. If, on the contrary, scandal breaks out— everyone turns against the guilty...». On the basis of this and other observations, Becker makes the trenchant point that «Whether an act is deviant, then, depends on how other people react to it» (11). This is very much what Feijoo tries to make Fortunata understand.

Isla and Guillermina whose morality best typifies that of Restoration Madrid. Second, I contest the notion that Feijoo is middle-class Madrid's truant officer on the lookout for errant and upstart members of the *pueblo*. Third, because I believe Fortunata already lost by the time she reaches Feijoo, fully socialized and thoroughly accepting of middle-class values. And finally, because I view Feijoo's primary function to be that of demonstrating to Fortunata the distinction between self and society, of enabling her in other words to develop a realistic sense of otherness. Montesinos and Gullón are representative of those critics who understand Feijoo's role as that of an advocate who fails. They do not put his failure in the context of educating Fortunata about herself and society, but they do see his «lessons» as subversive in the same vein as Mauricia's admonitions were subversive. Montesinos also makes what I consider to be an essential distinction about Feijoo's priorities and intentions: «El quiere enseñar a su chulita a ser libre, no a ser hipócrita».[3]

In the following pages, then, I want to suggest that current criticism notwithstanding Feijoo fails and Galdós tells us so. For example, after delivering his last lecture to Fortunata, Feijoo leaves forever the flat on the Calle de Tabernillas:

> Creyó que una desconocida lengua le gritaba: «¡Estúpido, vaya, vaya unas cosas que enseñas a tu hija...!» Extendió la mano para detener al cochero y decirle que volviera a la calle de Tabernillas; pero antes de realizar aquel propósito, cesó la trepidación que en su alma había sentido, y todo quedó en reposo... «¡Qué debilidades! —pensó—; éstas son chocheces y nada más que chocheces... ¿Pues no se me ocurrió volver allá para desdecirme? No te reselles, compañero, y sostén ahora lo que has creído siempre. Esto es lo práctico, es lo único posible... Si le recomendara la virtud absoluta, ¿qué sería? sermón absolutamente perdido. Así al menos...»
> Y siguió tan satisfecho. (III, iv, 10; 206-07)

At the very moment of Feijoo's ostensible victory Galdós shows it to be more apparent than real. Feijoo comprehends the impossibility of his teaching; his premonition of failure achieves the category of prophecy. I submit that every effort on his part was directed to one end: the preservation in society of Fortunata. It was not Feijoo who instructed Fortunata to give her fortune to Guillermina; in fact, he directed her to give her funds to Guillermina's antithesis, doña Lupe. Nor did he instruct Fortunata to give her son to Jacinta; rather, he taught her now to win

---

[3] CARLOS BLANCO's article is included in this group of essays. GEOFFREY RIBBANS, «Contemporary History in the Structure and Characterization of *Fortunata y Jacinta*», *Galdós Studies*, I, ed. J. E. Varey (London: Tamesis, 1970), pp. 90-113. RICARDO GULLÓN, «Estructura y diseño en *Fortunata y Jacinta*», *Papeles de Son Armadans*, 12 (febrero-marzo, 1968), 223-316, esp. 245-47; JOSÉ F. MONTESINOS, *Galdós*, II (Madrid: Castalia, 1969), 266-67. On Mauricia v LUCILLE V. BRAUN, «The Novelistic Function of Mauricia La Dura [sic] in Galdós' *Fortunata y Jacinta*», *Symposium*, XXXI (1977), 277-89.

the body of Jacinta's husband. Indeed, were it not that Juanito had begun an affair with her confidante, Aurora, Fortunata might have continued serenely on her own, having successfully undermined the *orden público* of the two families. It is in sum incorrect to see Feijoo as the emblematic arm of middle-class morality in the Spain of Fortunata and Galdós.

Nor is Fortunata socially, intellectually, or sentimentally a victim of Feijoo. Rather, as John Kronik suggests in this volume, she is a pupil who cannot learn her lessons well. Instead of subverting the order of the middle classes, she *becomes* middle class. Despite the best efforts of the retired colonel, Fortunata cannot learn to be devious. Furthermore, it is time we recognized that Feijoo and Fortunata share many of the same ideas about society, about life in society, and about love. Fortunata will find this hard to accept; prior to her liaison with Feijoo, she was effectively educated to believe in her own guilt. It is not that Feijoo sabotages her attempt to undermine social order and control her own life; rather, it is that by the time she meets him she is doomed to fail, forever unable to be «práctica». Moreover, Feijoo's wish to teach her to be «práctica» is nothing less than a desire that she be able to live her own life in society, if necessary by subverting it. His fears as he leaves forever the apartment on the Calle de Tabernillas intimate what by the end of the novel we know to be true: Fortunata is beyond his reach; he cannot help her because she is *a priori* a weapon disarmed.

This essay takes the view that Fortunata is able for a time to implement the ideas she shares with Feijoo. Eventually she fails to maintain them in practice. Those ideas have always been the practical basis of Feijoo's existence. They were not a means to an end but the means and end both. On the other hand, the basis of Fortunata's existence is her love for Juanito and the desire to bear his son. Feijoo's practicum is for her only a means. In the end, Fortunata and her teacher are unsuccessful because she is too self-centered, a sentimental bourgeois, an «apasionada» like Maxi (III, iv, 7; 172) who allows love and jealousy to drag her down into the street from the literal and metaphoric fastnesses of existence above the world in the Cava de San Miguel. Her battle with Aurora kills her, after all; in purely biological terms it is wasteful, ethically it is unnecessary.

Finally, I wish to resuscitate the notion of Galdós's neo-Hegelianism. Specifically, I should like to suggest in this essay that *Fortunata y Jacinta* is very much influenced by notions of the Hegelian system, and that the structure of the novel is rigorously dialectical.

II. THE DIALECTICAL JOURNEY OF LIFE: INDIVIDUAL REBIRTH AND SOCIAL RESTORATION

If it is misleading to see Feijoo as the oppressive weapon of the capitalist social order, it is also incorrect to see Fortunata as the victim of that society. Matters are more complex. Look, for example, at the rejection suffered by Fortunata at Juanito's hands in Part III, Chapter III, «La revolución vencida». In the socioeconomic sphere, the end of the Revolution of 1868 with the Restoration signified the consolidation, in power, of the bourgeoisie. And it is now, supposed victim that she is, that Fortunata also comes to power dominating Feijoo.

Galdós certainly does not wish to suggest that Fortunata has not suffered, or that she has not been abused by Juanito. But he does want us to know that every affirmation bears within it the seeds of its own contradiction, something which elsewhere I have called his «aesthetic of ambiguity».[4] Lucille Braun suggests that Mauricia is an excellent example of this ambiguity of character. Although there is no comparative study of the function of Mauricia and Feijoo, in many respects the two show a certain complementarity: spontaneity versus calculation, intuition versus intelligence, self versus other. They are not a pair, however; they exist in dialectical tension with Fortunata. Moreover, if Mauricia exists dialectically with Fortunata and Feijoo, she shows also a similar tension with Fortunata and Guillermina who (as Gullón first observed) is no more of a saint than Mauricia is evil.[5] The latter is constructive as the voice giving «expression to ideas fermenting deep within Fortunata's soul» (Braun, 282), just as she is destructive.

If *Fortunata y Jacinta* is a novel characterized by these traits of contradiction and compatibility, then surely we will find them in the protagonists. Fortunata's relationship with Feijoo is exemplary on this point. Recall that Juanito's rejection of her physically incapacitates the young woman; her weaknesses, her vulnerability, paradoxically give her the power to take possession of Feijoo, exercising over him a destructive effect. She literally saps his vitality; she rejuvenates, he enters an irreversible state of decline and decrepitude. At first Feijoo seems to be the dominant personality, asserting himself immediately. Visiting her in her flat, «Como D. Evaristo se preciaba de saber algo de medicina, tomóle el pulso» (III, iv, 1; 118). He then gives her a lecture, finally leaving. Later

---

[4] PETER B. GOLDMAN, «Galdós and the Aesthetic of Ambiguity: Notes on the Thematic Structure of *Nazarín*», *Anales Galdosianos*, IX (1974), 99-112 and «Galdós and the Nineteenth Century Novel: The Need for an Interdisciplinary Approach», *Anales Galdosianos*, X (1975), 5-18.

[5] BRAUN, *op. cit.* GULLÓN, *op. cit.*, 247-57.

he returns and begins to show —and realize— that he is coming under
her spell, and that she is beginning to overpower him with her passivity:

> —¿Y qué tal nos encontramos esta tarde? —dijo D. Evaristo inclinán-
> dose para verle la cara.
> Echábaselas de médico; pero examinaba la cara por lo bonita que le
> parecía, no por buscar en ella síntomas hipocráticos; y como avanzara la
> noche y no había luz, tenía que acercarse mucho para ver bien. Continuaba
> ella en el propio sitio y postura que por la mañana. (III, iv, 1; 123-24)

Fortunata's passivity is a critical factor; she does not wish to overpower
others, she is possibly unconscious of her effect on them. Her domination
of Maxi and Feijoo, for example, is not premeditated. But if she is a
victim, she also victimizes. If she is the subject which others mold and
form apparently as they wish, she also is possessed of innate powers which
operate important changes on those who pretend to work her to their
will. Therefore, from the very beginning of her amorous association with
Feijoo, Fortunata exercises a certain influence over him. At the end of
his afternoon visit that first day, «Esta mujer me vuelve loco —pensaba
Feijoo, experimentando, al oír a Fortunata, una sensación de inefable
contento—. Si estoy chocho, si no sé lo que me pasa... ¡Ay Dios mío, a
mi edad!... No hay remedio, me declaro... Pero no, refrénate, compañe-
ro, aún no es tiempo...» To which the narrator adds:

> Al buen señor se le ponían los ojos encandilados oyéndole contar aque-
> llas cosas con tan encantadora sinceridad. Sonrisa de alegría y esperanza
> contraía sus labios, mostrando su dentadura intachable. Su cara, que era
> siempre sonrosada, poníasele encendida, *con verdaderos ardores de juventud
> en las mejillas.* Era, en suma, el viejo más guapo, simpático y frescachón
> que se podía imaginar; limpio como los chorros del oro, el cabello rizado,
> el bigote como la pura plata; lo demás de la cara, tan bien afeitadito, *que
> daba gloria verle;* la frente espaciosa y de color de marfil, con las arrugas
> finas y bien rasgueadas. Pues de cuerpo, ya quisieran parecérsele la mayor
> parte de los muchachos de hoy. Otro más derecho y bien plantado no había.
> (III, iv, 1; 126-27; my italics)

Within a month of their becoming lovers, Feijoo spends most of his
time in the Tabernillas Street flat where Fortunata now lives. After meals
it is their custom to play cards or converse, Feijoo doing most of the
talking and recounting his own adventures. But if, in the early stages of
their affair, Fortunata's powers rejuvenate Feijoo, once she is definitively
installed as a permanent fixture in the life of the retired colonel she begins
to sap his vital energies. Their relationship has the biological characteristics of a classic case of parasitism. Fortunata's improvement shows
its inverse expression in the health of her lover:

> Y la verdad era que con aquella vida tranquila y sosegada, eminente-
> mente práctica, se iba poniendo tan lucida de carnes, tan guapa y hermo-
> sota *que daba gloria verla.* Siempre tuvo la de Rubín buena salud; pero

nunca, como en aquella temporada, vio desarrollarse la existencia material con tanta plenitud y lozanía. Feijoo, al contemplarla, no podía menos de sentirse descorazonado. «Cada día más guapa —pensaba—, y yo cada día más viejo.» (III, iv, 4; 142; my italics)

The reader does not fail to observe that the very same words with which the narrator praised Feijoo's good looks are now used in praise of those of his paramour. This occurs precisely when the old gentleman starts noting his own physical slowdown. Indeed, as they finish their discussion that evening Feijoo observes that his debility is more than negligible: «Y al levantarse, apoyándose las manos en los brazos del sillón, notó, ¡ay!, que el cuerpo le pesaba más; pero mucho más que antes» (III, iv, 4; 149). He is disintegrating rapidly, unexpectedly; he walks with difficulty (III, iv, 5; 150), his hearing fails, his body begins to pain him (III, iv, 5; 150-51). That same lordly aspect which we earlier observed is converted, almost from evening to following morning, into the macabre reflection of what once it was. Nor do these signs escape the notice of the two lovers (III, iv, 5; 151). It is Feijoo, moreover, who articulates what is happening physically to both himself and Fortunata: «Ya ves», he tells her one afternoon, «qué contraste; yo voy para abajo, tú para arriba. Cuando digo que tienes lo mejor de la vida por delante» (III, iv, 5; 158).

And so Feijoo comes apart and Fortunata comes together in this fourth chapter of Part III of the novel. She becomes the obsession of Feijoo who almost kills himself over her. Fortunata certainly is not his victim; she leaves Feijoo undone physically just as Maxi is left undone mentally. She is more complex a character than assumed, incarnating as she does contradictory powers and possibilities, powers which are simultaneously creative and destructive, voluntary and unconscious. Even her passion is thus; her love for Juanito, after all, is what makes Fortunata so attractive to Feijoo (III, iv, 1; 117-27).

i. *Rebirth and external renewal*

In this sense —which increases the dimension of complexity and therefore reality in this extraordinary novel— each life influences those which surround it, just as it demonstrates reciprocally the influence on itself of surrounding people and events. Thus Fortunata does not simply pass from one vital state to another; she also leaves traces of her existence on those who affect her. If Feijoo does not acknowledge the relationship as such, he does observe its manifestations. There is first of all the birth imagery which is introduced at the very beginning, on the day following her break with Juanito. Feijoo instructs Fortunata: «Se necesitan muchas lecciones... [...] Usted no sabe de la misa la media. Parece que acaba de nacer, y que la han puesto de patitas en el mundo» (III, iv,

1; 121). Subsequently, as we already have seen, she recovers physically while his body begins to cease functioning (III, iv, 4; 142-43). Finally, there is the encounter over dinner (III, iv, 5; 157-58). Feijoo by now is reduced to ingesting nothing more than a boiled egg and chocolate; his major dinner-time activity is watching Fortunata eat. During dessert he speaks while she listens, mechanically devouring some «pasas y almendras, cogiéndolas del plato una a una y llevándoselas a la boca sin mirarlas» (III, iv, 5; 158). Suddenly Feijoo surprises her, gripping her chin and telling her

> ¡Qué gruesa estás y qué hermosota, y yo... yo... concluido, absolutamente concluido [...] Yo acabé. El estómago me pide el retiro. Hay algo en mí que ha hecho dimisión; pero dimisión irrevocable; efectividad concluida, funciones que pasaron a la historia. (III, iv, 5; 159-60)

Feijoo swallows an egg at this meal; it is symbolic of the embryo which figuratively resides within him, the Fortunata to whom he will give birth, his «hija».[6] The effort will kill him just as subsequently his «daughter's» health will be destroyed by childbirth.

The long generation of Fortunata moves at this point from the biological and physical recovery to the development of social behavior. The phase she now enters is a repetition with modifications; that is, her growth is realized dialectically. The narrator informs us:

> Se visitaba con los inquilinos de la casa, y con alguna familia de la inmediata, gente muy llana, muy neta; como que a todas las visitas iba la prójima con mantón y pañuelo a la cabeza. En el tiempo que duró aquella cómoda vida volvieron a determinarse en ella las primitivas maneras, que había perdido con el roce de otra gente de más afinadas costumbres. El ademán de llevarse las manos a la cintura en toda ocasión volvió a ser dominante en ella, y el hablar arrastrado, dejoso y prolongando ciertas vocales, reverdeció en su boca, como reverdece el idioma nativo en la de aquel que vuelve a la patria tras larga ausencia. (III, iv, 5; 155-56)

Thanks to the scholarship of Stephen Gilman[7] the reader comprehends immediately the symbolic importance of this description; the image herein painted is very like that seen at the outset of Juanito's —and the

---

[6] Later he tells her (III, iv, 10; 206): «Aquello se acabó... y ahora soy tu padre, tú mi hija...» This reading of biological symbolism is in line with STEPHEN GILMAN's seminal but nevertheless controversial «The Birth of Fortunata», *Anales Galdosianos,* I (1966), 71-83, as well as subsequent elaborations such as ROGER L. UTT, «'el pájaro voló': Observaciones sobre un leitmotif en *Fortunata y Jacinta»,* *Anales Galdosianos,* IX (1974), 37-50, and AGNES MONCY GULLÓN, «The Bird Motif and the Introductory Motif: Structure in *Fortunata y Jacinta»,* *Anales Galdosianos,* IX (1974), 51-75. Nevertheless it is possible to maintain such a reading independent of the bird motif. First and foremost, after all, this is a novel of births and deaths, of biological generations and degenerations of our own species.

[7] GILMAN, «The Birth of Fortunata», 77-78. The phrase about bringing her hands up to her waist finds its analogue in the famous passage cited by Gilman:

reader's— first encounter with Fortunata (I, iii, 4; 98). But we observe also that this is not a birth; rather it is the *re*birth of Fortunata. As with so many other important episodes in this novel, there is really no such thing as replication: With the repetition of an occurrence or the reappearance of a character, there are also important, indeed essential, changes. The episode recurs, yet it is no longer the same. The Fortunata who is reborn here after the gestation with Feijoo is radically different; important changes in her personality and on her person have altered her. Aesthetically speaking, the dialectic of life is projected externally — i.e., physically and episodically as the product of internalization of experience.

As if to emphasize the point, Galdós suggests that she is about to enter society again, that she is developing a social self. For Fortunata, a social self is rooted in having a name, in being the señora de Rubín. At this moment, she is almost, but only almost, ready to be the wife of Maxi again. Feijoo counsels Fortunata to return to her husband; the reader is surprised at the possibility but even more stunning is the fact that Fortunata is not at all taken aback:

> —Resultado de lo mucho que cavilo por ti. Es preciso que te vuelvas a unir a tu marido.
> *Contra lo que el simpático viejo esperaba Fortunata no hizo aspavientos de sorpresa.* Puso, sí, una carita muy monamente apenada, y alzando la voz, dijo:
> —Pero eso, ¿cabe en lo posible? (III, iv, 6; 161-62; my italics)

Neither we nor Feijoo ought be surprised, since Fortunata has heard all this before. As he was about to leave her for a second time, Juanito had delivered up the same advice to his devastated mistress:

> —Nos separaremos como amigos —dijo Santa Cruz tomándole una mano, que ella separó prontamente—, y me retiro dándote un buen consejo.
> —¿Cuál? —preguntó ella más airada que dolorida.
> —Que te unas... que procures unirte otra vez con tu marido.
> —¡Yo...! —exclamó la señora de Rubín con indecible terror—. ¡Después de...!
> —Ya te serenarás, hija. ¡El tiempo! ¿Sabes tú los milagros que ese señor hace? Tú lo has dicho: no hay mal que cien años dure, y cuando se tocan de cerca los grandes inconvenientes de vivir lejos de la ley, no hay más remedio que volver a ella. Ahora te parece imposible; pero volverás. (III, iii, 1; 105)

However much a rascal he may be, Juanito has a certain vision of social realities which frequently is lucid and accurate. Perhaps it was Montesi-

---

«La moza tenía pañuelo azul claro por la cabeza y un mantón sobre los hombros, y en el momento de ver al *Delfín*, se infló con él, quiero decir, que hizo ese característico arqueo de brazos y alzamiento de hombros con que las madrileñas del pueblo se agazapan dentro del mantón...» (I, iii, 4; 98).

nos who said it best (II, 217): Juanito is a «grandísimo botarate, pero botarate brillante. Es el producto de aquella educación progresiva que practicaba y preconizaba Don Baldomero». Juanito is right when he temporizes «Solemos decir: "tal cosa no llega nunca". Y sin embargo llega, y apenas nos sorprende por la suavidad con que ha venido» (III, iii, 1; 105). But if with Feijoo Fortunata is no longer put off by the suggestion that she return to Maxi, she still believes that the Rubín family will not accept her. Feijoo's answer on the healing quality of time again echoes Juanito:

> —Todo se perdona, hija, todo, todo —dijo el enfermo con indulgencia empapada en escepticismo—. Por muy grande que nos figuremos la masa de olvido derramado en la sociedad como elemento reparador, esa masa supera todavía a todos nuestros cálculos. El bien y la gratitud son limitados; siempre los encontramos cortos. El olvido es infinito. De él se deriva el *vuelta a empezar*, sin el cual el mundo se acabaría. (III, iv, 6; 163, Galdós's italics)

To be noted is the fact that the same advice elicits distinct reactions from the same person. If the giving of the advice is a scene repeated, neither the subject —Fortunata— nor her context are what formerly they were. And this structural element, that is, a repetition with essential modifications, is characteristic of the novel.

ii. *Rebirth and internal development*

With these concepts in mind, it is worthwhile to discover why Fortunata, at the time of Feijoo's advice that she return to Maxi, is still not prepared for her next sally into society. If she is on the point of *volver a empezar,* she still lacks the actuation of certain internal changes. Under Feijoo's tutelage these alterations of her character are rapidly effected. Her physical renascence is followed by the development of a social self. On leaving the bed of her now ill and infirm lover she begins to become conscious of the distinctions and divisions between her private or interior self, her social self and the selves of others. Now this acuteness is an alteration which *seems* to crop up overnight, but which in reality is the legacy of her long and fertile affair with Feijoo. The new attribute in her character is a sharp social sensibility; it has developed out of the tension between what one wants and that which is possible given the limits of the social structure within which one functions. Therefore the description which Galdós devotes to this fundamental shift in Fortunata's personality is extremely important. Unsurprisingly the description also reveals Galdós's vision of the structural role —aesthetic and social— of the dialectic.

Fortunata leaves Feijoo in his own flat and returns to the one which the two had maintained together; her mind is full of new, disturbing ideas and possibilities: «Al verse otra vez en su casa y sola, Fortunata no podía con la gusanera de pensamientos que *le llenaba toda la caja de la cabeza.* ¡Volver con su marido!» (III, iv, 7; 169; the italics are Galdós's). She contemplates the new life which is about to begin, and confesses to herself that its possibility neither surprises her nor seems absurd. In truth, she had considered it earlier as totally impracticable; now it is undeniably feasible. Furthermore, resuming with Maxi is now not only inevitable but also «conveniente». The dissolution of her life with Feijoo signals the blossoming of a new life with Maxi; the latter is rooted firmly in the former, however much on the wane it may be. One phase of existence gives way to another which it generates; life experience is not a rosary of isolated events but a dialectic of actuation, in which no episode stands alone but exists, rather, in balance with those past in which it was generated and those future rooted in and developing out of it.

Galdós gives flesh to this scheme of existence as he describes the equally dialectical mental process of associative thought occurring inside Fortunata's mind:

> Así *como en las mutaciones de cuadros disolventes, a medida que unas figuras se borran van apareciendo las líneas de otras,* primero una vaguedad o presentimiento de las nuevas formas, después contornos, luego masas de color, y por fin, las actitudes completas, así en la mente de Fortunata empezaron a esbozarse desde aquella noche, cual apariencias que brotan de la nebulosa del sueño, las personas de Maxi, de doña Lupe, de Nicolás Rubín y hasta de la misma Papitos. Eran ellos que *salían nuevamente a luz, primero como espectros, después como seres reales* con cuerpo, vida y voz. Al amanecer, inquieta y rebelde al sueño, oíales hablar y reconocía hasta los gestos más insignificantes que modelaban la personalidad de cada uno. (III, iv, 7, 170; my italics)

Fortunata's memory begins to awaken and with it the power to integrate the past with the present. She contemplates that stage of her life which is coming to a close, that which included Feijoo. It was, she admits to herself, tranquil but also lacking in the vitality and excitement deriving from «ambicionar» (III, iv, 7; 170-71). She felt at times «encarcelada». Although she lived in compliance with that regimen, her conformity diminished daily and progressively; her imagination was agitated increasingly by «algo nuevo y desconocido que interesara profundamente su alma, y pusiera en ejercicio sus facultades, *que se desentumecían después de una larga inactividad*» (*idem,* my italics). If finally her mental faculties are again sharpening themselves, her newborn social understanding and judgment enable her to desire and to plan ahead. Feijoo, following Maxi's path-breaking work with her,[8] paves the way for Fortu-

---

[8] In addition to inciting Fortunata in the Cervantine sense employed by Gilman and Américo Castro, Maxi also has some profound and practical effects on Fortunata. On incitation *v* AMÉRICO CASTRO, «La estructura del *Quijote*», originally published in 1947 and subsequently in his *Hacia Cervantes* (Madrid: Taurus, 1957),

nata by reminding her that she has both a past and present; therefore she also must have a future (which ironically is denied him):

> —Tú déjate querer, grandísima tonta, y hazte cargo de que se te presenta un ancho horizonte de vida... si lo sabes aprovechar.
> Esto del horizonte avivó en la mente de la joven *aquel naciente anhelo de lo desconocido, del querer fuerte sin saber cómo ni a quién.* Lo que no podía era compaginar esperanza tan incierta con la vida de familia que se le recomendaba. Pero algo y aun algos se le iba clareando en el entendimiento. (III, iv, 7; 172; my italics)

Only now is Fortunata armed for her next sally into society. There remains the preparation of society to receive her; this task too Feijoo takes upon himself. In sum, the rebirth of Fortunata occurs chronologically in a direction from *exterior inwards*. First she recuperates and then blossoms physically; subsequently she recovers her former social manner and dress habits, then her memory, her mental capabilities and finally her capacity for feeling and passion. It is important to note that her external being, her appearance, if prettier and more robust, seems as it was previously. She appears to be the same person, but in reality is forever changed, having suffered fundamental internal alterations.

iii. *Restorations*

The importance of the interior metamorphosis experienced by Fortunata is emphasized by contrast in the same chapter. Her renascence complete, Galdós thereupon lays before us another «mutación», society's change of skin due to the Restoration. The latter essentially meant nothing new, something Galdós understood full well by 1886 when he was writing *Fortunata y Jacinta*.[9] The Restoration in Galdós's mind was a phenomenon which *seemed* to augur a substantive change but which, *in reality*, was

pp. 241-65; STEPHEN GILMAN, «Narrative Presentation in *Fortunata y Jacinta*», *Revista Hispánica Moderna*, XXXIV (1968), 288-301, esp. 295-96, and pp. 162-64 of his *Galdós and the Art of the European Novel: 1867-1887* (Princeton: Princeton Univ. Press, 1981).

[9] On Galdós's assessment of the Restoration, based on a reading of his own journalism dating in the majority from 1885, *v* GOLDMAN, «Galdós and the Nineteenth Century Novel...», 6-8. Part I of *Fortunata y Jacinta* was completed in January of 1886, Part II in May and Part III in December (I, 479; II, 447; III, 399). THOMAS E. LEWIS remarks about the failure of the Restoration and Galdós's reaction to it that *Fortunata y Jacinta* «signals a novelistic attempt to reopen debate surrounding the ideology for which the highest sectors of the Spanish bourgeoisie subsequently opted...». Hence the temporal reversion to the Revolution of 1868 and the eight years following; *v* «*Fortunata y Jacinta*: Galdós and the Production of the Referent», *Modern Language Notes*, XCVI (1981), 316-39, esp. 326. Ribbans's thoughtful essay becomes even more interesting in the light of Lewis's observation. The reader wishing to consult historical, political and cultural studies of the period 1868-76 may find an orientation in the scholarship acknowledged in the notes to the above three essays.

meaningless. This is the significance of Madrid's literal change of ward-
robe, as seen by the eyes of Feijoo a few days following his urging that
Fortunata reunite with Maxi. He leaves her one day and ventures out
to the Café de Madrid (III, iv, 7; 173). We must observe first of all that
the internal reawakening of Fortunata and Feijoo's visit to this cafe —for
the purpose of proposing to Juan Pablo Rubín that the family accept her
again— textually occupy the same section 7 of Part III, Chapter IV. The
implication on one level is that the restoration of Fortunata as the señora
de Rubín will be as lacking in fundamental change in her matrimonial
life as the Restoration of Alphonso XII was socially and economically
in Spanish national life. But, and this should be emphasized, the parallel
just drawn exists in strong tension with an undeniable contrast, which is
the following: If nothing has changed truly in Spanish society, the character
and personality of Fortunata, her inner self, are totally different though
hidden behind an outer self which, more developed and polished, is nevertheless the same. It is perilous business at best to attempt to discern
simple correspondences between the socioeconomic realities of Spanish
society, and the people and their society in this novel. At times —and
they are frequent— Galdós tells us clearly that life is as much dominated
by contrasts and contradictions as by points in common.

The working of parallels against contrasts presents itself, as we just
mentioned, at the end of section 7 of Part III, Chapter IV. Feijoo enters
the Café de Madrid and the reader, through the eyes of the retired
colonel, sees one of those timely characters who are glimpsed but briefly
in the novel but who remain indelibly imprinted in the mind because,
like Refugio with her absent tooth, they are «personaje de historia, aunque no histórico» (III, iv, 8; 186). Now the person in question is Basilio
Andrés de la Caña. Why, one wonders, does he capture the narrative eye
in the first place? In this volume Peter Bly demonstrates that de la Caña's
presence cannot be dismissed as narrative garnishing. Indeed, read closely
Bly shows it to be a powerfully drawn presentation, a descriptive *tour
de force*. I submit additionally that although at first glance de la Caña's
presence seems insignificant, it provides not only the parallels Bly elucidates, but also a sharp contrast against which we may evaluate the
alterations experienced by Fortunata.

Feijoo on this morning in search of Juan Pablo travels the streets of
Madrid; he considers the fact that Juan Pablo, with the rest of Restoration society, has gone out to buy new clothes and is planning also to
replace his infamously filthy cape with a new one (III, iv, 7; 173). The
narrator voices Feijoo's cynicism and affirms «Eso al menos iba ganando
el país». The intervention of the narrator is due to the necessity of bringing our attention into focus, for a moment and only for a moment, and
furthermore without our realizing it, on don Basilio. As soon as he is

portrayed the narrative point of view will again be Feijoo's. The description of de la Caña is this:

> Pero de todas las mejoras de ropa que publicaban en los *círculos políticos* y en las calles de Madrid el cambio de instituciones, ninguna tan digna de pasar a la historia como el estreno de levita de paño fino que transformó a don Basilio Andrés de la Caña a los seis días de colocado. Hundióse en los abismos del ayer la levita antigua, con toda su mugre, testimonio lustroso de luengos años de cesantía y de arrastrar las mangas por las mesas de las redacciones. Completaba el buen ver de la prenda un sombrero de moda, y el gran D. Basilio parecía un sol, porque su cara echaba lumbre de satisfacción. Desde que entró a servir *en su ramo* y en la categoría que le cuadraba, estaba el hombre que no cabía en su chaleco. Hasta parecía que había engordado, que tenía más pelo en la cabeza, que era menos miope, y que se le habían quitado diez años de encima. Se afeitaba ya todos los días, lo que en realidad le quitaba el parecido consigo mismo. No quiero hablar de las otras muchas levitas y gabanes flamantes que se veían por Madrid, [...] Este es un fenómeno histórico muy conocido. (III, iv, 7; 173-74, Galdós's italics)

As we see, this is the transformation of one person into another. But the transformation is only skin deep. Don Basilio, following his entrance, shows himself to be as presumptuous, as inflated and vacuous as before; he is the eternal public job seeker turned employee.[10] In contrast to the transformation undergone by Fortunata, he dresses in the most stylish and contemporary fashions. His alteration has occurred during the brief but symbolic period of six days, compared to the long birthing of Fortunata which took months. Vis-à-vis its biblical counterpart, the parallel and contradiction implicit in the six-day creation of an earthly paradise in Restoration Madrid provide a framework for further comparison of don Basilio to Fortunata. Although both persons have filled out physically, he seems different but is really the same; she on the other hand seems the same but has changed radically. Remaining the same as always, she is altered; changing, he progresses not a whit. As Galdós was to state in 1893, «No hay que burlarse de las paradojas, que suelen entrañar verdades».[11]

Nor can we doubt that don Basilio is emblematic of all of middle-class Madrid society. The narrator says of him when first we meet Juan Pablo's café cohorts: «D. Basilio descendía siempre a menudencias de personal [...] era vulgo [...] Gustaba de ocupar posiciones superiores a

---

[10] In addition to some brief but impressive paragraphs on this subject by C. A. M. HENNESSY, *The Federal Republic in Spain* (Oxford: Oxford Univ. Press, 1962), esp. p. 46, *v* also A. F. LAMBERT, «Galdós and the Anti-bureaucratic Tradition», *Bulletin of Hispanic Studies*, LIII (1976), 35-49.

[11] This passage is taken from the important article «Confusiones y paradojas» published 12 July 1893 in *La Prensa* (Buenos Aires) and subsequently in BENITO PÉREZ GALDÓS, *Obras inéditas de...*, ed. Alberto Ghiraldo, II. *Arte y crítica* (Madrid: Renacimiento, 1923), pp. 183-95; the quote is from p. 195.

las que merecía» (III, i, 1 and 2: 10; 13-14). Melchor Relimpio, another *tertuliano,* says of de la Caña: «El mejor negocio que se podrá hacer en estos tiempos, ¿a que no saben ustedes cuál es? Pues abrirle la cabeza a don Basilio y sacarle toda la paja que hay dentro para venderla» *(idem,* 14). That Galdós selects the supreme nonentity, as judged even by his intimates, to represent the new changes effected in Madrid by the Restoration speaks for itself as to his view of the «Restauración».

The narrator stresses de la Caña's exemplary significance in the phrases which open and close his description, and which indicate how generalized is the transformation effected on don Basilio, and just how (un)important it is. Thus the narrative *coup de grâce* which comments on the close relationship between changes in governments and changes in clothing fashions: «Por eso cuando pasa mucho tiempo sin cambio político, cogen el cielo con las manos los sastres y mercaderes de trapos, y con sus quejas acaloran a los descontentos y azuzan a los revolucionarios» (III, iv, 7; 174).

Indeed, we discern the traces of this transformation of Madrid society even in Maxi. According to Feijoo he no longer seems «tan raquítico» and «Ha engordado; ha echado carnes, y hasta me pareció que tiene un aire más arrogantillo, más...» (III, iv, 9; 199-200). Fortunata hears this incredulously and smiles in silence; not because she doubts that Maxi has grown more robust, but that in consequence of his physical improvement she may learn to love him. Like the reader she recognizes that physical change may be meaningless if it occurs without an internal metamorphosis; by itself, improvement in one's appearance is no renascence in any meaningful sense of the word.

III. THE DIALECTICAL STRUCTURE OF SOCIETY: RECURRENCE
    AND RELATIONSHIP AS VITAL EXPERIENCE

Now it is not precisely that Fortunata is rejuvenated. She is no elderly matron suddenly lightened physically in years. What she really undergoes is a transformation more akin to rebirth. This is a novel filled with births and deaths, with powerful biological reactions and expressions. For example, the sign of Feijoo's physical decay, like Fortunata's recovery, is a voracious appetite or its absence; food literally sickens Feijoo (III, iv, 5; 157). Moreover, in the novel life itself is not a simple linear process. The end of her love affair with Juanito inaugurates another stage in Fortunata's existence, the tranquil period with Feijoo. If something dies, something is also born, like the Phoenix rising from its own ashes. In our own lives, individually, the dialectic functions vertically, spiralling upwards from birth to death. In this novel its symbol appropriately is the famous stairway in the house at number 11, Cava de San Miguel, which we see in Part IV with Fortunata's eyes:

> ¿Pues y la casa? En ella, desde el portal hasta lo más alto de la escalera de piedra, veía pintada su infancia, con todos sus episodios y accidentes, como se ven pintados en la iglesia los Pasos de la Pasión y Muerte de Cristo. Cada peldaño tenía su historia, y la pollería y el cuarto entresuelo y después el segundo tenían ese *revestimiento de una capa espiritual* que es propio de los lugares consagrados por la religión o por la vida. (IV, iii, 7; 210, Galdós's italics)

In this moment two powerful images —heretofore described by characters but never before seen directly through their eyes as they live through the experience of the climb— fuse. There is first of all the building itself, a locale which Peter Bly persuasively suggests holds the key to a correct interpretation of Galdós's masterpiece.[12] Second and more important is the stairway itself. In his novels Galdós frequently uses the image of a stairway as a metaphor for society and life in it. One instance of this portrayal occurs at the end of Part I. Juanito learns that Fortunata has returned to Madrid. Villalonga's description of her is rather a close version of the words Miquis employs to describe the resurfacing, and in certain ways rebirth socially, of Isidora in Part II of *La desheredada*. But whereas Isidora will descend, Fortunata will ascend. Moreover, whereas Isidora is located with precision, Fortunata at this moment is lost to Juanito and the reader. He searches for her, going up and down the stairway of society: «No encontrando lo que buscaba en lo que parece más alto, descendió de escalón en escalón» (I, xi, 3; 476).

Analogously, when Jacinta visits the tenement on Mira el Río where Mauricia and Pitusín live, the metaphor again appears. She traverses an outer patio, studying the while those rooms which open on it. At the other end, she goes up six stairs and crosses through to an inner patio far uglier, more cramped, dirtier in aspect. Her movements and the sight she beholds are verbalized by the narrator in the same symbolic language:

> Comparado con el segundo, el primero tenía algo de aristocrático y podría pasar por albergue de familias *distinguidas*. Entre uno y otro patio, que pertenecían a un mismo dueño y por eso estaban unidos, había un escalón social, la distancia entre eso que se llama *capas*. (I, ix, 2; 299-300, Galdós's italics)

Like Juanito and Jacinta, Fortunata conceives of society in these terms. While an inmate of the Micaelas, we learn her perspective on work and the social structure:

[12] PETER A. BLY, «Fortunata and No. 11, Cava de San Miguel», *Hispanófila*, no. 59 (1977), 31-48. GILMAN, «The Birth of Fortunata», is not explicit on this point but the inference at least to me is clear; *v* also *Galdós and the Art*, pp. 307-09.

Las labores delicadas, como costura y bordados, de que había taller en la casa, eran las que menos agradaban a Fortunata, que tenía poca afición a los primores de aguja y los dedos muy torpes. Más le agradaba que la mandaran lavar, brochar los pisos de baldosín, limpiar las vidrieras y otros menesteres propios de criadas de escalera abajo. (II, vi, 1; 254-55)

If three of the most important characters assay socety and life in it in the metaphoric imagery of a stairway, a fourth, Maxi, unites that image with Fortunata's house at number 11, Cava de San Miguel. The linkage develops almost imperceptibly, as the half mad Maxi searches for a wife once presumed dead and now thought to be alive (Part IV, Chapter V). He frequents the Café del Gallo and overhears José Izquierdo complain one night of having to «go upstairs» to deliver some dates, the delicacy Maxi knows to have been Fortunata's favorite food. He times Izquierdo's absence and notes that *Platón* returns out of breath, concluding «debe de ser alta la escalera» (IV, v, 2; 249). Days later he observes Quevedo's weariness upon returning from a house call; he recollects that the obstetrician had gone to the Cava (*idem,* 252). Finally, Maxi again overhears Izquierdo complain about trudging upstairs «y de bajar rodando por los escalones de piedra». Whereupon he exults «Ya sé, pues, dónde está [...] Es en la casa de los escalones de piedra» (IV, v, 3; 258).

The identification of the house by its spiral stairway is total. Thus when Maxi boasts of his deduction to doña Lupe, rather than tell her (and the reader) the address of Fortunata's domicile, he simply repeats the description: «vive en la Cava de San Miguel, en la casa de los escalones de piedra» (*idem,* 262).

If the house and its famous stairs frame the novel and symbolize life in it, perhaps we might add that they serve too as the aesthetic armature of the entire work. Given her spiraling journey upwards literally and symbolically, it stands to reason that if Fortunata has returned to the house of her childhood, the pattern is not for this reason circular. Bly pointedly shows that Fortunata's position architecturally in that structure is different from what it was when in that edifice we first, with Juanito, met her. And from Stephen Gilman and, in this volume, Carlos Blanco and John Kronik, we have come to infer what is obvious yet unnoticed: That in body, mind and spirit Fortunata is also at once the same yet again radically and meaningfully transformed.[13] The socially, intellectually and emotionally infantile young woman of Part I has been transformed by the end of the novel into a mature adult about to give birth to her own child. To all this we must add her own self-assessment, which is made in *purely social and economic terms.* As Fortunata ascends the stairs to the top, the narrator reports:

[13] BLY, «Fortunata and No. 11...»; GILMAN, *Galdós and the Art,* pp. 345-48.

«¡Las vueltas del mundo! —decía dando las de la escalera y venciendo con
fatiga los peldaños—. ¡Quién me había de decir que pararía aquí otra vez!...
Ahora es cuando conozco que, aunque poco, algo se me ha pegado el señorío.
Miro todo esto con cariño; ¡pero me parece tan ordinario...!» (IV, iii,
7; 210, my italics)

Now Galdós does not stop here. These points, structured once again
dialectically and in the identical language used to describe her journey
up the one hundred twenty steps, are repeated by Fortunata as she settles
into her old yet new home. Socioeconomic mobility, personal growth, and
the flow of life all merge in the image of the upward spiralling staircase
and the building containing it. She slowly begins to experience a «resu-
rrección mental de lo pasado» (IV, iv, 1; 226); some time after learning
that her landlord is Guillermina Pacheco, Fortunata reconsiders —with
iterative precision— the notions which initially occurred to her on her
return to the building: «[¡] *quién me había de decir que viviría en su
casa! ¡Qué vueltas da el mundo!* En aquellos días, ni a mí se me pasaba
por la cabeza venirme aquí» (*idem*, 225, my italics).

Only by going back does she realize how far she has come, how much
she has changed; if in some way she is the same, in others she is unalterably
and irredeemably different.[14] The point is again in social and economic
terms. As she reaches the top of the stairs

Fortunata vió el cuarto. ¡Ay, Dios, qué malo era, y qué sucio y qué feo!
Las puertas parecía que tenían un dedo de mugre, el papel era todo man-
chas, los pisos muy desiguales. La cocina causaba horror. *Indudablemente
la joven se había adecentado mucho y adquirido hábitos de señora, porque
la vivienda aquella se le representaba inferior a su categoría, a sus hábitos
y a sus gustos.* (IV, iii, 7; 211, my italics)

Nor is it simply the narrator speaking here. Not long after this scene
Fortunata says of herself «Por más que digan, yo me he afinado algo.
Cuando pongo cuidado digo muy pocos disparates. [...] Las señoras Micaelas me desbastaron, y mi marido y doña Lupe me pasaron la piedra
pómez, sacándome un poco de lustre» (IV, iv, 1; 227-28). She may have
returned home physically, but in values, in awareness, in worldliness, in
tastes and in status she is elsewhere, just as her son will be taken elsewhere to live and grow.

Fortunata's progress out of the *pueblo* and into the middle classes is
gradual but deliberate. By the time she returns to Madrid at the end of
Part I, Fortunata's social pretensions have taken root if Villalonga's
description of her clothing and jewelry is to be believed. By the time she
has become the señora de Rubín, she is middle class though a member

---

[14] The *embourgeoisement* of Fortunata was first noted by GEOFFREY RIBBANS,
Pérez Galdós: Fortunata y Jacinta (London: Grant and Cutler, 1977), p. 68.

of its lower orders. When she first meets Juanito following her marriage, she betrays a self-awareness that she has become «civilizada». He observes «Estás ahora mucho mejor que antes». To which she responds «con cierta coquetería. —¿Lo dices porque me he civilizado algo? ¡Quia! no lo creas...» (II, vii, 6; 398). Her protestations that she still is *pueblo* and wants to turn the clock back, that she wants to be as she once was, underscore the progress of her transformation. And by the time she has terminated her affair with Feijoo, Fortunata is intermediate to upper middle class, recognizing her own pretensions and tastes as we saw in the description of her return to the Cava de San Miguel. Her self-awareness is expressed inversely in her speech and attire. Whereas once she affected middle-class ways, as she definitively rises, socially and economically Fortunata reverts to her old accent and habits of speech; she again wears clothing of the class to which she no longer belongs (III, iv, 5; 155-56).[15]

If Fortunata is climbing, then, to ever higher levels of existence —socially, economically, spiritually— nevertheless many of the key processes and episodes in her life repeat themselves, at times with the same people and circumstances. But each episode or process repeated is more than just a duplicate of its predecessor. It is an elaboration, with specific alterations and refinements, which at once give the new development the gross appearance of repetition but which, on closer examination, show it to be essentially distinct, thereby eliciting different reactions and results.[16]

i. *Recurrence*

For example, Juanito enters the building wherein he and Fortunata have their love nest; he is about to abandon her for the second time. As he climbs the stairs something so unusual occurs that the narrator calls

---

[15] On Fortunata's socioeconomic climb upwards, *v* also the remarks concerning her income in n. 59 below.

[16] What I am describing here is not so different, on the personal level, from the concept of history as the concatenation of events suggested in CARLOS CLAVERÍA's seminal essay, «El pensamiento histórico de Galdós», *Revista Nacional de Cultura*, XIX, 121-22 (marzo-junio, 1957), 170-77, esp. 173-74. JAMES WHISTON, «Language and Situation in Part I of *Fortunata y Jacinta*», *Anales Galdosianos*, VII (1972), 79-91, finds a repetition of «analogues of ironic patterns» wherein «situations derive out of their opposites» (90-91). Similarly J. J. MACKLIN speaks of «multiple images of similar experiences» on p. 198 of his «B. Pérez Galdós: *Fortunata y Jacinta* (1886-7)», pp. 179-203 of David A. Williams, ed., *The Monster in the Mirror: Studies in Nineteenth-Century Realism* (Oxford: Oxford Univ. Press, 1978). Such interpretations are rooted in an understanding of realism aligned, PETER DEMETZ insists, with a description of the ordinary rather than the unique, with the «rhythm of repetition» rather than the «unrepeatable event» («Über die Fiktionen des Realismus», *Neue Rundschau*, LXXXVIII [1977], 554-67). See the exposition of MARSHALL BROWN, «The Logic of Realism: A Hegelian Approach», *PMLA*, XCVI (1981), 224-41.

our attention to it. Juanito is absorbed by his plans to overthrow the
«república» of adulterous living. He reaches the landing and raises his
hand to lift the door knocker: «en el momento de poner la mano en el
llamador, un hecho extraño cortó bruscamente el hilo de sus ideas» (III,
iii, 1; 98). Unexpectedly the door opens and an elderly gentleman «de
muy buena presencia» exits, and he does so greeting Juanito. As we
know, it is Feijoo. But the incident has a larger importance. First, because it is part of the preparation for Feijoo's introduction later in the novel
as a major character. Second, the incident is a prime example of the
chain about which we have been speaking. We call to mind that the most
important encounters we witness in Fortunata's life occur in the entry to
a dwelling in which she resides: that in the Cava de San Miguel where
she and Juanito first meet (I, iii, 4); that in the Calle de Pelayo, third
floor, where she lived with Feliciana and where she meets Maxi for the
first time (II, i, 3); and this introduction to Feijoo.

Juanito's meeting with Fortunata is sufficiently well-known to most
readers, her first encounter with Maxi perhaps less so:

> Por la noche fue Maximiliano al *hotel* de Feliciana, tercer piso en la
> calle de Pelayo, y al entrar, lo primero que vio... Es que junto a la puerta
> de entrada había un cuartito pequeño, que era donde moraba la huéspeda,
> y ésta salía de su escondrijo cuando Rubín entraba. Feliciana había salido
> a abrir con el quinqué en la mano, porque lo llevaba para la sala, y a la
> luz vivísima del petróleo sin pantalla, encaró Maximiliano con la más extra-
> ordinaria hermosura que hasta entonces habían visto sus ojos. Ella le miró
> a él como a una cosa rara, y él a ella como a sobrenatural aparición.
> (*idem*, 29)

Maxi then goes into the sitting room and watches Olmedo play solitaire.

Obviously if there are similarities there are also differences. In the
first two encounters Fortunata is seen from without as an object of great
beauty. This time, Juanito and the reader ignore her in order to pay
attention to the man who is taking leave. There is furthermore the undeniable symbolism and symbolic function of the doorway. The latter is
not simply an entry to one's domicile but the threshold to another world.
Significantly Maxi and Juanito see Fortunata from without because they
never are able truly to comprehend and appreciate her. For them she will
always be an object contemplated from the outside. On the other hand,
Feijoo is seen by Juanito *and us* while leaving. Moreover, his first visit
to Fortunata's world is a story we never hear; that is, we never know
just how Feijoo and Fortunata came to meet and know each other. In
the Café de San Joaquín Feijoo tells Juan Pablo Rubín that he has visited
Fortunata several times in her own house (III, i, 6; 45). She adds a bit
to our knowledge when she informs Juanito that she has received the
old colonel three times (III, iii, 1; 99). But that is all. Recall also that
Juanito is on his way elsewhere (Estupiñá's flat on the top floor), an

encounter well described by Stephen Gilman.[17] Maxi is going in: «y al entrar, lo primero que vio...» (II, i, 3; 29). And Feijoo is coming out. In the first house, Fortunata lives with her aunt; in the second, with Feliciana, sometime prostitute and mistress of Olmedo, Maxi's friend; in the third flat, Fortunata is more emancipated, governing the space as Juanito's mistress. Of the three meetings, the first two are described in some detail; all that we see in this third incident is a polite farewell. The first two meetings are from Fortunata's perspective accidental, the third very clearly is not for she already has received her caller.

The narrative point of view establishes certain implied relations.[18] The reader, together with Juanito, is outside the interior and private world of Fortunata; on the other hand, Feijoo is within, admitted and an intimate. Galdós's technical device announces here a relationship which later is reinforced: Feijoo, and only Feijoo, comprehends and appreciates Fortunata for what she is. She is not Juanito's object of pulchritude; she is not Maxi's project for self-fulfillment; she is Fortunata, «la prójima», truly Feijoo's «compañera». Later of course, at that doorway to the top floor of the Cava de San Miguel, number 11, she is mistress of a world, her world, to which she and only she literally and figuratively has the key (IV, vi, 7). But for now it is she and Feijoo, the only one among all her friends and lovers who truly knows her and loves her for what she is. Hence the first time we see the two together they are already on friendly terms, the two together in their beliefs and isolated from the rest of the world. Whereupon Feijoo walks out her door and into the heart of this novel. Each doorway scene, then, between Fortunata and one of her lovers is emblematic of the role and relations which each affair plays in the novel.

First encounters, like other primary episodes, are repeated throughout the novel. But each repetition has as many dissimilarities and modifications as parallels. Further, each repetition establishes itself with reference to its predecessors and those which follow. A repeated episode posits a new and higher level of existence for Fortunata, setting down emblematically themes which later are developed. This structure is reflected even in what we might term ancillary scenes which grow out immediately from a repeated incident. Ancillary scenes frequently reinforce the ambiguity of the primary episodes, so that the latter, like every major character in

[17] «The Birth of Fortunata». Ribbans, *Pérez Galdós,* p. 52, is the only scholar to have studied Maxi's first encounter with Fortunata. He remarks that in the manuscript version Galdós originally set the meeting in the street.

[18] Two useful essays on Galdós's manipulation of point of view are BRIAN J. DENDLE, «Point of View in *Nazarín*», *Anales Galdosianos,* IX (1974), 113-21, and HARRIET S. TURNER, «Strategies in Narrative Point of View: On Meaning and Morality in the Galdós Novel», pp. 61-77 in *Homenaje a Antonio Sánchez-Barbudo,* ed. B. Brancaforte, R. Mulvihill and R. Sánchez (Madison: Univ. of Wisconsin, 1981).

the novel, contain their own contradictions. The meeting between the reader and Juanito, on the one hand, and Feijoo and Fortunata on the other, is an example. The reader, like Juanito, reacts similarly on seeing Fortunata in the company of the «elderly gentleman». Galdós manipulates us so that on first reading we share with Juanito the suspicions that she is being unfaithful. Galdós does this not merely to deceive us, but also so that in sharing the same point of view with Juanito we separate ourselves from Fortunata and her future preceptor-protector. In consequence, having read earlier that Feijoo had already visited Fortunata in her home (III, i, 6; 45-46), and that he declined to discuss the matter for supposed reasons of delicacy according to the narrator, we accept erroneously but totally as possible Juanito's opinion that she is unfaithful. Under the influence of this bias we watch as the farewell scene between Juanito and Fortunata unfolds. Elements in the scene not only resonate with events to occur subsequently during Fortunata's affair with Feijoo; more important, certain actions, reactions and even utterances (i.e., novelistically and aesthetically speaking, word groups) will recur later.

Juanito enters their flat as Feijoo descends the stairs:

> La salida de aquel señor le produjo en un instante dos sentimientos distintos que se sucedieron con brevedad. El primero fue algo de enojo, el segundo satisfacción de que el acaso le proporcionase un buen apoyo para el rompimiento que deseaba ... [...] «¡*Si tendremos gatuperio...*! Estaría bueno. Pero más vale así.» (III, iii, 1; 98, my italics)

Thereupon Juanito feigns jealousy; in response, Fortunata tells him that Feijoo is a decorous gentleman (98-99). Santa Cruz alters his tactics, finally telling her the truth: He is leaving her. While Fortunata goes to her bedroom to cry, Juanito works himself up into another false fit of indignation. Meditating on the possible ways to cut off the affair according to accepted rules governing amatory behavior,

> Pronto comprendió que no podía apetecer mejor coyuntura para plantarse rápidamente en la calle y dar por terminado el enojoso trámite de la ruptura.
> «Pero aún me falta la última parte —pensó echando mano a su cartera—. No puedo abandonarla así...» Después de meditar un rato, volvió a guardar la cartera y se dijo: «Mejor será que me vaya... Se lo mandaré en una carta... Adiós... No dirá Jacinta que...»
> *Salió de puntillas, como se sale de la casa en que hay un enfermo grave.* (*idem*, 106-07; Galdós's punctuation, my italics)

This image and the attitude of Juanito on taking his leave are later reproduced by the words of Feijoo. On the first day of their life together, following her installation in the apartment on the Calle de Tabernillas, Feijoo sets out his terms according to which their affair is to be regulated. In counterdistinction to Fortunata's scene with Juanito, the narrator intervenes frequently here to editorialize; the reader is given a full supply of qualifications and confidential value judgments concerning the retired colonel and his behavior. The narrator continually underscores the differences between her new lover and other men of his kind: «se portaba con ella como un caballero, y no tenía nada de quisquilloso, ni las impertinencias que suelen gastar los hombres. El primer día le leyó la cartilla, que era muy breve» (III, iv, 3; 137). On setting out before Fortunata his ideas about what initially will amount to a contractual relationship, the words of Feijoo evoke in the reader's mind the second farewell of Juanito. This occurs ironically, underscoring Santa Cruz's insincerity and inconstancy; moreover and by way of contrast the ironic counterpoint highlights the rectitude and openness of don Evaristo, who advises Fortunata, «Quiero que seas leal conmigo, como yo lo soy contigo. En cuanto te canses avisas... Aquí no me entres a ningún hombre, *porque si algún día descubro gatuperio, me marcho tan calladito* y no me vuelves a ver...» (*idem,* my italics). And immediately we recall Juanito's thoughts as he approached the door to Fortunata's flat; similarly we are reminded of how he left her, «de puntillas».

In sum, the encounter in the doorway to Fortunata's dwelling is first of all related directly to other episodes in the novel. Secondly, from it and its analogues grow other occurences which too are interrelated dialectically.

ii. *Relationship*

If the synthesis which the characters of this novel all desire eludes them, it does not for that reason follow that the novel itself is lacking such structure.[19] In fact the reader, by putting together the pieces of the novelistic puzzle, is quite able to formulate the synthesis which is always beyond the grasp of the characters. Hence *both* Gilman and Blanco are right in their contentions concerning Fortunata.[20] Her salvation, i.e., Gilman's «ethical and prophetic»[21] equivalent to synthesis, occurs outside the

[19] I am here thinking of ANTHONY N. ZAHAREAS, «El sentido de la tragedia en *Fortunata y Jacinta*», *Anales Galdosianos*, III (1968), 25-34. I am suggesting we take another look at his valuable insights from the perspective of dialectics. Individual «tragedies» or frustrations should be placed in a larger context.

[20] GILMAN, «The Birth of Fortunata»; CARLOS BLANCO AGUINAGA, «On 'The Birth of Fortunata'», *Anales Galdosianos*, III (1968), 13-24. See also SHERMAN H. EOFF, «Galdós in Nineteenth Century Perspective», *Anales Galdosianos*, I (1966), 3-9.

[21] Page 461, n. 10 of his review «SHERMAN H. EOFF, *The Novels of Pérez Galdós* (1954)», *Romanische Forschungen*, LXX (1958), 455-65. The full sentence reads «Similarly when Eoff remarks that Fortunata dies while still 'in process' leaving the novel curiously unfinished, it is probably because he senses that she has not yet been sociologically 'packaged'. He has, thus, misunderstood the ethical and prophetic climax.»

world of the novel, in the mind of the readers. But in her own world she is consigned to oblivion, something made starkly clear by the funeral scene and its aftermath (IV, vi, 16). Blanco, Zahareas, Rodríguez Puértolas and others [22] also are quite correct, therefore, in their pessimistic interpretation of Fortunata viewed strictly as a creature of her own world. Galdós was unable to forge a totally redeemed character until writing his trilogy *Nazarín, Halma* and *Misericordia*.[23]

This fact highlights another, which is his vision of the world, a vision which besides informs the narrative structure of *Fortunata y Jacinta*. A dialectical synthesis is discerned not within the confines of a single life, but across the encounters between various lives. In the misapprehension of this basic fact resides the confusion of critics who see the novel and its structure as triangulated,[24] or as a «series of contrasts» replete with «pairs of contrasts». The latter is the eloquent suggestion of Carlos Blanco Aguinaga in his contribution to the present volume. I do not disagree with either the triangle theories, or the theories of double natures and pairs or «binary dualism» argued with elegance by Blanco, Monroe Hafter and William Risley. What I am trying to suggest is that a poetics of ambiguity, informed by dialectics, coherently integrates all of these various —and among themselves, contradictory— theories. A dialectical vision here is not exclusive; rather, without conceptual or intellectual conflict it is inclusive.[25]

[22] JULIO RODRÍGUEZ PUÉRTOLAS, chs. I-II of *Galdós: Burguesía y revolución* (Madrid: Turner, 1975). See also JOHN H. SINNIGEN, «Individual, Class, and Society in *Fortunata y Jacinta*», *Galdós Studies*, II (London: Tamesis, 1974), 49-68, who concludes «Therefore the resolution offered by Fortunata's *idea* of the differences between the *pueblo* and the bourgeoisie can only be a potential solution to the problems of society, for those who must carry out this resolution continue, unlike Feijoo and Maxi, to live in the world of material reality where it does make a difference if one is in a palace or a dung heap and where idealist solutions cannot be realized» (68, his italics). See also n. 58 below.

[23] GOLDMAN, «Galdós and the Aesthetic of Ambiguity...», 108-09; «Galdós and the Nineteenth Century Novel...», 12-14.

[24] E.g., GULLÓN and MONCY GULLÓN.

[25] MONROE Z. HAFTER, «Ironic Reprise in Galdós' Novels», *PMLA*, LXXVI (1961), 233-39; WILLIAM R. RISLEY, «Setting in the Galdós Novel», *Hispanic Review*, XLVI (1978), 23-40. The phrase «binary or dualistic method of structuring» is Risley's (37). Other representative variants advocating a dualistic structure are SHERMAN H. EOFF, «The Deification of Conscious Process», pp. 120-47 of *The Modern Spanish Novel* (New York: New York Univ. Press, 1961), esp. pp. 130, 134-35; BRAUN; MACKLIN, p. 187. Favoring triangular constructs are, e.g., HARRIET S. TURNER, «Family Ties and Tyrannies: A Reassessment of Jacinta», *Hispanic Review*, LI (1983), 1-22, and RICARDO LÓPEZ-LANDY, *El espacio novelesco en la obra de Galdós* (Madrid: Cultura Hispánica, 1979). PHYLLIS Z. BORING, «The Streets of Madrid as a Structuring Device in *Fortunata y Jacinta*», *Anales Galdosianos*, XIII (1978), 13-22, posits a different structural pattern after demonstrating the deficiences in the others. Dualities and triangles, Boring argues, do not accord with the complexity of the work. RICARDO GULLÓN explores a more sophisticated approach reminiscent of his «cuadros disolventes» in «On Space in the Novel», *Critical Inquiry*, II (1975), 11-28, esp. 19. The conceptual shortcomings of the

The notion is not so distant from Zahareas's argument for irreconcilable extremes. But as we have also observed, each character and event bears within itself the seeds of its own contradiction. In full interaction with other people or events, the seeds sprout and flourish. There is no triangle described by Juanito, Maxi and Feijoo, for example; rather, each of the three exists in a dialectical tension not only among themselves, but also with various others. Is there not a similar relationship between the three *señoritos,* Feijoo, Juanito and Moreno Isla? Feijoo may love; his off-spring is spiritual, not biological. Juanito is loved but cannot love; he is biologically potent. Moreno Isla is sterile in the deepest senses of the word. If anyone in this novel personifies the hypocritical morality of Restoration Madrid, it is this *señorito.* He has nothing but contempt for his own national society and exploits it with foreign capital. He seeks only liaisons with married women in order to refrain from personal commitment, with of course the exception of Jacinta. But it is reasonable to assume that his desire for the latter is a product of her inaccessibility. His is a life as barren spiritually at it is biologically, for he is without even Juanito's ability to incite a Fortunata.

We discern an analogous relationship between Maxi (who creates lives), Ido del Sagrario (who creates fictions) and Ballester (who has no wish to create but to live; who invests as much energy in his own life as his counterparts do in the lives of others). And among the women we also find interlacing dialectics: Fortunata, Jacinta and Guillermina; Fortunata, Mauricia and Severiana; Guillermina, Bárbara and doña Lupe; Jacinta, Fortunata and Aurora; and so on. Now these are not all either «pairs» or «triangles»; rather, they constitute an extremely dense, interconnecting nexus of relationships which build out of each other, including across sexual lines (Fortunata, Maxi, Ballester; doña Lupe, Maxi and Juan Pablo; Juanito, Fortunata and Jacinta; etc.).

Galdós, a probable reader of Hegel,[26] understood that each person

various theories so far propounded are —implicitly— underscored by LEWIS and, in two articles, by GEOFFREY RIBBANS: «*Historia Novelada* and *Novela Histórica:* The Use of Historical Incidents from the Reign of Isabella II in Galdós' *Episodios* and *Novelas Contemporáneas*», pp. 133-47 of *Hispanic Studies in Honour of Frank Pierce,* ed. John England (Sheffield: The University, 1980); and «'La historia como debiera ser': Galdós' Speculations on Nineteenth-Century Spanish History», *Bulletin of Hispanic Studies,* LIX (1982), 267-74. Lewis's argument is aesthetic: The text of *Fortunata y Jacinta* has an underlying unity of structure which is «globally integrative» throughout, despite the variety, disparity, and conflict of images and characters (328-29). On the other hand Ribbans's point is in the strictest sense ideological. In the Pierce volume he insists that Galdós «offers little or no interpretation of history as such. What is conveyed, rather, is an acute awareness of the continuity of the past and the impact of the constant moral imperatives and physical demands it imposes on the present» (143).

[26] It is not simply that his characters mention Hegel by name, and at times employ «Hegelianism» improperly. Galdós does toy with Maxi (III, i, 6; 52) and Máximo Manso this way (*El amigo manso,* ch. III). But he also can get serious

who exists must perforce maintain social relationships, however elementary the level of interchange may be. The truly creative person in Galdós's world (Maxi, Fortunata, Mauricia, Jacinta), as against the truly *un*creative, ofttimes destructive individual (e.g., Juanito, Moreno Isla), is one who does not exist untouched in and by society. In Cervantine *and* Hegelian fashion —the compatibility is not coincidental— the creative person capitalizes on her vulnerability, changing and growing out of each encounter, affecting and being affected, taking as well as giving, forcing development in others as well as developing oneself.[27] The awesomeness of Fortunata's power is not that it is destructive, and it is that if we look at the trail of human debris which she leaves in her wake: Maxi, Feijoo, even Ballester who loses his job because he befriended her (IV, vi, 16; 431). What really make hers a fearful richness is that loving her, however costly emotionally and otherwise, is worth the price. Ballester, so often on target, states it with awful clarity on his way home from Fortunata's burial:

> Mire usted, amigo Ponce, yo estoy inconsolable; pero no desconozco que, atendiendo al egoísmo social, la muerte de esa mujer es un bien para mí *(bienes y males andan siempre aparejados en la vida)* [...] Me tengo por hombre de seso, *y sin embargo, yo me iba derecho al abismo.* (idem, 430; my italics)

The creative person works on, and is worked upon by, society; as they pass through the world, they and it are never quite the same.

As opposed to the stasis of pairs and triangles, the nature of a dialectic is described by open-ended, dynamic tension. Fortunata affects Feijoo who in turn acts on the Rubín brothers; Maxi helps Fortunata polish

---

about the German philosopher. For example, on 15 May 1872 Galdós applauded the appearance of Fabié's translation of the *Logic,* commenting: «La *Lógica de Hegel,* cuya traducción tan acertadamente ha llevado a cabo el Sr. Fabié, es libro oportunísimo, no sólo por su mérito intrínseco, sino porque los estragos que en entendimientos muy ilustrados hace la escuela positivista, exigen grandes esfuerzos para devolver a la metafísica el puesto que la corresponde entre los acontecimientos humanos.» These and other comments appear in William H. Shoemaker, ed., *Crónica de la Quincena by Benito Pérez Galdós* (Princeton: Princeton Univ. Press, 1948), p. 131. The most extensive treatment of Galdós's indebtedness to Hegelianism is still SHERMAN H. EOFF, *The Novels of Pérez Galdós. The Concept of Life as Dynamic Process* (St. Louis: Washington Univ. Press, 1954), ch. VII.

[27] Madariaga's concepts of «sanchificación de don Quijote» and «quijotización de Sancho» are perhaps the best examples of this phenomenon: SALVADOR DE MADARIAGA, *Guía del lector del «Quijote»* (Buenos Aires: Editorial Sudamericana, 1961), 5.ª ed., pp. 127-48. Acknowledging the Cervantine quality of Galdós's realism, EOFF, «Deification», pp. 127 and 141 observed that the social environment consisting of ideas, general background, and personal relationships sustained by a character, was essential for a realistic portrayal of that character. MACKLIN, pp. 179-92, says that relationships provide the «context of character». LEWIS, 332-39, in a particularistic scrutiny of café society in the novel shows just how rich and important that context is.

herself socially, thereby and inadvertently making her more attractive to Juanito; Moreno Isla's affair with Aurora has profound effects on Fortunata; and so on. There develops across this novel a vital chain of actuations, encounters, contemplations and reactions; all lead us with the characters along a dialectic of life. But it may be an ascendant or a descendant journey. It is true that the essentially negative aspect of life described by Zahareas weighs on most of the denizens of Fortunata's world; life for this populace is a constant frustration of attempts to achieve one's primary goal.[28] Yet this observation is factual only within the limits of each individual life. Individual failures nevertheless may constitute positive gains for others; hence the action of one life, e.g., Mauricia, on a second, e.g., Fortunata, may be mortally frustrating for the one yet fundamentally positive for the other. Aspects of each individual life have various and contradictory effects on oneself, on others, and on society generally. Hence the importance of those first pages of the novel, which not only establish a bourgeois-novelistic dynasty as Gilman demonstrates,[29] and portray the socioeconomic bases of commercial capitalism as Blanco and Rodríguez Puértolas add,[30] but also reflect Galdós's Hegelian interpretation of society.

Two final points must be clarified. The first is that Galdós, as far as can be determined, had no intentional plan to write novels based on an Hegelian conception of society. Whatever else it may be, the Hegelian underpinning of his novels is not the expression of a consciously formulated project. Rather, it reflects what we —in the good company of Sherman Eoff— might take to be the spirit of the age in which Galdós lived and wrote. Citing a number of eminent thinkers and doers, Eoff proves impressively that despite its setback earlier at the hands of positivism, Hegelianism was again rising in popularity in the final third of the century.[31] This might explain why in Galdós's more self-conscious attempts to reconstruct Spain's history, specifically in the *Episodios*, few traces of an Hegelian approach were found by Hinterhäuser, whereas Casalduero saw it recurring with increasing frequency in the *novelas contemporáneas* as the century came to a close.[32]

---

[28] «El sentido de la tragedia...».

[29] «The Birth of Fortunata», 71-74; *Galdós and the Art*, pp. 291-301.

[30] BLANCO AGUINAGA, «On 'The Birth of Fortunata'»; RODRÍGUEZ PUÉRTOLAS, ch. I (pp. 13-59). See also SINNIGEN, pp. 50-58 and LEWIS on the general socioeconomic roots and context of this novel.

[31] EOFF, «Deification», esp. pp. 123-26. Read Galdós's own words cited above, n. 26.

[32] HANS HINTERHÄUSER, *Los «Episodios nacionales» de Benito Pérez Galdós* (Madrid: Gredos, 1963), trans. José Escobar, pp. 116-29. JOAQUÍN CASALDUERO, *Vida y obra de Galdós,* 2nd ed. (Madrid: Gredos, 1961), pp. 127, 186, 234. GILMAN is right when he notes (*Galdós and the Art*, pp. 342-44) that the occasions of direct mention of Hegel are ironic in the novels. But an occasional specific naming of the German philosopher neither precludes, nor is qualitatively equivalent to,

Second, relationships do not exist in novels only as a reproduction of social facts and reality. They also serve aesthetically to remind the reader of the depth and complexity of characters like Juanito, who spiritually do not grow or change. Even these, the uncreative individuals, nevertheless *progressively reveal themselves* to us as we read of their various doings in society. They do not grow as persons, but they do, as their multifaceted personalities are made manifest during social intercourse, grow in our minds. We continually discover even the shallow Juanito as we witness his complex interactions with the social world. Juanito, the faithful son, the unfaithful husband and lover, the neglectful father, the social philosopher who whether we like it or not has the gift of accurately perceiving social reality (as we saw when he abandoned Fortunata for the second time [III, iii, 1]), this Juanito is always Juanito. He is not some inchoate character made up of various *personae* who inhabit the same body; nor is he a psychological aberration comprising various and pathologically separate personalities much like a schizophrenic. He is, simply, an individual composed of a multitude of aspects and possibilities which are seen to be stimulated or repressed by another multitude of individuals and socioeconomic relationships.[33]

iii. *The ambiguity of vital experience*

The general failure to appreciate Galdós's absorption of Hegel [34] is due to three major misapprehensions of the latter's ideas. In the first place,

a general responsiveness to his ideas absorbed both directly from his work and from day to day living in a society in which those ideas are discussed and dissected.

[33] On the creation of ironically ambiguous perspectives, see two helpful studies of *Miau*: EAMONN RODGERS, *Pérez Galdós: Miau* (London: Grant and Cutler, 1978), and MARY LEE BRETZ, «The Ironic Vision of *Miau*», *The American Hispanist*, IV (1978), no. 29, 16-19. Rodgers in essence shows Galdós's efforts to avoid a single perspective of a character or situation, and Bretz demonstrates that this effect often is produced by developing the interactions of a pair of characters to reveal the complexity of a third.

[34] E.g., RODRÍGUEZ PUÉRTOLAS states «el proceso dialéctico es incompleto, por falta de la apropiada síntesis final» (55, n.). STEPHEN GILMAN, «The Consciousness of Fortunata», *Anales Galdosianos*, V (1970), 55-66, esp. 60: «Hegelian consciousness is ultimately intellectual while Fortunata's is axiological — a vessel not of ideas but of undistorted perception and value judgement.» See also *Galdós and the Art*, pp. 343-44. Gilman here expands on points first made in 1966 and 1968 in «The Birth of Fortunata» and «Narrative Presentation in...». One overlooked study which senses what other critics have missed, and correctly views Galdós's use of history and social context as a vehicle for the dialectical unfolding of his novels, is JUAN LÓPEZ-MORILLAS, «Historia y novela en el Galdós primerizo: En torno a *La Fontana de Oro*», *Revista Hispánica Moderna*, XXXI (1965), 273-85. His analysis of the early novel compels López-Morillas to observe: «Adelantándose a su procedimiento habitual en las *Novelas españolas contemporáneas,* Galdós desdoble a sus entes de ficción con el fin de revelárnoslos en dos planos complementarios: lo que esos personajes son para el mundo y lo que quisieran ser para sí mismos,

as suggested the dialectic functions not only within each life but in society across all lives. We recall the example of Mauricia, whose powerful emotions have a destructive effect on herself but a positive effect on Fortunata.[35]

The second misapprehension of Hegel and the dialectic assumes that the synthesis represents only a transcendent state, whereas in fact transcendence and/or apotheosis are but varieties of synthesis. Fortunata's liaison with Feijoo is a synthesis of her earlier affairs with Juanito (like Feijoo, a *señorito*) and Maxi (like Feijoo, an educator, a *filósofo*); yet also it is but one more step in a *continuing* process of life. Hence Fortunata will return to Maxi, will have yet another amorous interlude with Juanito, will become Ballester's friend. The synthesis is not only an endpoint; it is as much a beginning and a middle as well. As such, the synthesis is not an absolute, but simply a higher stage out of which comes a new thesis, thereby perpetuating the dialectical process. Critics who seek in a novel the transcendent or absolute variety as the only synthesis possible may thereby deprive themselves of a richer reading.[36]

Finally, if transcendence is one form of synthesis, destruction, death, even effacement are others. They are negative in quality, that is all. Hence the true implications of the title to Part II, chapter xvi of *La desheredada,* which reads «Las ideas de Mariano. La síntesis». Now a positive and transcendent synthesis in novels is by definition of the genre almost impossible, at least if we agree with Lukács who reminds us that the protagonist of a novel is *a priori* doomed to failure. Transcendence, such as it is, derives from struggling for meaning in a meaningless world, knowing all the while that one is doomed to be frustrated: [37]

haciendo de la tensión o 'dialéctica espiritual' así creada la 'imagen de la vida' que es para él la sustancia misma de la novela» (282).

[35] BRAUN, *op. cit.*

[36] The most important elucidation of Hegel's philosophy, as a philosophical system, is CHARLES TAYLOR, *Hegel* (Cambridge: Cambridge Univ. Press, 1975). In terms of social theory and political science, HERBERT MARCUSE's *Reason and Revolution. Hegel and the Rise of Social Theory* (New York: Oxford Univ. Press, 1941). The second edition (Boston: Beacon, 1960) contains an important preface, «A Note on Dialectic». See also his development of the negation as a stage in the dialectic in *Negations. Essays in Critical Theory* (Boston: Beacon, 1968). On Hegel, I acknowledge with gratitude the orientation provided me by my colleague, C. L. HARDIN.

[37] GEORG LUKÁCS, *The Theory of the Novel,* trans. Anna Bostock (Cambridge: MIT Press, 1971), pp. 85-86. Gilman himself observes that «the theme of *Fortunata y Jacinta* is the theme of all great novels ever since the *Quijote*: the creation of significance out of insignificance or, as Lukacs [sic] tells us, a search for values which in apparent failure nevertheless succeeds» («The Consciousness...», 59). But he then makes a jump which I believe is incorrect, an unwarranted imposition of his own values on Galdós's novel: «Hence, Fortunata's carnal death and angelic resurrection in the consciousness of those she leaves behind» (59-60). Besides the reader, who counts for nothing in Fortunata's world, there are the insane Maxi and Ballester who admits *as he is returning from her burial* «Esta imagen [...] vivirá en mí algún tiempo; pero se irá borrando, borrando, hasta que enteramente

> Indeed, the irony is a double one in both directions. It extends not only to the profound hopelessness of the struggle but also to the still more profound hopelessness of its abandonment — the pitiful failure of the intention to adapt to a world which is a stranger to ideals, to abandon the unreal ideality of the soul for the sake of achieving mastery over reality.

It is in this that Gregor Samsa, Ivan Denisovich, Jean-Baptiste Clamence, are united with Fortunata and don Quijote.

Marcuse's notions about negations [38] are particularly useful in helping us understand the relationship of the dialectic to ambiguity in the novel: Every positive characteristic contains intrinsically the very qualities which can and may undercut and reverse it. If Fortunata is an angel in the satanic-bourgeois world of Madrid, she also is an *exterminating* angel employed as one instrument of the middle classes against those who do not conform to the socioeconomic strictures of society. She is ineffectual against the like of «good» *señoritos* such as Juanito and Villalonga; she cannot and does not hurt them. She can only harm those who are not full-fledged members of the middle classes, such as Maxi, Feijoo and Ballester. They are deviants, outsiders, against whom she is dangerous indeed.[39]

Fortunata is dangerous because she is, after all, a product of Madrid too. If she is in opposition to her society, she is also of it. She is so marvelous a figure of life because she never escapes, although she indeed transcends, this vital ambiguity, this overpowering attraction for a world which she knows to be inhospitable and which she detests as powerfully as she desires it. Readers tend to forget that she constantly seeks validation in Madrid society. That is the essence of her wish to be «honrada». Like Lazarillo de Tormes, Fortunata presents us with the dilemma of a person who wants to «arrimarse a los buenos». Fortunata's spirit transcends the brutal process of socialization whereas Lazarillo's does not.[40] Yes this in no way can obscure her constant desire to be accepted in the bourgeois world of nineteenth-century Madrid.

Ambiguity then is a function of the dialectical vision. The very nature of an ambiguous world is dynamic; everything is precarious, fluctuating. There is definition to every person and every situation, but definition changes in direct response to circumstance. In 1885 Galdós observes that

desaparezca» (IV, vi, 16; 429). Everyone forgets Fortunata; that is her earthly destiny. See also the text below.

[38] *Reason and Revolution* and *Negations*. Refer also to SUSAN BUCK-MORSS, *The Origin of Negative Dialectics* (New York: Free Press, 1977).

[39] Maxi is a deviant because of his physical and biological state. Ballester is isolated socially, Feijoo morally. See definitions of deviance in the early pages of BECKER, *Outsiders*.

[40] See, e.g., STEPHEN GILMAN, «The Death of Lazarillo de Tormes», *PMLA*, LXXXI (1966), 149-66; and JAVIER HERRERO, «Renaissance Poverty and Lazarillo's Family: The Birth of the Picaresque Genre», *PMLA*, XCIV (1979), 876-86.

the very measures liberating the middle classes make them a new dictator enslaving others. What is good for one individual or class is another's bane: «Todo ha cambiado. La extinción de la raza de tiranos ha traído el acabamiento de la raza de libertadores. [...] ahora resulta que la tiranía subsiste, sólo que los tiranos ahora somos nosotros, los que antes éramos víctimas y mártires, la clase media, la burguesía, que antaño luchó con el clero y la aristocracia [...] los desheredados de entonces se truecan en privilegiados».[41] In a similar vein, but going one step further, we may observe that the same characteristic in a person may be sequentially distinct in its effects. Fortunata's belief that she and Jacinta have common bonds is equally the cause of her fight with Aurora and the delivery of her son to Jacinta, which redeems her aesthetically while effacing her socially. Finally, ambiguity may exist simultaneously: Feijoo's love for Fortunata is his great passion yet also the cause of his physical decline. Whatever the mode of ambiguity, it is always characterized by the blend within a single characteristic or situation of dissimilarities and contradictions out of which is developed a synthesis. In an ambiguous world, therefore, all three of the following conditions obtain: (a) things are what they seem; (b) things are not what they seem and may even be the opposite; (c) the merger of (a) and (b) leads to a situation in which our appreciation of both is heightened, and which yet is richer in possibilities than either considered separately. Since all three conditions coexist, we have a situation far more complex than the commonplace of the whole being more than the sum of its parts. Ambiguity therefore surpasses a merely relativistic view of existence; rather, it is an acceptance of and testimonial to the rich complexity of life.[42]

[41] «El 1.º de Mayo», 15 de abril, 1885, reprinted in BENITO PÉREZ GALDÓS, *Política española*, II, ed. Alberto Ghiraldo, vol. IV of the *Obras inéditas* (Madrid: Renacimiento, 1923), 268-69; see also n. 9 above.

[42] In a perceptive essay HAROLD L. BOUDREAU, «The Salvation of Torquemada: Determinism and Indeterminacy in the Later Novels of Galdós», *Anales Galdosianos*, XV (1980), 113-28, suggests a somewhat different understanding of ambiguity. I will be pleased if our differences of definition are offset by similar readings of the Galdós text. Essentially I see ambiguity with the neo-Hegelian vision described by EOFF, «Deification», pp. 134-35 and 139. Eoff stresses the fundamental quality of paradox in Galdós's work, reasoning that Galdós, like Hegel in *Phenomenology of Mind,* brings «meaning into the paradoxes of life» (139). This of course is what Galdós means in «Confusiones y paradojas» cited above, n. 11. Boudreau here and in «Máximo Manso: The *molde* and the *hechura*», *Anales Galdosianos*, XII (1977), 63-70, describes the capacity of Galdós to combine «opposites and his related talent for creating dichotomous characters» («Manso», 68). See MACKLIN, pp. 191-94, and ARNOLD M. PENUEL, «The Ambiguity of Orozco's Virtue in Galdós' 'La incógnita' and 'Realidad'», *Hispania*, LIII (1970), 411-18, and «The Problem of Ambiguity in Galdós' *Doña Perfecta*», *Anales Galdosianos*, XI (1976), 71-88. Using a model of ambiguity based on EMPSON's *Seven Types of Ambiguity*, Penuel finds it present in all of Galdós's work but «immature» (72) in the earlier novels. Two who examine the manifestations but not the concept itself are (in Galdós) ROBERT E. LOTT, «From Irony to Empathy and Ambiguity in

IV. THE FAILED REVOLUTION AND THE AESTHETIC OF AMBIGUITY:
SUBVERSION AS LIFESTYLE

Fortunata's affair with Feijoo is an eloquent case in point. When he warns Fortunata of her own weaknesses and danger, Feijoo unwittingly prophesies her fall. It is a radical, perhaps revolutionary interpretation of life which he preaches and Fortunata *does* grasp. Yet at first his notions seem rather commonplace:

> Tienes tú en ti misma poca defensa contra los peligros que a la vida ofrece continuamente el entusiasmo. Si te dejo sola, aunque te asegure la subsistencia, te arrastrarán otra vez las pasiones y volverás a la vida mala. Necesita mi niña un freno, y ese freno, que es la legalidad, no le será molesto si lo sabe llevar... si sigue los consejos que voy a darle. Tonta, tontaina, si todo en este mundo depende del modo, del estilo... (III, iv, 6; 163-64)

Now it could be and has been argued that this is equivalent to accepting the middle-class hypocrisy which Feijoo, Fortunata and Galdós all abhor.[43] But in reality what Feijoo and Galdós go on to suggest is the necessity of understanding just how society works, and how one like Fortunata may function freely, with autonomy, within the social structure using that same structure paradoxically to subvert itself. Put another way, author and character coincide here in the latter's discourse on social action and socioeconomic relations. Their object is that Fortunata learn how to manipulate society for her own ends. It is Feijoo for example who understands the best way to approach doña Lupe so that Fortunata

---

Galdós' Use of Free Indirect Style in *Misericordia*», pp. 255-60 of *Studies in Honor of Tatiana Fotitch*, ed. J. M. Sola-Solé (Washington: Catholic Univ. Press, n. d. [1978]), and (in general) KEITH ELLIS, «Ambiguity and Point of View in Some Novelistic Representations of Jealousy», *Modern Language Notes*, LXXXVI (1971), 891-909.

[43] Such is the argument put forward by Carlos Blanco in his essay included in the present collection. Others, Montesinos (II, 262-63, 266-67) among them, see Feijoo as irredeemably cynical. Perhaps, but only prior to his involvement with Fortunata; thereafter he grows considerably as a person. It may be that he possesses selfless qualities even before we watch his personality unfold; we must remember that until Part III, Chapter IV we see Feijoo only as a product of café society because of the narrator's and Galdós's artistic selection. They choose not to discuss him except when imbibing and conversing about politics with Juan Pablo and his cronies. For example, Galdós titillates us with the revelation that Feijoo has visited Fortunata at home (III, i, 6; 45-46), and then allows the narrator to editorialize about Feijoo's refusal to discuss the matter further: «Era sin duda cosa delicada para dicha delante de testigos» (*idem*, 46). The reader should proceed cautiously rather than rush to judgment with the narrator. Is Feijoo really an amoral cynic, or are parts of his personality simply undisclosed to the reader? The essays by ALAN S. TRUEBLOOD on the *Quijote* are instructive in this sense: *v* «Sobre la selección artística en el *Quijote*: '... lo que ha dejado de escribir' (II, 44)», *Nueva Revista de Filología Hispánica*, X (1956), 44-50; and «El silencio en el *Quijote*», *Nueva Revista de Filología Hispánica*, XII (1958), 160-80.

finally dominates her. Fortunata, we remember, gives her own funds —a gift from Feijoo— to doña Lupe. Note how the latter reacts:

> Lo más particular era que doña Lupe, por impulsos de tolerancia que habían surgido bruscamente en su espíritu, se esforzaba en suponer a aquel caudal una procedencia decente. ¡Fascinación que la moneda ejerce en ciertos caracteres, porque para éstos lo bueno tiene que tener buen origen! (III, v, 2; 225)

And of the fact that on Feijoo's advice Fortunata gives her so much money to invest while refusing to accept any receipt for it, the narrator observes: «Tal prueba de confianza le llegaba al alma, porque no sólo era confianza en su honradez, sino en su talento para hacer producir dinero al dinero...» (*idem*). This kind of successful manipulation depends on knowing exactly the most susceptible areas of a person's character, and how to touch them to elicit the desired result; it is managing people so that they do what we wish, thinking all the while that they are doing their own bidding; it is the stimulation of their self-esteem so that blinded by their own conceits, they work in our interest. Each person, like every socioeconomic relationship and every element of the social structure, has her peculiar pressure point and functions on the basis of distinct requirements and impulses. An acute sense of the variegated nature of these elements is what Feijoo is trying to teach Fortunata. He wants her not subjugated but autonomous. For indeed, the domination of socioeconomic relations so that our result is contrary to the ends for which such relations were formed is to subvert them. Ultimately Fortunata controls doña Lupe, queen of the bourgeois economic nexus, in order later to circumvent the «orden público» by maintaining it in appearance as the restored señora de Rubín; she uses one social convention to undermine another. This is the revolution which Feijoo preaches, and which Fortunata can implement but not sustain in practice.

But there is more. At one point during their numerous and protracted discussions, Feijoo admonishes Fortunata

> *Nada es bueno ni malo por sí.* ¿Me entiendes? Ojo al corazón es lo primero que te digo. No permitas que te domine. *Eso de echar todo por la ventana en cuanto el señor corazón se atufa, es un disparate que se paga caro.* Hay que dar al corazón sus miajitas de carne; es fiera y las hambres largas le ponen furioso; pero también hay que dar a la fiera de la sociedad la parte que le corresponde, para que no alborote. Si no, lo echas todo a rodar, y no hay vida posible. (III, iv, 6; 164, my italics)

The foreshadowing of Fortunata's ultimate «disparate» and the high price it exacts is really incidental to the social analysis provided by Feijoo. We must not allow our twentieth-century values to cloud our readings of his view of nineteenth-century society, or to obscure the possibility that Feijoo himself does not care for the reality he is describing. What we must bear in mind is that his is an accurate study of Madrid in the last half of the century, when relativity had come of age and absolute values were by and large absent from social relations. His notion that life consists of a balance between personal wants and the requirements of society is not the least outlandish. In fact it is rather timely, especially since his philosophy places a premium on the final goal of personal autonomy, a freedom within society which permits individuals to do as they please so long as they attend to the limits imposed by decorum. In effect, Feijoo wants Fortunata to learn how to be «honrada» and simultaneously to have a lover (III, iv, 9; 198-203. III, iv, 10; 204-06). Appropriate manipulation of social convention in the guise of the «orden público» and the «paz del matrimonio» will enable Fortunata to enjoy extramarital affairs (*idem*). For Feijoo, the key is the awareness that one is both, and at the same time, a private individual and a social animal. The task set before Fortunata is to be conscious of this division of existence and, subsequently in her own life, to exploit this reality to her advantage.

An understanding of Feijoo's notion of self, other and society resolves for us also the seeming contradiction —which has drawn critical comment— surrounding his decision to take last rites. We are informed that Feijoo «siempre hizo alarde de libre pensador» (III, iv, 10; 208). When in what ostensibly are his final moments, everyone is amazed that he acquiesces and takes last rites: «Todos los presentes se maravillaron al oírle» (*idem,* 209). Subsequently we remember that Feijoo rapidly and unexpectedly gets well (*idem*). Many readers consider Feijoo's behavior hypocritical at best. I am not persuaded however that Feijoo's state of mind and own words ought to be discounted. Moreover I agree with James Whiston who finds Feijoo's observation of last rites consistent with the man's character.[44] When advised by his friends that he will die shortly, Feijoo prepares himself admirably: «mas con gran sorpresa de todos, oyó la indicación del modo más sereno y amable, diciendo que él tenía sus creencias, pero que al mismo tiempo gustaba de cumplir toda obligación consagrada por el asentimiento del mayor número» (III, iv, 10; 208-09). Why make one's own dying more unpleasant than it is by upsetting not only oneself but also everyone else? Feijoo is truest to himself when he states —*repeating* what the narrator has just told us— «Por el respeto que los hombres nos debemos los unos a los otros, no quiero dejar de cumplir ningún requisito de los que ordena toda sociedad bien organizada. [...] No descomponerse; ése es mi tema» (*idem,* 209). It may be ill advised to doubt the sincerity of a dying man, or of one who is convinced that he is dying.

As far as I am aware only Kay Engler and Michael Nimetz appreciate

[44] «The Materialism of Life: Religion in *Fortunata y Jacinta*», *Anales Galdosianos,* XIV (1979), 65-81, esp. 72.

Feijoo as Galdós intended. Engler observes that his perspective is «the most comprehensive and all inclusive vision of reality. Only his interpretation allows for the accommodation of passion and reason, instinct and decorum, spirit and flesh, individual and society. His observations most clearly and explicitly represent the norms of the novel...»[45]

i. *Varieties of revolutionary experience: The romantic revolt*

Just as she is not Feijoo's victim biologically, we see too that he fails to reverse the socialization of Fortunata. This is all the more ironic given that their views exhibit a remarkable coincidence. It is true that concerning love the ideas and opinions of Feijoo and Fortunata are not identical, but they do show a basis in the same social ethos. Put another way, ideologically Feijoo and Fortunata are from the very first in accord; only in amorous theory and practice do they exhibit differences. Certainly the divergence on matters of the heart is important because love is very much a motive force in this novel. Yet also fundamental is ideology, because social and economic values are the prism through which Fortunata increasingly views her world and its affairs. On her return to the Cava de San Miguel, for example, Fortunata muses:

«Falta saber de quién es ahora la casa... ¿La habrá heredado doña Guillermina?...» *Quedóse meditando en que su destino no le permitía salir de aquel círculo de personas que en los últimos tiempos la había rodeado. Era como una red que la envolvía*, y como pensara escabullirse por algún lado, se encontraba otra vez cogida. «No; habrán heredado la casa los señores de Ruiz Ochoa, o la mujer de Zalamero... Y después de todo, ¿a mí qué me importa que herede la finca Juan o Pedro? *Yo no la he de heredar*.» (IV, iii, 7; 212; my italics)

The passage just cited occurs moments after her realization that «Ahora es cuando conozco que, aunque poco, algo se me ha pegado el señorío» (*idem*, 210). Whether we like it or not, Fortunata's political and economic consciousness, just as her social consciousness, has been raised by the end of the novel. Her ideological compatibility with Feijoo, a matter which Galdosian criticism seems to have left unexplored, therefore deserves closer scrutiny.[46]

The strands of love and ideology are intertwined in a complex pattern in *Fortunata y Jacinta*. If we are to isolate the social and economic values

[45] «Notes on the Narrative Structure of *Fortunata y Jacinta*», *Symposium*, XXIV (1970), 111-27; see 126 for this explanation of Feijoo. MICHAEL NIMETZ, *Humor in Galdós* (New Haven: Yale, 1968), pp. 85 and 195.
[46] Primarily this oversight is due to the traditional location of Fortunata among the *pueblo* (e.g., BLANCO, ENGLER, GILMAN, RODRÍGUEZ PUÉRTOLAS, SINNIGEN). This despite the fact that at the end of her life Fortunata is irredeemably bourgeois (*v* Part III of this essay and n. 59 below).

of Feijoo and Fortunata, they must first be separated from the notions concerning love to which each character ties them. My point ultimately is this: Even prior to meeting Feijoo Fortunata was incapacitated for her own salvation because she was already socialized, corrupted by what perforce must be called bourgeois sentimentality. The phrase, however distasteful it may be to those critics who eschew ideological commonplaces, nevertheless is fitting if we read closely: «Lo que Fortunata había pensado era que el amor salva todas las irregularidades, mejor dicho, que el amor lo hace todo regular, que rectifica las leyes, derogando las que se le oponen. Lo había dicho varias veces a su amante» (III, iii, 1; 103). Now this belief is constantly criticized by Feijoo; he calls Fortunata a victim of «un romanticismo impropio de estos tiempos» (III, iv, 1; 119). The criticism moreover is repeated frequently throughout their love affair (i.e., all of Part III, Chapter IV) by Fortunata's preceptor-protector when discussing her «corazón» or «rasgos» (e.g., III, iv, 4; 149. III, iv, 6; 164. III, iv, 7; 172; etc.). Fortunata's tranquillity, and later her life, are continually menaced by her conviction that the laws of society ought to be subordinate to those of the individual. Indeed, because of her beliefs Fortunata is correctly diagnosed by Feijoo as irredeemably romantic. In this she mimics an earlier tutor, Maxi. According to the latter, who engages Papitos in a discussion which she cannot comprehend, «el amor es la ley de las leyes, el amor gobierna el mundo» (II, ii, 6; 93). Such an expression of pure romanticism reflects Maxi's own desire to employ love for the purpose of transcending the *laws of nature* which bind his spirit to a body that is both ugly and sterile. This same romanticism afflicts Fortunata; it is a contagion which she catches from her teacher-husband as soon as she learns to articulate (II, ii, 1; 58): «por más que dijeran, nada que se relacionase con el amor era pecado». She subsequently informs Juanito that she expects love to enable her to transcend not the laws of nature *but of society:* «estoy dudando siempre, y al fin me hago este cargo: *querer a quien se quiere no puede ser cosa mala*» (II, vii, 7; 404; Galdós's italics).[47] As we are told later by Feijoo, Maxi and Fortunata are «apasionados», «unos sentimentales» (III, iv, 7; 172). Juanito appreciates her weakness. In consequence, on reuniting with her for the last time he encourages her by pleading: «Y ahora gocemos del momento presente, sin pensar en lo que se hará o no se hará después. Eso depende de las circunstancias.» To which she replies:

—¡Ah! esas señoras circunstancias son las que me cargan a mí. Y yo digo: «Pero, Señor, ¿para qué hay en el mundo circunstancias?» No debe haber más que *quererse* y a vivir. (III, vii, 5; 397; Galdós's italics)

[47] On this phrase and its importance *v* p. 263 of JAMES WHISTON, «Las pruebas corregidas de *Fortunata y Jacinta*», pp. 258-65 of vol. I, Segundo Congreso Internacional de Estudios Galdosianos [1978], *Actas* (Las Palmas: Cabildo Insular, 1979).

Her convictions further endanger Fortunata because, in addition to believing love supreme, she is unable to restrain her egocentrism and root her own passions to any social context. As she herself confesses, «¡qué indecente he sido! Todo por querer más de lo que es debido, por querer como una leona» (III, iv, 1; 120). Her self-criticism is consonant with the warnings of Feijoo and Juanito. Indeed, the several points of similarity between Santa Cruz and Feijoo are more numerous than are accepted by most readers; recall for example that Juanito is the first to admonish Fortunata:

> ... estamos pateando todas las leyes divinas y humanas. Si hubiera muchos como nosotros, pronto la sociedad sería peor que un presidio, un verdadero infierno suelto. [...] No se puede uno sustraer a los principios. [...] Las conveniencias sociales, nena mía, son más fuertes que nosotros, y no puede uno estar riéndose de ellas mucho tiempo... (III, iii, 1; 103-04)

Feijoo's counsel is more than coincidentally similar: «Al mundo hay que tratarlo siempre con muchísimo respeto. [...] hay que tener formalidad y no dar nunca malos ejemplos. [...] la dignidad siempre por delante, compañera» (III, iv, 3; 139).

The basic difference between their conceptions of love is that for Fortunata it is something noble and grand, whereas for Feijoo love is merely a biologically necessary amusement. This is both a theoretical and a behavioral distinction, even though on the level of practice love becomes for Feijoo one of life's great passions. Conceptually as well as concretely, love is for Fortunata everything; as we will see, for Feijoo even after he is taken with Fortunata, neither love *nor* laws matter unless they be put to use in the governance of beings.

With the help of the rationale based on her «romanticismo impropio de estos tiempos» as Feijoo calls it (III, iv, 1; 119), Fortunata comes to believe that she and not Jacinta is the natural wife of Juanito. The progression of events is well-known to all readers of this novel. But her ideas on love lead her in this process to the formation of another notion which is this: that vis-à-vis criminal law which does matter, the civil laws of society have no intrinsic morality or importance. This is far more advanced than merely expecting that the latter may be subordinated to true love; it is a realization that they are severely limited and may be manipulated independently of amorous matters. On this point she finds herself in agreement with Feijoo, the two against the rest of the world. And so, in the matter of the «valor social de las leyes»,[48] *Feijoo and Fortunata coin-*

---

[48] This was a matter of some importance in the last years of the nineteenth century and first years of the twentieth; *v* the important work by PEDRO DORADO MONTERO, *Valor social de leyes y autoridades* (Barcelona: José Gallach, n. d.), Manuales Gallach núm. XXXVIII. AMÉRICO CASTRO provides an interpretation of this phenomenon on pp. 301-19 of *La realidad histórica de España,* ed. renovada (México: Porrúa, 1962).

cide; he does not have to teach her anything about *theory*, because Fortunata already has all the information she requires. It is for this reason that Chapter IV of Part III bears the title «Un curso de filosofía *práctica*» (my italics).

Therefore if on the conceptual level the ideas of the two differ on the matter of love, they nevertheless *are identical* on the matter of laws and social strictures which pretend to regulate the amorous conduct of men and women. Fortunata —and not only in this long chapter, but throughout the novel [49]— is tormented by contradictory thoughts and feelings about love and correct social behavior. She does not wish to believe herself culpable or bad for having fallen in love. After being abandoned by Juanito and rescued by Feijoo

> ... tuvo horas de melancolía intensísima, en las cuales su conciencia, confabulada con la memoria, le representaba de un modo vivo todas las maldades que cometiera en su vida, singularmente la de casarse y ser adúltera con pocas horas de diferencia. Pero de repente, sin saber cómo ni por qué, todo se le volvía del revés allá en las cavidades desconocidas de su espíritu, y la conciencia se le presentaba limpia, clara y firme. Juzgábase entonces sin culpa alguna, inocente de todo el mal causado, como el que obra a impulsos de un mandato extraño y superior. «Si yo no soy mala —pensaba—, ¿Qué tengo yo de malo aquí *entre mí*? Pues nada.» (III, iv, 3; 135-36, Galdós's italics)

She recognizes that she is, or believes herself to be, innocent. On the other hand she also acknowledges that she has hurt others.[50] Her obvious problem is the reconciliation of opposing impulses. Hers is a dilemma articulated by Zahareas as «extremos de las realidades en conflicto..., el hombre no puede escoger sin pena entre cosas vitales que le hagan falta...».[51] Another way of stating this would be to say that the characters of *Fortunata y Jacinta* are enmeshed in a dialectic which on the level of the individual lacks its most important component: the transcendent synthesis (*v* Part III above).

ii. *Varieties of revolutionary experience: Dignity as subversion*

We should understand that Feijoo's world view derives not from an inveterate romanticism like that of Fortunata, but from an ascetic and paradoxically ethical utilitarianism as reflected concretely in the description of his rooms, the physical projection of his character (III, iv, 4;

---

[49] For example, *v* the chapters treating her stay in the Micaelas (II, v and vi) and BRAUN's article «The Novelistic Function of Mauricia...».

[50] As she declares to Feijoo, «a los que me habían hecho decente les di una patada! [...] a los que me querían afinar y hacerme honrada les di con su honradez en los hocicos... ¡Qué ingrata, ¿verdad?, qué indecente he sido!» (III, iv, 1; 120).

[51] «El sentido de la tragedia...», 33.

144, and 6; 164-65).[52] Of importance are Feijoo's «program» and Fortunata's reaction on hearing it. The two have been lovers for some time
when the retired gentleman reveals his ideas in the following scene.
Feijoo is inordinately content now for having achieved the «paraíso» in
which he has found not only a heated passion but also «la tranquilidad
dentro, el decoro fuera» (III, iv, 3; 139). Thereupon he articulates the
meaning of the word «práctica». Above all, it is a word which is eminently
social:

> Aquí tienes lo que yo te quería enseñar, ser persona práctica. Al mundo
> hay que tratarlo siempre con muchísimo respeto. Yo bien sé que lo mejor
> es que uno sea un santo; pero como esto es dificilillo, hay que tener forma-
> lidad y no dar nunca malos ejemplos. *Fíjate bien en esto; la dignidad siem-
> pre por delante, compañera.* (*idem*; my italics)

Now Feijoo is not the first to have expressed such thoughts to Fortunata, although no one previously had done so with the sincerity, the
forethought and the concern for her. In the most recent past Feijoo's
words replicate in their essence the same idea, more hollow in its cynical
enunciation, articulated by Juanito in his second farewell to Fortunata
(III, iii, 1; 103-04). Further, Feijoo's «program» also echoes superficially,
while contradicting in essence, that proclaimed by Maxi when he first
began «instructing» her. We recall that when Rubín initiated his amorous
relationship with Fortunata, she told him all about her first child and
its death. When mother and child had returned to Madrid, the baby
died and Santa Cruz paid for the funeral. To this bit of information
Maxi —more concerned in truth with his rivalry than with Fortunata's
feelings— reacts by exclaiming: «Primero le dejo yo insepulto, que recurrir... *La dignidad, hija, es antes que todo. Fíjate bien en esto*» (II, ii, 2;
62-63; my italics). The near identical use of words and phrases fixes in
contrast the differing context and real message of each utterance. These
distinctions indicate substantial differences between the three men who
speak to Fortunata. Maxi, a prisoner of his own romanticism, reacts much

---

[52] In his essay «Galdós and Realism» RODOLFO CARDONA reminds us of Galdós's
contention that one's living quarters are an extension of the individual (pp. 71-94
of *Galdós. A Symposium at Mary Washington College* [Fredericksburg, Va.: The
College, 1967]). The intimate physical environment one creates for oneself is in
Galdós's mind a faithful reflection of values, ethos, beliefs, etc. (CARDONA, pp. 79-
80). Pathbreaking work on this subject has been published by CHAD C. WRIGHT
in four articles: «The Representational Qualities of Isidora Rufete's House», *Romanische Forschungen*, LXXXIII (1971), 23-45; «Artifacts and Effigies: The
Porreño Household Revisited», *Anales Galdosianos*, XIV (1979), 13-26; «*Lo prohibido:* 'Las cuatro paredes de la Restauración'», *Modern Language Notes*, XCVII
(1982), 391-400; and «Secret Space in Pérez Galdós' *La de Bringas*», *Hispanic
Review*, L (1982), 75-86. See also RISLEY, «Setting in the Galdós Novel», and the
interesting view of GUSTAVO CORREA on pp. 56-58 of his *Realidad, ficción y símbolo
en las novelas de Pérez Galdós* (Bogotá: Instituto Caro y Cuervo, 1967).

as Fortunata will later when Juanito offers her money on abandoning her (the four thousand *reales* [III, iv, 1; 119]): He emits a *thesis* with little consideration of its consequence for Fortunata or of his motivations for doing so. The *Delfín* on the other hand uses the *words* as a formulaic response because his mind is focused entirely on the desired consequence of extrication without fuss from an embarrassing situation. He therefore preaches the *antithesis* of his rival; against Maxi's affirmation of «la dignidad personal» at any price Juanito posits complete submission to the social will. The irony and the paradox here are that Juanito advocates this subordination of the individual will to society as one who in practice lives according to an absolute antisocial individualism. No one in this novel is more self-centered and self-gratifyingly motivated than he. Only Feijoo with his ethical utilitarianism can maintain in synthetic balance both social and individual criteria.

Verification of this reading is made manifest subsequently when we hear Feijoo's theories resonate in the mouth of doña Lupe. At the time this occurs Fortunata is beginning to break away forever from Maxi; intellectually and emotionally she is already unfaithful to him, although she has not begun her final affair with Juanito. Doña Lupe recognizes that Fortunata is preparing an infidelity, but she is resigned not to interfere because she understands that in reality there is nothing she can do. The validity of Feijoo's counsel and its accuracy are borne out in doña Lupe's admonition to Fortunata:

> La taimada viuda de Jáuregui comprendió que una sujeción absoluta sería perjudicial, y *empezó a darle* [a Fortunata] *libertad. Un día le leyó la cartilla en estos términos:*
> —*Puedes salir;* no eres una chiquilla y ya sabes lo que haces. Yo creo que no nos darás ningún disgusto, y que has de mirar por el decoro de la familia lo mismo que miro yo. *La dignidad, hija, la dignidad es lo primero.* (III, vii, 5; 390; my italics)

The italicized words are a link between this narrative moment and that in which Feijoo elucidates his conception of «la dignidad». Doña Lupe's terms also indicate that Fortunata has progressed to a higher level of existence and experience; each time someone gives this «lecture» to Fortunata, she is on the threshold of a new stage in life. Hence the repetition here, almost word for word, of those which Feijoo recited when he and Fortunata were about to begin their life together:

> El primer día [Feijoo] le leyó la cartilla, que era muy breve:
> —Mira, yo te dejo en absoluta libertad. Puedes salir y entrar a la hora que quieras, y hacer lo que te dé tu real gana. (III, iv, 3; 137; my italics)

In each of these incidents the effect on Fortunata is that of initiating another leg of her dialectical journey through life. The confrontation with doña Lupe marks the moment in which Fortunata definitively determines to put into «la práctica» the principles of «la dignidad» learned from Feijoo. Following doña Lupe's remonstrance, Fortunata immediately leaves the house. With undeniable symbolism, Galdós propels her into the streets to the Plaza del Progreso where she witnesses a *funeral procession* which she follows at a distance. The narrator portentously reflects on the pregnant atmosphere, both literal and figurative:

> El cielo, el horizonte, las fantásticas formas de la sierra azul, revueltas con las masas de nubes, le sugerían vagas ideas de un mundo desconocido, quizás mejor que éste en que estamos; pero seguramente distinto. (III, vii, 5; 392)

Whereupon the wind carries to her the sound of the bells tolling the death knell, which sound *makes her think of Juanito* (*idem,* 393). She finds a white button with four holes in it, accepts it as an augury of *good things* to come,[53] and returns home. The following morning by chance she meets Juanito; the two begin their last and for Fortunata fatal liaison. The latter is marked for some time by «la dignidad» in «la práctica», and as such clearly indicates Fortunata's success in having subverted the social order at least in terms of its matrimonial injunctions.

To be a «practical» person means to be one who maintains «la dignidad», one who does not «descomponerse», thereby compromising «el decoro». The «dignidad» of Maxi is pure post-adolescent, romantic ingenuousness; it is self-destructive. That of Juanito is anti-social opportunism employed for society's benefit only when the exigencies of the latter coincide with personal caprice; as such, Juanito's «dignidad» is an instrument in service to the lowest form of egoism. But the «dignidad» according to Feijoo is quite another matter. He makes this fact clear during the same chat with Fortunata in which he had first broached the notions of «la dignidad», individual and society, and love. Immediately following his disquisition on «dignidad» and its importance he adds that he has no wish or intention to advise Fortunata to disobey laws, or even to insinuate such behavior. He explains:

---

53 GULLÓN, «Estructura y diseño...», 261-63, is especially enlightening on the subjectivity of Fortunata's and Mauricia's interpretations of auguries. Our point is that what Fortunata interprets as good for herself can be seen by us to be deadly. However, Galdós leaves the interpretation pregnant with all possibilities. After all, Fortunata could not realize her «pícara idea» without coupling yet once more with Juanito in that loving but mortal embrace foreshadowed in their very first encounter (so well interpreted by GILMAN, «The Birth...», 75-79, esp. the description of the *pollería*): «A la derecha, en la prolongación de aquella cuadra lóbrega, un sicario manchado de sangre daba garrote a las aves. Retorcía los pescuezos con esa presteza y donaire que da el hábito, y apenas soltaba una víctima y la entregaba agonizante a las desplumadoras, cogía otra para hacerle la misma caricia» (I, iii, 4; 97).

... no predico yo la hipocresía. En cierta clase de faltas, *la dignidad consiste en no cometerlas. No transijo*, pues, con nada que sea apropiarse lo ajeno, ni con mentiras que dañan al honor del prójimo, ni con nada que sea vil y cobarde; *tampoco transijo* con menospreciar la disciplina militar: *en esto soy muy severo;* pero en todo aquello que se relaciona con el amor, la dignidad consiste en guardar el decoro... (III, iv, 3; 140; my italics)

Feijoo continues, and explains to Fortunata his opinion that nothing derived from «el amor verdadero» is criminal or, for that matter, bad. He is on this point in agreement with Fortunata. But it is also clear that he would never consider love as the supreme law, nor does he believe that love governs the soul of human conduct.

iii. *Varieties of revolutionary experience:*
    Decorum and disintegration

Here is where Feijoo fails: He can teach Fortunata how to behave, but he cannot teach her what to believe. Only her social conditioning, most of which has occurred prior to their becoming lovers, can do that.[54] Possibly, friends and lovers could also were it not for the fact that Fortunata is isolated as she lives in and travels through a remarkably conflictive world. There is virtually no consensus of values here, except perhaps in the Santa Cruz household. In other words, for Fortunata there is no community, in the sense that community means shared values and lifestyles.[55] In the Rubín household as in the apartment shared with Maxi, when there was calm there was also solitary existence; in the Micaelas where community might have existed there was the disruptive factor of Mauricia and hence little peace for Fortunata. Only in the house on the Calle de Tabernillas do we read that Fortunata not only relaxes but also mingles, that she has people with whom she passes the time in visits or idle conversation, that she feels comfortable with self and surroundings (III, iv, 3-5; esp. III, iv, 5; 155-56). The lack of community on any socioeconomic level except in the Plaza de Pontejos where Fortunata forever

---

[54] GILMAN is only half right when he states that Fortunata is «impervious to pedogogy» (*Galdós and the Art,* p. 349; *v* also «The Consciousness of Fortunata», 63). In my opinion she is not all the «truthfulness and freedom» he suggests (*idem*); Fortunata has been educated quite well by society. It is her social conditioning and her efforts to transcend it that constitute her struggle. Gullón observes that she «siente el peso de la culpa. La sociedad, sobre propiciar las circunstancias condicionantes, la instituye culpable y la fuerza a reconocerse como tal. No será ella quien ponga en duda la tabla de valores conforme a la cual se la ha clasificado» (234). But if she is the «víctima eterna» as Gullón believes, then ultimately she falls victim to herself. Feijoo gives her the wherewithal to be independent; her decision to leave the safety of the Cava de San Miguel and descend once more into society in search of Aurora is purely her own.

[55] This is a different albeit not unrelated view of conflict as explored by Zahareas.

will be unwelcome, the lack of any harbor —until she meets Feijoo— in which to repair her damaged psyche and reflect in tranquillity, comprise the circumstance of isolation in society which forms the basis of Fortunata's social conditioning. She is unintegrated except in her role of paramour; until she meets Feijoo her body is her key to society's door (would Maxi, for example, have noticed and attempted to «save» an ugly or even plain woman?).[56]

Hence Fortunata grows up in society free not only of its restraints, which is all to the good, but also free of any sense of, and value for, community, which is her great misfortune. She must depend on herself alone and on her conditioning in order to formulate the values and beliefs which motivate her behavior. Additionally, her isolated circumstances leave her utterly without defense each time she sallies forth into society. The fact that she is fortunate enough —the play on words is intentional— to encounter three such men as Maxi, Feijoo and Ballester, should not obscure from us the second fact that like Refugio and Mauricia and Segunda she just as easily, in fact more probably, could have ended up —as for a time she does in Parts I and II— as they do via a chain of corrupt and corrupting social relationships. She is saved socially and economically not because of herself, but in spite of herself. This temporary and temporal redemption, due to others, is what enables her finally to achieve her spiritual redemption; let us never forget that.

Feijoo, then, is engaged in an uphill battle in the education and social integration of Fortunata. His efforts do not for that reason flag; he is impelled by his passion for his young lover to accelerate her formation. He does so, we may argue, out of motives not entirely associated with altruism. If he wishes to instruct Fortunata, he also desires to justify his own point of view; after all, even were she single, Feijoo would not marry Fortunata (III, iv, 5; 156-57). Feijoo loves Fortunata deeply, but he does not believe in either the supremacy or the durability of love and its institutions (*idem*). Society, he observes, is ruled by ten commandments, but only eight of them are valid in truth; the two which pretend to govern love and matrimony

... no me entran a mí. ¡Ah!, chulita, dirás que yo tengo una moral muy rara. La verdad, si me dicen que Fulano hizo un robo, o que mató o calumnió o armó cualquier gatería, me indigno, y si le cogiera, créelo, le ahogaría; pero vienen y me cuentan que tal mujer le faltó a su marido, que tal niña se fugó de la casa paterna con el novio, y me quedo tan fresco. (III, iv, 3; 140)

---

[56] The question may be thought to be artificial. Yet virtually everyone who sees Fortunata is first attracted to her by her appearance. Physiognomy was important to Galdós —aside from his own proclivities— because it was so important to his society. *Marianela* (1878) is more than sufficient verification.

The rules concerning love are no more useful than to «contener algo a la gente y asustar a los viciosos» (*idem*), but even in this they have little force and slight importance. As to constancy in any love relationship, «decir *humanidad* es lo mismo que decir *debilidad*» (*idem,* 141; Galdós's italics). How great then really is the passion itself? Indeed, the social self must keep all laws relative to social conduct save those regarding love; in matters of the heart individuals, according to Feijoo, have every right to do as they please so long as they create no scandals or otherwise violate decorum:

> Verdad que por el decoro debido a la sociedad, hago que me espanto, y digo: «¡Qué barbaridad, hombre, qué barbaridad!» *Pero en mi interior me río y digo* «ande el mundo y crezca la especie, que para eso estamos...» (*idem,* 140; Galdós's italics)

Therefore, to state that Feijoo is a bourgeois instrument which contributes to the socialization and repression of Fortunata is to miss the complexity of their affair. Feijoo, in the words of the narrator, is an «original moralista» (III, iv, 10; 206). He seeks for Fortunata the most comfortable and convenient means by which she might live contentedly, so that she may benefit as fully as possible from every opportunity which in future presents itself including adulterous love. He wishes to teach her what society is and is not, and how to take advantage of it without hurting herself or being coopted by middle-class preoccupations. All of which, in effect, Fortunata realizes, until the fateful moment when «se descompone» and she goes forth in search of Aurora (IV, vi, 6). In the end bourgeois society conquers as Maxi, the *loco-cuerdo,* announces to his bed-ridden wife:

> ... lo que has hecho esta tarde favorece a tu enemiga [...] Tú eres tonta y *no conoces la naturaleza humana.* Yo, desde que entré en esta gran crisis de la razón, todo lo veo claro, y la naturaleza humana no tiene secretos para mí.
> *Fortunata no comprendía.*
> —Me explicaré mejor. Quiero decir que al maltratar a tu rival le has dado la victoria sobre ti. [...] Ahora [Juanito] no vacilará. *Entre una que se descompone y hace las brutalidades que tú hiciste y otra que padece y es maltratada, el amor tiene que preferir a la víctima.* Toda víctima es por sí interesante. Todo verdugo es por sí odioso. (IV, vi, 9; 363; my italics)

Any reader who knows Juanito in the slightest degree knows also that Maxi here describes exactly how Santa Cruz will react. More to the point, Maxi is right when he tells Fortunata that she has no understanding of human nature, to which Galdós might add that it is a very specific kind of human nature: that prevalent in the modern society of commercial capitalism. Fortunata's openness and directness have no place in a milieu where spontaneity must always be checked, where one must plot every move as if one were engaged in a chess game of the emotions. While it would be interesting to speculate on the moral issues which the existence of such a society presents —and clearly Galdós is not in sympathy with it— there is also the second question, morality being the first, of the reality of the situation. The clock cannot be turned back, nor the revolution precipitated; one must accept the fact therefore, as Fortunata does *not,* that modern society is the world in which one exists and with which one must cope, like it or not. There is no getting around this essential fact, and no moral imperative, however weighty it may be, can alter this fundamental reality of Fortunata's situation.

Galdós in the end comes down not on the side of the angels, but on that of reality. I am convinced that he loves his creation, Fortunata, but sees also —as do Maxi and Feijoo— that her destruction is inevitable. Her own pride, her hurt feelings, her indignation on behalf of Jacinta and her sense of betrayal by her friend and confidante, Aurora, all lead her to disobey the most important rule learned from her teacher, Feijoo, and reiterated by her insanely lucid husband. Feijoo had warned her: «*Lo primero que has de tener presente es que siempre, siempre, en todo caso y momento, hay que guardar el decoro*» (III, iv, 6; 167; my italics). This admonition, we recall, occurs when the two have decided to put an end to their love affair. Feijoo has begun to prepare the way for Fortunata's return to the Rubín household when suddenly he falls ill and takes to his bed. Fortunata visits him there and he urges her, «Como un dómine que repite la declinación a sus discípulos, machacando sílaba tras sílaba, cual si se las claveteara en el cerebro a golpes de maza» (*idem*). His message is explicit and simple. He begins with the warning —just cited— to maintain public decorum at all times. And how and to what end does one maintain decorum? Feijoo, at intervals deliberately pausing for emphasis, goes on:

> —Guardando... las... apariencias, observando... las reglas... del respeto que nos debemos los unos a los otros... y..., *sobre todo, esto es lo principal... no descomponiéndose nunca, oye lo que te digo... no descomponiéndose nunca...* [...] *no descomponiéndose nunca, se puede hacer todo lo que se quiere. (idem,* 168; my italics)

Maxi's words to Fortunata on her sickbed declare to us ironically that Feijoo has failed and that his pupil has undone not only her teacher but also herself. Lest we rush to make light of Maxi's repetition of Feijoo's words and call it coincidence, we should bear in mind that Maxi's announcement of Fortunata's «descomposición» is framed also by two additional reiterations of Feijoo's assertions. When Fortunata could not believe that Maxi would take her back, it was Feijoo who told her «*tú no conoces la naturaleza humana*» (III, iv, 7; 172, my italics). It is exactly with this phrase that Maxi begins his verbal assault in those final scenes in the Cava de San Miguel. And he closes off his attack, the truth cutting like a scalpel into Fortunata's consciousness, advising Fortunata that «En un pleito de amor, la víctima gana siempre. Esta es una verdad que está escrita en el corazón humano como en un libro, y yo *leo en él tan claro como leemos una noticia en "El Imparcial"*» (IV, vi, 9; 363; my italics). Maxi's exultantly proclaimed superiority has an unexpected source of power in the fact that we heard his words before: Feijoo had boasted to Fortunata, upon thoroughly manipulating doña Lupe,

> ¡Oh! entiendo bien a mi gente. [...] Conozco las callejuelas de la naturaleza humana mejor que los rincones de mi casa. [...] ¡Ah!... *Leo en ella como leo en ti.* (III, iv, 8; 182-83; my italics)

The verbal parallels and outright replications are not accidental. The insights of an insane husband at the deathbed of his wife may be inopportune in their timing but are not for that reason less correct in their analysis.

The words spoken by the two «filósofos»,[57] both teachers of Fortunata, strike home. Fortunata indeed begins to decompose psychologically and physically in direct response to having done so emotionally and spiritually. She gives money to Maxi to buy a revolver and kill Juanito and Aurora (IV, vi, 9; 368); her moods are thoroughly erratic (IV, vi, 8; 12). Her body can no longer manufacture the milk which will give life to her son (IV, vi, 10; 13) nor retain the blood which supports the life of the mother (IV, vi, 13). As her body fails to respond to the commands of her brain, Fortunata understands that she is going to die. She is overcome by this conviction which is articulated as follows: «Sentía la herida allá dentro, sin saber dónde, *herida o descomposición irremediables,* que la conciencia fisiológica revelaba con diagnóstico infalible, semejante a inspiración o numen profético» (*idem,* 403; my italics).

As we saw earlier, Feijoo on his own «deathbed» had declared «No descomponerse; ése es mi tema» (III, iv, 10; 209). The lesson is not lost on Fortunata, nor even the words themselves. Fortunata confronts Jacinta in the house of the moribund Mauricia and declares herself with the two shattering words, «Soy Fortunata». In the face of Jacinta's dignified silence Fortunata is half enraged, half wounded. The narrator tells us that «su acción *descompuesta* y brutal le gravitó en el alma como si la casa se le hubiera desplomado encima!» She flees the house: «Bajó y se puso en la calle, acordándose de una de las principales recomendaciones que le había hecho Feijoo: *"No descomponerse nunca."* Pues bien *se había descompuesto* aquel día... "Pero verdaderamente —discurrió tratando de serenarse, —Yo ¿qué he hecho? nada... Unicamente decirle quién soy, para que me conozca..."» (III, vi, 5; 305-06; my italics). Never-

---

[57] Galdós calls Feijoo «el filósofo práctico» (III, iv, 10; 209).

theless after she returns home and calms down she reflects «Hubiera sido mucho mejor [...] decirle aquello de *yo soy Fortunata,* con calma» (III, vi, 6; 307; Galdós's italics). Moreover, when doña Lupe describes Mauricia's final seizure, she states «De repente, *se descompuso,* hija; ¡pero de qué manera!... se quedó amoratada, empezó a dar manotazos y a echar por aquella boca unas flores, unas berzas... Era un horror» (III, vi, 9; 332; my italics). Finally, when she and Juanito accidentally meet at the end of Part III, to begin the liaison eventuating in her death and the birth of a new *Delfín,* she recalls Feijoo's advice. His words, in particular, hang portentously in her mind: «Y en el acto se acordó de las amonestaciones de Feijoo. *Claro; no había necesidad de descomponerse ni de faltar a la religión de las apariencias*» (III, vii, 5; 396; my italics). Twice more in the brief but intense scene she remembers Feijoo's lessons, the narrator informs us. *Descomponerse* therefore is a process laden with negative value, a negative value which even Fortunata appreciates.

iv. *The failed revolution*

It is only now out of the developing negation of her body and her physical being, in perfect dialectical fashion, that Galdós tells us Fortunata's spirit begins to take flight. The affirmation is unequivocal:

> Pero mientras la personalidad física se extinguía, la moral, concentrándose en una sola idea, se determinaba con desusado vigor y fortaleza. En aquella idea vaciaba, como en un molde, todo lo bueno que ella podía pensar y sentir; en aquella idea estampaba con sencilla fórmula *el perfil más hermoso y quizás menos humano* de su carácter... (IV, vi, 13; 403; my italics)

If Fortunata finally redeems herself, it is not in her world that such an action occurs. This fact ultimately is what is most important to Galdós the man and citizen, even if not to Galdós the novelist. Her redemption in the world of the reader is what matters to the latter, and that redemption does occur. Yet his subsequent novels all bear witness to the fact that if aesthetically Galdós approves of Fortunata's achievement, as a man of his time he found the cost of such greatness prohibitively expensive. Fortunata's sacrifice is too much and in her world solves nothing. In her world, it is no sacrifice at all but a waste. Not only is she blotted out in memory; even her son's resemblance to her fades and dissolves. The *Delfinito* comes to look like his middle-class stepmother (IV, vi, 15; 427).[58]

[58] On the pessimistic tone of the ending *v* n. 22 above and the text to section III, ii. The ending and Galdós's ultimate vision of society pose a problem still preoccupying many scholars, e.g., BLY, «Fortunata and No. 11...», 45; MACKLIN, p. 202; BLANCO AGUINAGA, «On 'The Birth of Fortunata'», *passim.*

Fortunata y Jacinta may be an exhilarating reading experience but it is a terribly depressing novel. It is so because the aesthetic solutions are antithetical to the social and economic solutions, to the historical solutions, to reality itself. And so we come full circle back to Feijoo, whose ideas represent a synthesis of the possibilities of Madrid and Fortunata: If she had followed his teachings, Fortunata would not have lost, or rather surrendered her self, her worldly goods and her child to bourgeois society.

We must always bear in mind that Feijoo presented the one solidly anti-bourgeois, subversive solution and that Fortunata was too heavily conditioned to take advantage of his teachings. Feijoo believed that nothing deriving from love was sinful (III, iv, 3; 140); and as one who put into practice that which he preached, Feijoo was able to enjoy throughout his life all manner of love affairs, many of which were adulterous (III, iv, 4; 146-47). It was also Feijoo who repeatedly declared that infidelity was no more than «el fuero de la naturaleza» (III, iv, 5; 157) for the simple reason that everything attendant on affairs of the heart was the «reclamación de la especie» (III, iv, 5; 158. III, iv, 10; 204). Feijoo was of the opinion that all law supposedly governing relations between the sexes was «fuera de las bases inmortales de la Naturaleza» (III, iv, 5; 159). And it was he who informed Fortunata:

> Por eso me río yo de ciertas leyes y de todo el código penal social del amor, que es un fárrago de tonterías inventadas por los feos, los mamarrachos, y los sabios estúpidos que jamás han obtenido de una hembra el más ligero favorcito. (*idem*)

Most important of all, Feijoo tried to make Fortunata understand that in appearing to obey convention she could subvert it; she could make of the restraints of bourgeois society the very keys to her own revolutionary freedom. By being married and seeming to be a good wife she could have her illicit relationships. Marriage provided her at once with security, a name, *and the shelter* of its protection; a well-managed and manipulated spouse would leave Fortunata with complete liberty. It was Feijoo who told Fortunata

> ... no sabes la ganga que es tener un nombre y una chapa decorosa en el casillero de la sociedad. [...] Casi estoy por decirte que mejor te cuadra un marido como el que tienes, que otro de mejor lámina, porque con un poco de muleta harás de él lo que quieras. (III, iv, 7; 171-72)

BRIAN J. DENDLE's look at the last three series of *Episodios* concludes that in these novels Galdós's pessimism about nineteenth-century Spanish society is «all-pervading» (pp. 183-84 of *Galdós. The Mature Thought* [Lexington: University Press of Kentucky, 1980]). Ranged against this formidable host is the equally formidable STEPHEN GILMAN, *Galdós and the Art*, pp. 229-30, 244-45, 337-38, who denies that Fortunata's death is a «triumph for the bourgeoisie» (338). In my view we must recognize that in order to edify us, the readers, Galdós allows the world of nineteenth-century Madrid to annihilate his heroine.

According to Feijoo, marital fidelity was always preferable to adultery. Nevertheless he recognized the uncommon nature of Fortunata and her situation and he was always nothing if not a realist. If it was necessary to «transigir con las formas» and «tomar las cosas de la vida como son», if it was essential to «transigir con las leyes sociales» and «sacrificar el gusto... y la ilusión», it was equally essential that one never lose one's «gran sentido de la realidad» (III, iv, 9; 200). And for Feijoo, reality was defined as the synthesis of «lo práctico» and «lo posible». In the case of Fortunata, Feijoo understood the impossibility of living a life centered on Maxi, for this would leave her without any desire to live at all. It was important that her «sacrificio» be limited to a bearable extent, that in other words Fortunata have some outlet and some joys against which the drudgery of the Rubín household might be balanced. Hence he also was compelled to tell Fortunata:

> No se deben imponer sacrificios superiores a las fuerzas humanas. Si el corazón se te conserva en el tamaño que ahora tiene, si no hay medio de recortarlo, si se te pronuncia, ¿qué le vamos a hacer? Dentro del mal, veamos qué es lo mejor entre lo peor... (III, iv, 9; 202)

For Fortunata, «lo mejor entre lo peor» was to be the *señora de* Rubín and secret lover of Juanito. Feijoo pointed out to her that any other person was preferable to Juanito, given the latter's ability to destroy her equilibrium; but in any case she must never fail to respect decorum regardless of the identity of her lover: «Es cuestión de estilo y habilidad. [...] Dirás que es difícil; pero ahí está el talento, compañera» (III, iv, 10; 205). For a time she succeeds. Hence readers are not astonished that Fortunata was able to do violence to her marital life and still accomplish her desired ends. Until she threw everything away Fortunata had been managing quite well: She had her own home, her child, and an independent income thanks to Feijoo.[59]

[59] The development of Fortunata into a full-scale member of the middle classes is described in Part III and in PETER B. GOLDMAN, «Feijoo and Mr. Singer: Notes on the *aburguesamiento* of Fortunata», in Francisco Márquez Villanueva, ed., *Estudios filológicos dedicados a Stephen Gilman*, forthcoming. Feijoo we remember presents Fortunata with a handsome gift consisting of stocks and 20,000 *reales* in cash which she invests through the mediation of doña Lupe (III, iv, 10; 210. III, v, 2; 225. IV, iii, 5; 198). By the time she leaves Maxi forever, Fortunata's cash assets have increased fifty percent to 30,000 *reales* (*idem*). Even before she left the Rubín household, Fortunata was supporting her aunt, Segunda Izquierdo (IV, i, 11; 95). Her cash is employed in usury to soldiers (IV, iii, 5; 198) and yields interest of 1,252 *reales* every three months (*idem*, 197 and IV, v, 1; 242). Her annual income therefore is 5,000 *reales plus* an undisclosed semi-annual dividend on her stock (IV, iii, 5; 199). This income is rather comfortable though certainly not luxurious. But it is continually growing, and of course is founded both on money-lending, the trade of doña Lupe and Torquemada (who helps her invest Feijoo's gift — *idem*, 198-99), and on the parasitic speculation which we find so loathsome in the Santa Cruz family. The

In sum, Feijoo wished not to oppress or otherwise limit his lover, but give her means for achieving in future the widest latitude within the limits of the possible. It was his wish and intention to demonstrate to Fortunata that great personal liberty existed *if* she could appreciate the ambiguity of her situation, learning thereby how to take advantage of society and its rules, how to subvert them while employing and obeying them, how to contravene them while appearing to live in accordance with them. Feijoo's failure was due to never having realized that Fortunata was already too socialized by bourgeois society and was, therefore, beyond help. But her self-destruction was as much her own doing as that of a corrupt world. Feijoo together with Maxi gave Fortunata a multitude of opportunities, each of which was obstructed or overcome, thanks to her collusion with middle-class Madrid, which beforehand pushed Fortunata towards her own ruin. Feijoo and Fortunata were in perfect agreement in so many of their interpretations of the dynamic of society; despite such concordance in theory, Fortunata could not in practice maintain herself as Feijoo advised. When for example Feijoo expounded on his ideas concerning love, matrimony, social behavior and strictures, human nature, and «dignidad», Fortunata reacted according to the narrator in a revealing and significant fashion:

> Todo esto le pareció a Fortunata muy peregrino cuando lo oyó por primera vez; pero a la segunda, encontrólo conforme con algo que ella había pensado. ¿Pero no sería un disparate? Porque era imposible que ella y Feijoo tuviesen razón contra el mundo entero. (III, iv, 3; 141)

In contrast to the fact that Fortunata and Feijoo are —as she correctly perceives— on the same side from the very beginning, there is the startling revelation of Fortunata's own pessimism. She believes herself wrong and society right; it is impossible in her opinion that her instincts are accurate, that her feelings are healthy, that her ideas are sound. That is, Fortunata cannot believe it possible to overcome her past and her present because society has already incapacitated her to believe in herself. She doubts the possibility of her own autonomy, even when it is beginning to take shape. She is doomed beforehand, conditioned as she is to accept on blind faith the rightness of society's judgments. Feijoo at one point says that he is rational and that society is frail when not nonsensical; his faith in himself never wavers. By contrast Fortunata may —after the death of Mauricia— come to believe in her «pícara idea», but she never for a moment doubts either the sanity of society or that she is in the wrong.

fortunes of the latter rise as the health of the country declines (*v*, e.g., I, x, 6; 430-32). The price of Fortunata's redemption is not inconsequential. On salaries during the period, *v*, e.g., ANDRÉ BARTHE ET BARTHE, *Le Salaire des ouvriers en Espagne* (Madrid: Richard Fe, 1896), and JUAN JOSÉ MORATO, «La vida obrera en Madrid», *Nuestro tiempo*, III: 28 (abril de 1903), 540-49.

She is even ashamed that she is pregnant, although she has wanted to have Juanito's child (IV, iii, 5; 194). In this sense truly Fortunata is an outsider or deviant as Becker defines the term, insofar as she accepts the rules of a society which judges her deviant and yet decides to break them anyway (*Outsiders,* chs. 1-2). Worse still, in her death throes she reaffirms those rules by surrendering her child and wealth to middle-class society and the Church, to the very persons and institutions which branded her as deviant. From the point of view of the reader, the act confirms her isolation; from that of the society which cast her out, it emphasizes her contrition, thereby also validating the very world which oppressed her. Thus Guillermina characterizes Fortunata's final actions as «un rasgo feliz y cristiano» (IV, vi, 14; 414). *Rasgo,* we recall, was a word favored by Feijoo when he wished to comment negatively on Fortunata's behavior.[60]

Ricardo Gullón masterfully observed one of the greatest ironies of this novel: Fortunata, despite the anti-social nature of her fervent wish for a child, never loses faith in a mindless society which she always contemplates with awe and respect. It is herself whom she doubts until the very end of her life.[61] Hence, it is great, but also pathetically fitting, that her transcendent act of will must be one of complete abnegation. All the efforts of Feijoo are *a priori* useless because they have arrived too late; Fortunata is beyond salvation in her own society. And it is only as she is taking leave of *her* world that she redeems herself in *ours.*[62]

Syracuse University.

[60] On the importance of the word «rasgo» both to Galdós and his times, *v* GILMAN, «La palabra hablada y *Fortunata y Jacinta»*, *Nueva Revista de Filología Hispánica,* XV (1961), 542-60, esp. 558-60; *Galdós and the Art,* pp. 286-88; and RIBBANS, «Contemporary History...», 94, n. 5.

[61] «Estructura y diseño...», 234.

[62] The John Simon Guggenheim Memorial Foundation liberated the author from his customary professional obligations in 1976-77 in order that he might spend a year devoted to reading and research. Some of the spadework for this project was begun at that time; I am pleased therefore to acknowledge the help of the Guggenheim Foundation. My greatest debt, however, is to my three collaborators, Carlos Blanco Aguinaga, Peter A. Bly, and John W. Kronik. The latter two read earlier versions of this paper; their suggestions for improvement were invaluable, their red penciling savage but enlightened, their tact and patience saintly.